INSIGHTS

General Editor: Clive Bloom, Princi̟
Polytechnic

Editorial Board: Clive Bloom, Brian D ̠, ̠a̠ y Day, Lesley Bloom and
Hazel Day

Insights brings to academics, students and general readers the very best
contemporary criticism on neglected literary and cultural areas. It consists
of anthologies, each containing original contributions by advanced scholars
and experts. Each contribution concentrates on a study of a particular work,
author or genre in its artistic, historical and cultural context.

Published titles

Clive Bloom (*editor*)
JACOBEAN POETRY AND PROSE: Rhetoric, Representation and the
 Popular Imagination
TWENTIETH-CENTURY SUSPENSE: The Thriller Comes of Age
SPY THRILLERS: From Buchan to le Carré

Clive Bloom, Brian Docherty, Jane Gibb and Keith Shand (*editors*)
NINETEENTH-CENTURY SUSPENSE: From Poe to Conan Doyle

Dennis Butts (*editor*)
STORIES AND SOCIETY: Children's Literature in a Social Context

Gary Day (*editor*)
READINGS IN POPULAR CULTURE: Trivial Pursuits?
THE BRITISH CRITICAL TRADITION: A Re-Evaluation

Gary Day and Clive Bloom (*editors*)
PERSPECTIVES ON PORNOGRAPHY: Sexuality in Film and Literature

Brian Docherty (*editor*)
AMERICAN CRIME FICTION: Studies in the Genre
AMERICAN HORROR FICTION: From Brockden Brown to Stephen King

Rhys Garnett and R. J. Ellis (*editors*)
SCIENCE FICTION ROOTS AND BRANCHES: Contemporary Critical
 Approaches

Robert Giddings (*editor*)
LITERATURE AND IMPERIALISM

list continued on next page

The British Critical Tradition

A Re-evaluation

Edited by

GARY DAY

MACMILLAN

First published 1993 by
THE MACMILLAN PRESS LTD
Houndmills, Basingstoke, Hampshire RG21 2XS
and London
Companies and representatives
throughout the world

ISBN 0–333–53275–9 hardcover
ISBN 0–333–53276–7 paperback

A catalogue record for this book is available
from the British Library.

Printed in Hong Kong

Series Standing Order

If you would like to receive future titles in this series as they are published, you
can make use of our standing order facility. To place a standing order please
contact your bookseller or, in case of difficulty, write to us at the address below
with your name and address and the name of the series. Please state with which
title you wish to begin your standing order. (If you live outside the United
Kingdom we may not have the rights for your area, in which case we will
forward your order to the publisher concerned.)

Customer Services Department, Macmillan Distribution Ltd
Houndmills, Basingstoke, Hampshire RG21 2XS, England

For Hazel, Tony and Sharon
because the past matters as well as the future

Contents

Preface

This collection offers a re-interpretation of the history of British criticism by exploring the work of neglected as well as celebrated critics. It contextualises the current crisis and shows how traditional criticism anticipates and to some extent parallels the concerns of post-modern critical theory. The issue of value is also addressed as is the question of the future direction of criticism, making this volume an important contribution to contemporary critical debate.

I should like to thank Clive and Lesley Bloom and Brian Docherty for all their help and encouragement. I should also like to thank Janet Dudley for her work on the index compilation. Thanks are also due to Frances Arnold for her patience and support, and special thanks go to Deborah Griffiths.

Notes on the Contributors

Helena Blakemore is currently researching contemporary fiction at Middlesex Polytechnic. She has contributed articles to *Readings in Popular Culture* and *Twentieth-Century Suspense*, both in the *Insights* series.

Clive Bloom has edited several books for the *Insights* series. His latest is *Spy Thrillers: From Buchan to le Carré*. He is currently a principal lecturer in English at Middlesex Polytechnic.

Anthony Crabbe lectures in history of art and design at Trent Polytechnic. He has contributed articles to *Readings in Popular Culture* and *Perspectives on Pornography*, both in the *Insights* series.

Barry Cullen is a senior lecturer in English at Middlesex Polytechnic. He is currently writing a book on F. R. Leavis.

Gary Day has edited *Readings in Popular Culture* and co-edited *Perspectives on Pornography* with Clive Bloom, both in the *Insights* series. He is one of the editors for the forthcoming Longman's series *Literature and Culture*.

Michael Hayes teaches at Lancashire Polytechnic. He has published widely on literary theory and popular fiction.

Barbara Helm is doing research at Lancashire Polytechnic. Some of her short stories have been broadcast by the BBC.

Graham Holderness is Head of Drama at Roehampton Institute, London. He has published extensively in Renaissance and modern literature and drama. His most recent publications are *Shakespeare out of Court* and *The Politics of Theatre and Drama* (editor) in the Insights Series. He is also the author of *Shakespeare Recycled: The Making of Historical Drama*.

Laura Kranzler teaches feminist theory at Oxford. She has just completed her thesis on violence in the Gothic novel.

Bart Moore-Gilbert lectures at Goldsmith's College. He is the author of *Kipling and Orientalism* and is the co-editor of *Cultural Revolution? The Challenge of the Arts in the 1960s.*

Christopher Norris is Professor of English at the University of Wales. He is the author of numerous articles on critical theory. His latest books are *Spinoza and the Origins of Critical Theory, What's Wrong with Post Modernism* and *The Gulf War and the Politics of Theory.*

Adrian Page is a principal lecturer at Luton College of Higher Education. He is editor of *The Death of the Playwright? Modern British Drama and Literary Theory* published in the Insights Series.

Noël Parker lectures for the Open University. He is author of *Portrayals of Revolution: Images, Ideas and Patterns of Thought in the French Revolution.*

Tony Pinkney lectures in English at the University of Lancaster. He is the author of *Women in the Poetry of T. S. Eliot: A Psychoanalytic Approach* and *D. H. Lawrence.* He has also edited *Raymond Williams: Postmodern Novelist* and *Introduction to Literary Theory.* He is a member of the editorial board of *News from Nowhere.*

Jim Reilly lectures at Cambridge University and for the Open University. He has published on Conrad, George Eliot and Alasdair Gray.

Andrew Smith is currently researching into the Gothic novel. He has contributed to *Readings in Popular Culture* and *Twentieth-Century Suspense,* both in the *Insights* series.

Ross Stuart has taught at universities in Canada and Morocco. His research interests are in early modernism.

1

Introduction: Criticism in Crisis

GARY DAY

As Chris Baldick has pointed out, criticism has always been in a state of crisis.[1] The present one centres on the problem of legitimation and, closely related to it, the question of criticism's proper object of study: literature – itself a highly contentious and unstable term – or society, an equally suspect word.

The problem of legitimation is part of the landscape of post-modernism and may be expressed as follows: where does critical theory[2] find the authority for its pronouncements when it has effectively demonstrated that all texts, including its own, are riddled with errors, unconscious assumptions, contradictions, slippages and rhetorical machinations?

In the eighteenth century, criticism was legitimated by the existence of a public sphere governed by the exercise of reason.[3] To inquire into matters of taste, to discuss the issues of the day and to discourse about literature all reinforced the commonality of reason and confirmed those who participated in this civilised intercourse as rational enlightened subjects. The nineteenth century saw the disappearance of this public sphere and the corresponding isolation of the critic. Criticism's new task was no less a one than the prevention of anarchy. Literature was to have a softening and humanising influence on the masses and the study of poetry was to wean them from class conflict.[4] This view was also apparent in the work of the Leavises who urged the study of literature as a means of combating what they saw as the destructive forces of mass culture. Critics were keepers of language and guardians of a tradition which was ultimately located in the organic community of the English Village. This tradition was under threat from the banality and sensationalism of the mass media, particularly advertising. If it was to be safeguarded it was imperative that a sense of 'experience' be cultivated, a sense of the concrete which literary criticism alone was able to instil. Traditional values could be renewed by concentrating on the relations between language and concrete experience in a way that recalled the natural rhythms of village life.

The legitimacy of criticism then, to simplify somewhat bluntly, came first from its sense of shared values and, secondly, from its sense of itself as a force for salvation or social renewal. As criticism was gradually institutionalised in the universities, the public sphere diminished and with it so did criticism's legitimacy: the critic was now an expert rather than an equal, and criticism had to find a new justification for itself. This it did with its sense of social mission which perhaps received its most robust and passionate expression in the prose of F. R. Leavis. However, this missionary fervour, especially as it appeared in literary criticism, was itself premised on a number of philosophical assumptions which Leavis notoriously refused to explicate. As Baldick comments, his literary judgements were made in the 'corroborative mode – "This is so, is it not?"[5] It was precisely to the extent that these assumptions were unspoken that they could act as a legitimising force, a force which evaporated once their contradictions and incoherencies were brought to light.

For the past twenty years or so critical theory has targeted the assumptions not just of its own but of other discourses too. The effect of this has been to render them unworkable; they are shown to be compromised or self-defeating and any authority they have derives not from themselves, as they fondly imagine, but from elsewhere, showing them to be partial, flawed and dependent at the very moment they assert their transcendence. Lacking legitimation they can say nothing of worth and all they can aspire to is, firstly, a consciousness of how they are constrained and, secondly, a reflexivity to be able to operate within those constraints.

Chris Norris is one critic who takes issue with the view that it is impossible to legitimate critical theory. His objection is that if everything is either a 'will to power' or a hermeneutic circularity then we can never learn anything new nor have objective standards of truth and falsehood, and this flies in the face of our social and political experience, even bearing in mind the extent to which it is constructed.[6] Norris' solution to the present critical impasse is to look for its origins in the work of Spinoza and see whether or not his concepts can be usefully brought to bear on current problems. He also stresses the rigours of deconstruction to show that we can break the hermeneutic circle and gain new insights and knowledge. Terry Eagleton's proposal is to create a 'counter public sphere, one based upon those very institutions of popular culture and education which failed to emerge in post-war Britain'.[7] As well as giving criticism a larger audience than it at present has this would also give it a new role: the demystification of symbolic systems through which political power is deployed.

Both these critics resist the idea that criticism lacks any means of legitimation. Norris' case is slightly weaker because he looks for the rationale and justification of criticism through logic and truth and, powerful though his argument is, it never quite succeeds in overcoming recent attacks on such concepts. Eagleton has more of a case because he sees criticism as a potential social force and though this is not without its problems – in particular how the counter public sphere is to be created – it does at least seek to ground criticism in something other than the quicksand of language.

Another way of legitimating criticism is the one taken by this collection of essays which, together, suggest that criticism needs to have a more thorough understanding of its own history. One feature of post–1968 criticism is its contemptuous dismissal of earlier work and this jettisoning of its own history is ironic for a criticism which, at least in part, has tried to bring the question of history to the forefront of its thinking. This volume tries to develop the view of criticism, suggested by critics as far apart as Eagleton and Washington, that contemporary literary theory is a continuation of the past rather than a break with it.[8] Each essay deals with one critic and, by showing how congruent some of his/her ideas are with contemporary criticism, brings out the radical dimension of his/her work. It is through such an examination of its own history that criticism can shift from its present crisis to its next and hopefully more profitable stage of development. As has been remarked in another context, those who do not come to terms with the past are condemned to repeat it.

Although this collection offers a way of legitimating criticism, the question arises as to why we should worry about criticism being legitimated or grounded at all. The rigorous demands made by contemporary critical theory make it impossible for any discipline to be legitimate, either because of internal incoherence or because of its dependence on an outside authority. But this very insistence on the impossibility of legitimation betrays a desire for it. Indeed, critical theory derives its legitimacy from exposing the fictitious character of legitimacy elsewhere. Moreover, in the progress of its argument, critical theory betrays a belief in standards of reason and logic whose existence it claims to deny. In other words, critical theory detects the problem of legitimation everywhere, yet by being legitimated itself, through its own assumptions and operations, the problem is greatly diminished.

But the problem of why something needs to be legitimated still remains. This desire for legitimation, for justification, seems to belong to the Benthamite tradition which asks what is the use of something. This legacy is still apparent today as writers like Eagleton and Norris attempt to find a use for criticism. Perhaps it could be argued that this shows their capture by the very ideology they seek to overthrow for the question of the use of something is germane to capitalism; it acted as a motor for economic development in the nineteenth century and helped to usher in reforms benefiting manufacturing industry. 'What is the use of it?' can be seen as the official question of capitalism even though, ironically, its production processes are based not on use but exchange value and its commodities are not as necessary as they are superfluous.

The question of the use of literature and criticism articulates with the Puritan tradition in the writing of the Leavises[9], which means that pleasure becomes a factor in the debate if only to be instantly repressed. Pleasure, in the form of happiness, is implicit in the Benthamite approach to criticism and literature but there too it is a problem, first because it is seen as quantifiable and second because it is ultimately subsumed under the category of the useful, which becomes more of a means to the smooth running of the capitalist system than a means to the greatest happiness of the greatest number. Both the Benthamite and Puritan traditions ensure that pleasure is not a part of literary discussion. And thus criticism with its roots in these traditions, particularly the latter, becomes a discourse of guilt – which is, of course, the essence of Puritanism.

In this context, it is significant to note that, with the exception of Barthes, little has been written about literary pleasure. Instead, critical response has concentrated on the morally uplifting qualities of literature or, from a different camp, how it can give knowledge of the ideology in which it is bathed. Nowhere is there a tradition of writing about literature as pleasure and it is too easy to say that it is impossible to write about pleasure for that ignores the point that no discourse of pleasure has either been developed, or allowed to develop. It is worth recalling here that one of the objections to the novel was that it was an idle, frivolous pastime, neither productive nor socially useful, and therein lay its threat. The problem of legitimation then may arise as a defence against the disruptive nature of pleasure. In capitalist ideology, all revolutionary discourses can be tolerated since they can be accommodated within the prevailing institutions of discourse; pleasure cannot.

As mentioned earlier the problem of legitimation is closely related to criticism's lack of an object. This rather cumbersome way of stating the case overlooks the fact that an object is not just out there in the world, waiting to be discovered and studied. On the contrary, the object is constituted by the methods and aims of study as much as they are constituted by the object; it is an ongoing dialectical relationship. Different types of literary criticism constitute and are constituted by different types of literature in a mutually affirmative relationship. Hence there is no essential truth of the text, only an equivalence between two different discourses.

The problem of the critical object, if such a phrase may now be permitted, has been compounded by deconstruction, which has argued persuasively that there is little difference between literature and criticism, with the result that critics now write as much about each other as they do about authors. Criticism has become its own object and it is doubtful whether it can get enough distance from itself, no matter how self-reflexive it is, to say anything worthwhile. It cannot escape its own boundaries so it is socially marginal, even redundant, except perhaps as a symptom of the society it inhabits.

An even greater problem, however, is the fact that criticism is a *bricolage* of other discourses: semiotics, psychoanalysis, film studies, cultural theory and so on. Each one is a specific discourse for a specific object and this can only hinder criticism's quest for its own object. It cannot construct one as long as others haunt it.

Lacking an object, criticism operates as a free-floating discourse. It seems to want to function in the manner of traditional philosophy as a short of clearing house for the ordering of ideas and values. It has shifted further and further away from its original object, the individual text and, by extension, from society too. It is now more interested in the world of language than in the relation between language and the world and, in this respect too, it seems to be trying to usurp philosophy. Of course this does not mean that criticism no longer scrutinises the social and political field but its observations are now more analytic and localised than prescriptive and general. Moreover, the language in which these observations are couched has a quasi-scientific character, which confers a sort of absoluteness on what is described, making it difficult to imagine that it can be changed.

Furthermore, it is a language removed from 'ordinary' human experience and, while pre-1968 criticism had many vices, its one virtue was the cultivation of a discourse concerned with choice, discrimination and value.

Of course, this was open only to a few; nor is there any question that literary criticism functioned as an agent for the construction of a subjectivity suitable for the bourgeois state. However, it always contained within it the potential for 'opposition to that state. It believed in its capacity to effect change and it spoke in a comprehensible language that connected with 'real' experience. By contrast, present day criticism is crippled by its own knowingness and sophistication, resembling Hamlet in its procrastinations and musings. It may dismiss opposition as naive or idealistic but that misses the point; it doesn't matter if choice is a fiction, what matters is the *effect* this and other fictions have to enlighten and mobilise against oppression and exploitation.

Another feature of pre-1968 criticism is its concern to construct a hierarchy of texts based on a scale of values, and the most obvious example here is Leavis's 'Great Tradition'. Again, this worked in a conservative manner. In poetry, for instance, Keats is preferred to Shelley on the basis of the maturity of his verse when in fact this was more to do with the latter's radical politics than with his talent or otherwise for versification. However, just because mistakes were made there is no reason to dismiss the enterprise out of hand. The current trend for seeing no real difference between, say, Jackie Collins and George Eliot is hardly an improvement and in the long run spells the death of value. True, value systems are never innocent, but to dismantle them utterly leaves criticism without a meaningful framework for its analyses. A concept of value is necessary and inevitable and criticism, particularly as it relates to literature, is one of the few discourses where such a concept can receive rigorous examination and development. Without a language of value social policy becomes more cynical and expedient than it already is and criticism has a vital role to play, if not in improving the situation, at least in preventing it from deteriorating further.

Perhaps one way of doing this would be for criticism to abandon some of its pretensions and return to the literary text. However, this is easier said than done. Literary criticism has always 'policed' the text, using it to confirm rather than explore, but the revolution in communications, the growth of mass culture and a multi-racial society mean that the assumptions and shared values which sustained the study of literature no longer exist. This doesn't mean that literature should be abandoned, rather that its status in a hi-tech computerised society needs to be re-thought. The next stage should be to find some way of talking about literature that combines the developments of critical theory with the best of traditional writing in a discourse that balances analysis, value, knowledge and commitment. Having returned, as it were, to literature (its proper object?) criticism should then be better placed to reassess its relationship with and its role in society.

One final word about selection. The aim has been to include writers as well as critics in order to challenge the orthodox view of critical history. Hopefully, this will raise questions about the nature, purpose and future of criticism as they relate to its object and its quest for legitimacy; and certainly one component of that legitimacy will always be crisis.

NOTES

1. C. Baldick, *The Social Mission of English Criticism* (Oxford: Oxford University Press, 1987) p. 1.
2. There is some confusion between literary criticism, criticism, critical discourse and critical theory. Obviously there is an overlap and I shall exploit that to use 'criticism' and 'critical theory' more or less synonymously, except where the context demands more precision. What should be borne in mind, is that the former belongs more nearly to literary criticism whereas the latter, though it incorporates the former, covers a much wider field – feminism, Marxism, psychoanalysis, discourse theory and philosophy to mention but a few. In part, the crisis of 'criticism' lies in trying to clarify exactly what it is that is in crisis.
3. See T. Eagleton, *The Function of Criticism from 'The Spectator' to Post-Structuralism* (London: Verso, 1984), esp. pp. 9–27.
4. Baldick, *The Social Mission*, esp. pp. 59–75.
5. Ibid., p. 174.
6. Norris's argument is developed at length in C. Norris, *Spinoza and the Origins of Modern Critical Theory* (Oxford: Basil Blackwell, 1991).
7. Eagleton, *The Function of Criticism*, p. 112.
8. See P. Washington, *Fraud: Literary Theory and the End of English* (London: Fontana, 1989): '[Literary theory is] a continuation by other means of what it most dislikes, ie., traditional literary criticism' (p. 25); and Eagleton: 'The role of the contemporary critic, then, is a traditional one' (*The Function of Criticism*, p. 123).
9. Baldick, *The Social Mission*, pp. 176–8 and p. 182.

2

Carlyle's Metaphorical Dynamic of History: or How to Trace a Grand Narrative in the French Revolution

NOËL PARKER

Apart from specialists in literature and Victorian cultural history, not many people refer to Thomas Carlyle as an authoritative literary critic. He is not many people's idea of a historian either – though his *The French Revolution: A History* was republished in a new edition in the recent bicentenary year.[1] Yet, he was an enormous figure in the nineteenth-century intellectual world and he has continued to intrigue a considerable band of analysts and students. Erudite, severe, dogmatic and latterly bigoted almost to the point of insanity, he was a sage, a prophet of ills in the modern world of urbanisation, democracy and mass culture. He was not afraid to put himself on the line in questions of literature, history, politics or philosophy. And his writings set the terms for an entire Victorian generation of intellectuals.

There are obvious similarities between the situation of intellectuals in the 1830s and the post-modernists of today. Like then, they were confronted by a rapidly changing social world in which regressive authoritarianism looked the most powerful ideological current. History, for them too, had a gloomy or threatening direction. Intellectuals looked and felt vulnerable and unsure of their ground. What makes Carlyle's case potentially instructive for today's critics and historians is that he stuck to his guns as an intellectual.

Of particular interest is that Carlyle did not shrink from writing history. He did this even though he seems almost to have anticipated post-modernism's reasons for suspecting the historical 'grand narrative' – that is, accounts of history showing that it is directed towards some end. In his 1830 essay 'On History', he wrote that history 'is a real Prophetic Manuscript and can be fully interpreted by no man'.[2]

8

But he was not to be put off from the task, taking it merely as 'the lot of man' to miss perfection in history-writing, as in other endeavours. (*CME*, 'On History Again', vol. III, pp. 181–2). He confronted the topic of the French Revolution and wrote a progressive history of it, followed later by works on Cromwell and Frederick the Great. The question this essay poses, then, is: if Carlyle could do that sort of thing with history, why can't we?

Carlyle studies offer a considerable body of literary biography, cultural history, analysis of specific works and debate on his place in the formation of nineteenth-century thought.[3] A number of critics have considered Carlyle's historical writing. They argue that it constituted a version of the epic adapted to the modern world, where multiple values and voices contend.[4] My argument runs somewhat parallel to that line of thought. I want to argue that in writing the history of the Revolution, Carlyle successfully attempts what post-modernism regards as suspect, if not impossible: a grand narrative.

However, Carlyle builds his 'grand narrative' without the foundationalist grounding which post-modernism derides.[5] The trick is to interpret human action in history by what it symbolises, or means metaphorically, rather than by any ineluctable direction. To show how he does that, I shall draw on a reading of Carlyle's own work and the findings of various recent studies. I shall also, I confess, do some violence to Carlyle's way of thinking by stripping away its religious idealism.[6] In my submission, Carlyle first explores how to write history in his *Sartor Resartus*, and then executes that very task in *The French Revolution*.

The extraordinary rhetoric of *Sartor Resartus* has already been a particular object of modern critical attention.[7] The book is a spoof selection from the writings of an imaginary peripatetic German intellectual called Diogenes Teufelsdröckh – the surname means God-born Devil's dung, by the way. It was serialised in a journal during 1833 and 1834, to 'almost unqualified disapproval'.[8] (Later, however, following the enormous success of the *French Revolution* (1837), it was much better received in book form.) *Sartor* is thus a good place to start a reflection on how Carlyle writes.

The French Revolution, too, has a special place. It is the archetypal component in the narratives which, for post-modernists, ground history in the specious foundation of progress and 'dishonestly legitimate' Western rationality and ascendancy. In Carlyle's nuanced account, the Revolution is indeed a great story of human progress, but one in which rationalist ambitions tragically over-reach themselves in pain and bloodshed. However, it is not the story that Carlyle tells which interests me, but his manner of formulating it.

THE STYLE OF *SARTOR RESARTUS* AND ITS PHILOSOPHY

First, then, let us look at the way Carlyle thinks about human life and history in *Sartor Resartus*. Whatever is said in the book, is mediated through at least two fictional interpreters: Teufelsdröckh himself and his anonymous English editor. In addition, from time to time we hear about Dr Teufelsdröckh's scarcely credible life and work through the editor's German contact and informant, Hofrath Heuschrecke. All these characters possess at best dubious identity as human beings; they are sketchily and playfully drawn. Teufelsdröckh's autobiographical notes and souvenirs arrive in mid-text in six bags, each marked with a sign of the zodiac. Teufelsdröckh himself disappears at the end of the story amidst hints that he has gone off to the revolutionary events of 1830 in Paris, and that he may anyway be one and the same person as the editor.

It is never clear how these people, or their different voices relate to each other. The editor continually breaks in to bemoan the all too evident lack of order, style and even good sense in Teufelsdröckh's work. He directs a fussy indulgence on Teufelsdröckh. The man is in some ways rather unpleasant, but with redeeming features: 'so sly and still, so imperturbably saturnine . . . with some half-visible wrinkle of a bitter sardonic humour', yet possessing 'rapt earnestness' and 'untutored energy'.[9] On the other hand, the editor's narrow-minded objections and his own fuddy-duddy way of speaking hardly inspire confidence. 'Than which paragraph on Metaphors.' he once cuts in, 'did the reader ever see a more surprisingly metaphorical? However, that is not our chief grievance' (*SR*, 1: xi, p. 50). Anyway, if he is so critical, why does he sit 'daily and nightly . . . deciphering these unimaginable Documents' (*SR*, 1: xi, p. 54)? Both Teufelsdröckh and his editor seem equally errant and bizarre. Just for good measure, near the end (*SR*, 3: iv) the editor pulls out a pamphlet from Heuschrecke and mercilessly ironises on its Malthusianism. The substance of *Sartor*, whatever it may be, is delivered to us through a plethora of unreliable and discordant voices. It all leaves the reader perplexed and hungry for the assurance of a fixed substantive view.

What is the substance of *Sartor*? It is a 'philosophy of clothes': reflections on how Man makes clothes and clothes make Man. Preposterous and implausible, you might think. Indeed, you are encouraged to think that, by the medley of voices and a persistent irony in the tone. The editor's laboured hard-sell at the start gets off on that footing:

> Considering our present advanced state of culture, and how the Torch of Science had now been brandished and been borne about . . . for five-thousand years . . . it might strike the reflective mind with some surprise that hitherto little or nothing of a fundamental character . . . has been written on the subject of Clothes. (*SR*, 1: I, p. 1)

Heuschrecke's over-blown expectations of the editor's mission compound the bathos:

> the whole Philosophy and Philosopher of Clothes will stand clear to the wondering eyes of England (and) finally conquer great part of this terrestial planet! (*SR*, 1: XI, p. 52)

And yet, Teufelsdröckh means his ramblings on the subject of clothes to be taken seriously. He jokes that Montesquieu should have written not about laws and *customs*, but about *costumes* (*SR*, 1: V, p. 23). 'Rightly understood', the philosophy of clothes includes 'all that men have thought, dreamed, done and been' (*SR*, 1: XI, p. 50). Indeed, it progressively embraces the grand themes of European social and political thought: humans in the state of nature, human development and perfectibility, power, the relationship with God. These extensions usually happens thus: Teufelsdröckh whips himself up to some heady, far-fetched statements and the editor then tries to trim them. 'The first spiritual want of a barbarous man is Decoration', writes Teufelsdröckh, and then goes on to apostrophise about the 'continual growth, regenesis and self-perfecting vitality' of mankind, and to sweep over the growth of social, economic and industrial institutions (*SR*, 1: V, pp. 26–7). The editor butts in to pick out and commend the idea of man as a tool-maker. Later, Teufelsdröckh observes that men can produce the strange effects of obeying one another by virtue of one man's wearing red and another blue (*SR*, 1: IX, p. 40). Sometimes, he continues, he imagines what it would be like if the holders of power and dignity were naked.

'Would to heaven,' inserts the editor, 'thou hadst thought right to keep it secret!' (*SR*, 1: IX, p. 41). Elsewhere, Teufelsdröckh agonises:

> Who am I; what is this Me? . . . Sure enough, I am; and lately was not: but Whence? How? Whereto? The answer lies around . . . but where is the cunning eye and ear to whom that God-written Apocalypse will yield articulate meaning? . . . . The secret of Man's Being is still like the Sphinx's secret: a riddle that he cannot rede (*sic*)   (*SR*, 1: VIII, pp. 35–6)

This section the editor has scuppered in advance, calling it 'an untried, almost unspeakable region, or chaos'.

> He [Teufelsdröckh] says in so many words, 'Society is founded upon Cloth;' . . .
> By what chains . . . of Meditation the grand Theorem is here unfolded, and innumerable practical corollaries are drawn therefrom it were perhaps a mad ambition to attempt exhibiting.   (*SR*, 1: VIII, p. 34)

There is much to be said for the conclusion that Gerry Brookes draws from his detailed, and extremely useful analysis of the rhetoric of *Sartor*. The book's different voices do draw the reader in, persuading him or her to believe the implicitly stated doctrine.[10] The elaborate play, and the unconvincing mock anonymity are there to get the reader involved. But in my view, there is still more to it. The view of human life and society that *Sartor* expresses cannot be stated outright. It is beyond good sense, decency, logic and language – what Jacques Derrida has referred to as 'exorbitant'.[11] For a number of reasons it can only be pointed to through images embedded in an ironic web of incomplete statements by diverse voices.

Teufelsdröckh's ruminations lead him to feel that questions of the ultimate meaning and purpose of life lead only to angst-ridden 'dreaming' and to 'dream-theorems': humans are mere 'somnambulists', 'light-sparkles floating in the aether of Deity'. He hit on the philosophy of clothes, he tells us, when 'wearied' by thoughts like that. Clothes stand for all the antidotes to this existential nakedness. Yet, they are deeply ambivalent antidotes.

> Day after day, I must thatch myself anew; day after day, this despicable thatch must lose some film of its thickness . . . frayed

away by tear and wear, must be brushed off into the Ashpit. . . .
Am I a botched mass of tailors' and cobblers' shreds, then; or a
tightly-articulated, homogeneous little Figure, automatic, nay
alive?   (*SR*, 1: VIII, pp. 36–8)

The devices by which humans cover the ultimate questioning of
their existence are, it seems practical, transient, shallow and
inauthentic: 'there is something great in the moment when man first
strips himself of adventitious wrappages; and sees that he is indeed
naked . . . yet also a Spirit, and unutterable Mystery of Mysteries'
(ibid.). Yet, if clothes hide our naked identity from us, the realisation
that this is so is both admirable and deeply disturbing: 'Oh Heaven,
it is mysterious, it is awful to consider that we not only carry each a
future ghost within him; but are, in very deed, Ghosts! (*SR*, 3: IX,
p. 184). Consciousness of the absurd lies close to the surface: 'Thus,
like a God-created, fire-breathing Spirit-host, we emerge from the
Inane; haste stormfully across the astonished Earth; then plunge
again into the Inane' (*SR*, 3: VIII, pp. 181–4). Or again: 'In every the
wisest Soul lies a whole world of internal Madness . . . out of which,
indeed, his world of Wisdom has been creatively built together' (*SR*,
3: VIII, p. 180).

Those are the existential reasons why the clothes philosophy cannot be spoken outright. There are reasons of logic, as well. Carlyle
claims (in idealist terms) that humankind covers its metaphysical
nakedness with institutions of all sorts, investing them with significance : 'All things are emblems. . . . Matter exists only spiritually, and
to represent some Idea, and *body* it forth. Hence clothes, as despic-
able as we think them, are unspeakably significant' (*SR*, 1: XI, p. 50).
With the idealism stripped away, it amounts to this: the imagination
articulated in human life, individual or collective, invests all those
things we know of with the meaning by which we understand our
world and live in it. All our understanding of the world is, in that
sense, the product of our imagination.

The signifying tool of language is the medium of this process, so
this makes it difficult to state the clothes philosophy.

Language is called the garment of Thought: however, it should
rather be, Language is the Flesh-Garment, the Body of Thought.
. . . Imagination wove this Flesh-Garment . . . Metaphors are her
stuff . . . what, if you except some primitive elements (or natural
sound) what is it all but metaphors, recognised as such, or no
longer recognised?   (*SR*, 1: XI, p. 49)

Language must rely upon imagination and metaphor to establish an understanding of our world. The clothes philosophy which expresses that reliance, could only be part of that understanding. Thus to state the clothes philosophy without these devices would exceed the capacities of language. If we crudely assert our need for 'clothes' – that is, our reliance on the creative strategies of the imagination – we may undermine them. We would be reaching into the exorbitant – or, as Carlyle terms it, the infinite. Almost Teufelsdröckh's last words to us are: 'O Heaven whither? Sense knows not; Faith knows not; only that it is through mystery to mystery' (*SR*, 3: VIII, p. 185).

Finally, there are social reasons why the clothes philosophy cannot be stated. First, its view of human society imaginatively created would contradict the eighteenth-century's favoured way of grounding social life: in Nature. 'Nature is good,' the editor expostulates, 'but she is not the best: here truly was the victory of Art over Nature' (*SR*, 1: IX, p. 40). However, even this claim remains unsure. An open statement of the clothes philosophy could make social institutions appear the product of *mere* art, and so undermine them in their totality. As the editor observes: 'Men are properly said to be clothed with Authority' (ibid.). What price clothes, then?

In the 1830s, challenges to social institutions of course referred implicitly to the French Revolution. This only makes the clothes philosophy more subversive socially. So the editor feels he must step in to distance the book from the 'pestilential . . . Bog of Sansculottism' (*SR*, 1: X, p. 43). Though he acknowledges that Teufelsdröckh is 'a Sansculottist', he reassures readers of a nervous disposition that he is 'no Adamite' – i.e. he does not advocate a return to the state of nature (*SR*, 1: IX, p.40). And, anyway, even if he is a sansculottist, he is 'probably the politest man extant' (*SR*, 3: VI, p. 165)!

In spite of all these reasons for obscuring the clothes philosophy, there are unfortunately countervailing reasons why its truth has to be spoken. It has, in the end, to be both stated and not stated. Firstly, it is a profound truth of the human condition. Secondly, in Carlyle's mystical and early Victorian view of matters, the experience of its truth will restore the sentiment of wonder, the worship of God and the celebration of life, or 'the Everlasting Yea' to life (*SR*, 2: IX). For man, custom is 'a kind nurse, guiding him to his true benefit', but 'we are false, foolish nurselings, when, in our resting and reflecting hours, we prolong the same deception' (*SR*, 3: VIII, p. 179). Thirdly – and of greatest interest to me – its effects described by the clothes philosophy are experienced in history, for it is not enough to be content to stay with the emblems our imagination generated in the past.

In short, the clothes philosophy contains an exorbitant and disturbing knowledge of the human social condition to which it is impossible, dangerous and yet necessary to refer. That is why *Sartor Resartus* can only allude to it ironically, through shadowy intermediaries. It comprises an awareness of how human imaginative effort bounds and structures a liveable world for us, by ascribing meanings to what that world contains. It is now time to consider the consequences of this for the reading of history.

LOOKING AT HISTORY THROUGH THE PHILOSOPHY OF *SARTOR*

Chapter 5 of Book 3 of *Sartor Resartus* sets out a philosophy of history in the conventional sense: an account of history moving forward from one phase to another through cycles of belief and scepticism. Carlyle's philosophy of history is intended to demonstrate that history is a 'unifying, corporate process by which man gradually achieves his desire for spiritual freedom'.[12] In form, it resembles many similar nineteenth-century theories, so it is not of great interest to me here. Rather, I want to focus on how, according to Carlyle, we are to read such broad processes in specific histories.

As I said earlier, the effects of clothes are experienced in history. That is so in both personal and social history. The philosophy of clothes insists that human imaginative effort gathers the content of our lived world, ascribing meanings to what is in that world. Even if it cannot be directly stated, the truth of the philosophy can nonetheless be experienced in that lived world. And insofar as the meaningfulness of the world is the product of human imaginations, it is irredeemably associated with particular, historical persons or people. As the editor puts it, 'the demonstration lay much in the Author's individuality; as if it were not Argument that had taught him, but Experience' (*SR*, 1: VIII, p. 35). This thought underlies the whole structure of *Sartor*, because 'no Life-Philosophy . . . which originates equally in the character, and equally speaks thereto, can attain its significance till the Character itself is known and seen' (*SR*, 1: XI, p. 51). In the light of that second observation, the second book gives a personal history of Teufelsdröckh, the prophet of the philosophy; and the third book shows how 'clothes' are put on, *and changed* by particular societies in historical time.

Chapter III of Book 3 describes, in theistic terms, how human beings live 'in and through *Symbols*' which are an 'embodiment and revelation of the Infinite' (*SR*, 3: III, pp. 152–3). Since, for Carlyle, the universe is God's creation, to render it into symbols is naturally to convey something of Him'. All this is in line with his clothes philosophy and its religious idealism as I have outlined it. One reason for acknowledging a clothes philosophy is then the fact that 'Symbols, like all terrestrial Garments, wax old' (*SR*, 3: III, p. 155). Carlyle goes on to speculate on what sort of being can make our symbols anew.

He has already made it plain in the previous chapter (shocking the editor) that he holds contemporary religious symbolism to the outworn: 'Meanwhile, in our era of the World, those same Church-Clothes have gone sorrowfully out-at-elbows: nay, far worse, many of them have become mere hollow Shapes, or Masks, under which no living Figure or Spirit any longer dwells' (*SR*, 3: II, p. 149). Furthermore, in the first chapter of Book 3, he has told us of an 'incident in Modern History': the instructive story of George Fox, a mere cobbler whose questions of faith were unresolved by the established church. Fox took himself off to discover his own answers, dressed only in the garments his own skills could vouchsafe him: a leather suit. Carlyle's point is plainly that it was a show of self-reliance which gave Fox (the founder of the Quakers) his place in the great historical movement of the Reformation – a movement to find faith outside Church hierarchy.

So, as regards clothes effects in contemporary history, Carlyle is saying that there is a continuing crisis of faith in the old religious symbolism, which it is within the power of ordinary human beings to resolve. Chapter 5 is more explicit about the crisis: 'Society' is, according to Teufelsdröckh, 'as good as extinct', because 'there is no longer any Social Idea extant' (*SR*, 3: V, p. 160). In short, history is in a period of scepticism which is undermining the given imaginative construction of our lived world. This process will 'annihilate the past Forms of Society' (*SR*, 3: V, p. 162).

But what will replace them? Of course, Carlyle cannot set out the emblems that may contain our lived world in the future.[13] It would be beyond sense – exorbitant – to do so. Instead, he leaves the reader looking forward to an undeterminable future, balanced between the attitudes of his two intermediaries: the sansculottist Teufelsdröckh, who refers to Napoleon and expects an 'old sick Society', once burnt down, to rise phoenix-like from its own ashes; and the editor, who 'restricted to the duty of Indicator', forebears to comment (*SR*, 3: v, p. 164). The only reassurance Carlyle can offer his reader is the religious mysticism of his chapter on Natural Supernaturalism,[14] where 'generation after generation' are envisioned, each adopting its own form of meaningful life, but with the presence of God, the supernatural 'lost Friend' conveyed in Nature (*SR*, 3: VIII, pp. 181–4).

NARRATIVE STYLE AND METAPHYSICS IN *THE FRENCH REVOLUTION*

Sartor Resartus's philosophy of clothes puts centre-stage the human need to form a lived world by imagination – alongside the human necessity to destroy the forms created in the past. It suggests that these processes are happening in history. But it cannot show us much of the historical route through them – though there are indications: the processes are advanced through specific human beings, it seems, and through the medium of metaphor.

The narrative of the *The French Revolution* places the historical process – at least up to the limits of what can be said about it – in a historical universe that matches that suggested by *Sartor*. The history unfolds within metaphysical chaos: 'Our whole Universe,' remarks Carlyle in a lengthy aside, 'is but an infinite complex of Forces' (*FR*, I, p. 407). The book shows the Revolution, by the power of imagination, destroying and recreating forms for human life. It does this by means of three related elements of style that will come as no surprise given the above analysis of *Sartor*: irony; referring to a multiplicity of narrative strands, characters, voices and points of view, and, finally, metaphorical structures integrating the whole.

Granted that many thousands of people were involved in the Revolution, it is nonetheless remarkable that Carlyle seems at times obsessed with gratuitously enumerating them. During the protracted death-bed scene of Louis XV, for example, he lists, with some irony, a string of noble personnages (complete with their sometimes risqué personal histories) whose lives are seemingly *not* involved in the event (*FR*, I, p. 5f.). When Carlyle does this, his narrator's voice may knowingly point out (though we are probably aware of it already) those who will have a place later in History: Napoleon studying in the Ecole Militaire next door to where Loménie Brienne struggles with the finances of state (*FR*, ɪ, p. 112), Madame de Staël glimpsed watching the Estates-General (*FR*, ɪ, p. 141), and so on. The Festival of the Federation offers a particularly rich occasion for the narrator to sweep, almost wearily, over the historical scene: so many Héberts, Henriots, Ronsins, Rossignols, let us, as long as possible, forebear speaking' (*FR*, ɪ, p. 321).

When embracing such a plethora of *dramatis personnae*, Carlyle's tone is often ironic. He seems to suggest, even as he does it, that he ought not to be telling us about these characters. This, I would argue, is the same rhetorical posture that we see in *Sartor*: ironically stating realities which it is impossible either to embrace or to ignore. In this case, the impossible is this world bursting with historical actors, where the events take place. As narrator, Carlyle is in amongst this bustling mass, frequently speaking directly to the historical participants, even sympathising with them, as a warm-hearted bystander might: 'poor Louis' (*FR*, ɪ, p. 300), 'poor Camille' (*FR*, ɪ, p. 143), 'Hapless de Brézé' (*FR*, ɪ, p. 174) and so on. Yet all these people are too much to take in: 'the Life-sea, or onlooking unnumbered Multitude' at the Festival, for example, which in the narrator's and reader's gaze 'is unfortunately all-too dim' (*FR*, ɪ, p. 141). John Holloway has argued that there is in Carlyle's writing style a vibrancy that suggests 'life in the universe'.[15]

The historical universe is also ungraspable because in it space and time appear fractured and overlaid upon themselves. In Carlyle's history, the narrative centre moves constantly. In the account of the king's ill-fated attempt to leave France (*FR*, ɪ, pp. 455–95), for example, the royal entourage, various nobles, the hussars, the national guard, and peasants living in far-flung hamlets pass and repass helter-skelter before our eyes. The lead-up to the battle of Longwi is a triumph of this type of narration. Republicans hasten to root out fifth-columnists. But we are concurrently made aware of the royalist armies, beyond the margin of each present scene, hastening towards France: 'Prussian Brunswick, "over a space of forty miles", with his war-tumbrils, and sleeping thunders . . . coming, coming!' (*FR*, ɪɪ, p. 132).

As regards time, Carlyle's narration is fractured by continual changes of time-frame. Individuals can be scattered confusingly across historical time. Brienne, for example, introduced in a comparison between *past* and present, is promised us for the *future*: 'Some twenty years ago . . . your Loménie Brienne (a rising man, whom we shall meet with yet) could . . . insist . . .' and so on (*FR*, ɪ, p. 39). Again, though the battle of Longwi is recounted in the present tense, the immediate next chapter, reports in the pluperfect how the politicians in Paris try to counter the danger (*FR*, II, p. 136). It seems that they were dreadfully out of step with events. Likewise, the threat of imminent battle is used to pull us sharply from contemplating the slow wave of mass rebellion: 'If indeed that dark living chaos of Ignorance and Hunger, five and twenty million strong, under your feet, – were to begin playing. /For the present, however, consider Longchamp' (*FR*, I, p. 50)

In short, Carlyle seems deliberately to confuse any sense of the present and the steady, linear movement of time. His doing so expresses his view of the metaphysics of history. History happens, he wrote in the essay 'On History', in a 'Chaos of Being' (*CME*, II, p. 172). The forces at work exceed any single one-directional, or 'successive' time-sequence of the kind that human beings experience in ordinary life.

He takes us, his readers, into the multiplex lines of action in this historical universe by addressing imperatives and questions on equal terms to us and to the historical participants. We are frequently enjoined to see, to imagine, to consider, even to 'glance into the interior' (of the Jacobin Club) (*FR*, I, p. 333). We are confronted with questions which place us on a par with people present at the scene being described: 'why do the citizens shut their shops?' we wonder, as the sansculottes prepare for the rebellion that will overturn the monarchy (*FR*, II, p. 86). Our inclusion may even become physical incorporation: Louis XV 'kisses the Dubarry hand; so we, from the anteroom, can note' (*FR*, I, p. 18). By speaking in the same terms to readers and participants, Carlyle embraces three categories of human as participants in the historical universe: literal participants, the writer and the readers. This can only expand the plethora of human life that I spoke of earlier.

It also provides a rich base for multiple points of view. Carlyle is able to move his narrative rapidly to different points between the narrow, immediate perception of individuals and what C. F. Harrold calls the 'synoptic view',[16] that overlooking an entire society. Yet, there is no privileged, authoritative level from which this universe can be viewed and understood. As H. M. Leicester has demonstrated, the book's final rhetorical strophe even integrates Carlyle himself into 'the continuing dialectic of historical process'.[17] Many of the book's rhetorical questions convey the lack of a privileged level to view historical events – except that of History as a whole, or the

Almighty. For they are often unanswerable at *any* level. Early on, we may smile at the courtiers as they ask themselves whether to administer the last rights to the dying Louis XV. But the questions soon get harder to answer: 'What to do with the Finances?' (*FR*, I, p. 48); or again, 'What are we to do? Surely to adopt healing measures; such as the magic of genius will unfold; such as, once sanctioned . . . all men must, with more or less reluctance, submit to' (*FR*, I, p. 73). We know this is a vain hope. The vanity of human enterprises is frequently to the fore in Carlyle's historical universe. Yet, as he comments on the first flight of a hot-air balloon (which took place in Paris as the state fell into crisis): 'What will mortals not attempt?' (*FR*, I, p. 53). Human endeavour surfaces, in spite of the bustling, fractured universe in which Carlyle's history takes place.

METAPHOR AND METAPHYSICS IN *THE FRENCH REVOLUTION*

Human endeavour does make sense in Carlyle's historical universe. Direction is insinuated into the welter of participants' actions by metaphor. This is so not only in the sense that metaphors can discreetly hold the story-telling together. As the clothes philosophy explained, it is by metaphors that the imagination of human beings gives meaningful form to their lives. So, in the same way, within Carlyle's historical universe, the metaphorical interpretation of human acts conveys the coherence they possess at the imaginative level.[18] We can trace the hidden direction of the Revolution through metaphors that thread their way through the text, going through transformations as they do so.

Take the metaphors for the diffuse but crucial body of participants: the people.[19] In Books 3–7 of the first part, evolution in the role of the people is indicated through water, fire and animal images. The people, for example, 'inundate' the courtyard of the conservative Old Regime Parlement (*FR*, I, p. 105 and p. 132). They flow from towns and villages in 'subsidiary rills' to form up into 'a very sea of men' around the opening of the Estates General: 'one vast suspended-billow of Life' (*FR*, I, p. 139). The image dovetails with Carlyle's description of that first meeting, which will begin the Old Regime's constitutional collapse, as the 'baptism day of Democracy' (*FR*, I, p. 139). Later, when the Bastille is stormed by the mob, 'the tide of men' swells, 'welling through every street' (*FR*, I, pp. 198–9). This metaphorical sequence carries on through the history: when the people bring the monarchy down on 10 August 1792, they are an *'ocean*-tide' (*FR*, II, p. 107; my emphasis) that leaves the legislature 'water-logged' (*FR*, II, pp. 97 and 118). The metaphor makes the people's evolution as natural and as comprehensible as the different forms and and effects of water.

With the passage of time, the character and actions of people and leaders is also manifested in the metaphor of fire. So long as he is alive, Mirabeau, under whom the wild multitudes 'move . . . as under the moon do billows of the sea' (*FR*, I, p. 131), speaks on behalf of the people's wish for progress. Carlyle describes him as a 'fiery fulginous mass' which 'has got *air*' after years of smouldering, and will now blaze 'heaven-high . . . for twenty-three months' and 'fill all France with flame'. The parallel from chemistry is clear: hot, combustible material had been prevented from igniting only because it had lacked sufficient oxygen until collapsing absolute power and widespread constitutional debate gave it the oxygen of opportunity.

Even as work on the doomed 1791 constitution gets underway, Carlyle lets us know of a greater, and perhaps more efficacious fire: in due course Sansculottism will take over and proceed more radically in an activity like that of smelting. It will smelt away the shallow forms hiding reality in contemporary society. (In terms recalling *Sartor*, Carlyle refers to the latter as mere 'buckram'.) Sansculottism 'will burn much; but what is not combustible, it will not burn' (*FR*, I, p. 223). Sure enough, when the mob intervenes to take the king from Versailles to Paris, 'Rage, which has brewed itself in twenty thousand hearts . . . has taken *fire*' (*FR*, I, p. 290). Like Mirabeau, the people had long had the potential to flare up; now the crisis would give them the oxygen for an historic, purifying process like that of fire.

Likewise, animal metaphors integrate the particularly paradoxical character and role of the people. Like a growing cat, it turns from 'the merriest' into 'the cruellest thing known' (*FR*, I, p. 305). Through animal metaphors, the relationship of authority to the people is progressively inverted. Louis XVI going to force through unpopular edicts in 1787 is hunting 'two-legged unfeathered game' (*FR*, I, p. 95). But, 'unhappily', wild horses are only provoked by the whip. So the narrator wonders what whip will serve 'when a team of Twenty-five Millions begins rearing' (*FR*, I, p. 97). Indeed, during the Estates-General elections, 'the whole People shakes itself' and awakes (*FR*, I,

p. 128). Its animal nature changes. Gathered around the Bastille, 'it brays', but then it also 'roars'. It becomes the 'enraged National Tiger' (*FR*, I, p. 191). When the storming of the Bastille is let loose, the people finally seems 'more ravenous than famished lions over dead prey' – an image which hints at that long suffering in silence suggested by the metaphor of smouldering fire. Finally, Carlyle turns to address the French populace as a whole, marking the point where they rise to take history into their own hands with an expression that unites fire and animal images: 'Roar with all your throats . . . ye sons of Liberty' (*FR*, I, p. 199).

The evolving nature and deeds of the people, then, are contained and rendered comprehensible by metaphors. But I am not just speaking of a skilful skein of images added by Carlyle to hold the narrative together or explain the processes by analogy. Recall that, according to the clothes philosophy, metaphors are the medium by which human imagination creates the lived world within the formless 'infinite', it therefore follows that metaphorical description can bring out in human action greater direction and meaning than is immediately apparent; angrily challenging enfeebled political values can tease out new, legitimate ones. Thoughtless destructiveness can be a training for a maturer grasp of political power. Some human deeds permit a metaphorical description with that effect.

This is what Carlyle has in mind when he refers to some acts as 'transcendent'. It is not merely a matter of appealing description or clearer causal explanation. Certain deeds properly possess an historical meaning beyond that which their agents are immediately aware of. Just such a deed can be disentangled from the seething action when the king is taken from Versailles to Paris: 'Transcendent things of all sorts, as in the general outburst of multitudinous Passion, are huddled together; the ludicrous, nay the ridiculous, with the horrible' (*FR*, I, pp. 292–3). The greater meaning of this tumult of immediate, individual deeds and emotions is that, without their necessarily grasping it, the crowd is challenging an entire order of precedence and power: 'For here all seems fallen asunder, in wide-yawning dislocation. The highest, as in down-rushing of a World, is come in contact with the lowest: the Rascality of France beleaguering the Royalty of France' (*FR*, I, p. 280). In that example, it is not clear what meaning the participants themselves attribute to their deeds. One must suppose that there are various meanings: some broad, political ones, but many others besides – and many of them unarticulated. There are cases where Carlyle also gives us his view of the meaning that the deeds have to the agents. For the crowd gathered when the Estates General are assembling, for example – on 'the baptism day of Democracy', as Carlyle describes it (*FR*, I, p. 139) – something special is happening, though they know not what. Why else, indeed, would they have thronged there? 'Rejoice nevertheless . . .' says Carlyle, having rehearsed the enormous future outcomes – good and bad – 'to you, from whom all this is hid, the glorious end of it is visible' (*FR*, I, p. 140).

In yet other cases, Carlyle indicates how the agents and other contemporaries attribute *different* meanings to the same deeds. When the Old Regime Parlement challenges the king's procedure for forcing through edicts (*FR*, I, pp. 87–8), the Parlement for its part is *re*interpreting its own past practices as void. To others it is saying, by default, that a different body is constitutionally necessary; namely, the Estates General, which the king now proceeds to summon. For the excited crowd gathered outside the court building, on the other hand, the Parlement is expressing a looser 'universal spirit of a Nation'.

It is all pretty confusing, of course. But in *Sartor Resartus*, Carlyle had already confronted this very confusion in the meaning of human life. And his manner of writing history has been crafted to accommodate it. Anticipating post-modernism, Carlyle conveys an historical universe full of *contending* meanings with no privileged position from which to say authoritatively : this is the one definitive direction that supervenes our actions.

HISTORY AND HUMAN ACTION

I have explained Carlyle's way of attributing to human action meanings beyond those which are immediately apparent. I should like also to defend it – though still resisting its idealism. It merely belongs to ordinary human interpretative practices. We often take deeds to indicate unwittingly more than they appear to mean to the doer, or at first sight to anyone. Turning up late may mean you do not really want to come at all. A man's opening the door for a woman may be a gesture of welcome or an attempt to put her in her place. My complementing my boss on his clothes may be taken as an impertinence challenging his superior status. In writing this, I may be showing that history can be understood, or that writing history is futile. It is quite normal that different meanings cluster around human acts: Carlyle's writing ingeniously partakes of this aspect of human existence.

To find the 'transcendent' in events in history is, likewise, not so far-fetched a proceeding as one might at first think. We are often happy to claim that 'in the light of subsequent events', such-and-such a deed marked some new stage of life – personal or social – or some new way of acting. I may go on to challenge my boss in committee meetings, or apply for a job over him. This essay may be a turning point: I may put the final full-stop to it and never write another word. As agents, our awareness of these long-term meanings varies. We may naively suppose we are doing nothing unusual; or feel that something is afoot, we know no what; or expect things to change, whilst being mistaken about how they do so; or foresee the future clearly. Perhaps the last of these is the least common; for there are many by-ways and unexpected outcomes in human enterprises.

What turns out to be the long-term meaning of our actions is not merely a function of subsequent events or of causal factors as yet hidden from us. The later meaning depends crucially upon how present action, and all the subsequent developments, are interpreted. In short, the meaning of the present is up for negotiation between participants and observers present and future. In writing history, Carlyle joins in this negotiation quite openly, imaginatively building the coherence and direction from the meanings that can be imaginatively attributed to actions.[20] Carlyle's clothes philosophy refers, on a global, historical level, to just this aspect of human action: the confused, and ambivalent meanings and outcomes, within which human imagination can somehow find purposeful intentions.

Confusion and uncertainty of outcome is never more to the fore than when established patterns are being broken down. Hence the Revolution, because of its comprehensive challenge to the social order, is the very apogee of unpredictable human action. But Carlyle can claim that, even though its future outcome is so profoundly unpredictable, this destruction has a sense. Challenging the validity of everything leads at least to one kind of outcome; namely, that the patterns that emerge are likely to be less vulnerable to challenge as false and hollow. Carlyle alludes to this prospect (alongside his metaphor of sansculottism smelting away what is false) when speaking of the ill-fated post-revolutionary constitution-writing. The process of challenge is what he calls:

the Death-Birth of a World. . . . Whereby, however, as we often say, shall one unspeakable blessing seem attainable. This, namely: that Man and his Life rest no more on hollowness and a Lie, but on solidity and some kind of Truth. Welcome the beggarliest truth, so it *be* one, in exchange for the royallest sham! Truth of any kind breeds ever new and better truth.   (*FR*, I, p. 223)

The Revolution's challenge to the inherited social order is a question posed to the present, in hope of an answer in the future. It is Carlyle's claim (which I support) that this is the character of much profound human action. 'And thus in perpetual abolition and reparation, rending and mending, with struggle and strife, with present evil, and the hope and effort towards future good, must the Constitution, *as all human things do*, build itself forward' (*FR*, I, p. 226; italics added).

When human action is up against such a level of doubt, hope must be a major component in its motivation. In that sense, Carlyle describes the Revolution as 'the Era of Hope', which will 'dawn on towards fulfilment' (*FR*, I, p. 55). 'Hope is but deferred; not abolished, not abolishable. It is very notable, and touching, how this same Hope does light onwards the French Nation through all its wild destinies. . . . Hope, though in the saddest sense, – when there is nothing left but Hope' (*FR*, I, p. 61). Again, we have here a widespread feature of human action – as Carlyle realises full well. Even when it incites only unrealisable possibilities, hope is generating human aspiration. It is, as Carlyle puts it, the 'sole boon of man: whereby, on his strait prison-walls, are painted beautiful far-stretching landscapes' (*FR*, I, p. 337). Though critical of the content of the Revolution's hopes, Carlyle explains them and acknowledges them as proper to the humans in history who cleave to them.

Man, as is well said, lives by faith; each generation has its own faith, more or less; and laughs at the faith of its predecessor, – most unwisely. Grant indeed that this faith in the Social Contract belongs to the stranger sort. . . . The world has perhaps seen few comparable to that.   (*FR*, I, p. 341)

Certainly, Carlyle's history of the French Revolution is profoundly hostile to much of the specifics of what the Revolution did. But I have chosen to put to one side much of its *content* in order to concentrate upon the *form* in which it conceives human action and human history. Against the reasoning of modern opponents of history with a grand narrative, Carlyle writes one. In his history, human beings are shown moving forward by their own creative efforts, even though neither they, nor anyone else could authoritatively specify their direction.

With the passage of time, Carlyle placed more and more emphasis on the need for charismatic, autocratic leadership, and thus became ever more cynical about the democratic aspirations of the Revolution. Yet, even in the 1840 lectures which expounded that theme to the full, he praises the form of the Revolution so as to suggest exactly the model of human historical action that I have explained and defended.[21] In spite of everything wrong with the Revolution, he says, 'we have to return to truth. Here is . . . a Truth clad in hellfire' (*H*, p. 200). For Carlyle, the Revolution continues to have a meaning beyond all the specifics and immediate outcomes. It was both a question and a statement. It was a question to all the contemporary forms created for human life and, like many questions, it could not anticipate what would answer would come. It was a statement 'testifying once more that Nature is *preter*natural; if not divine, then diabolic; that Semblance is not Reality; that it has to become Reality . . .' (*H*, p. 201).

The French Revolution: A History describes, with great subtlety and inventiveness of style, how human beings construct a dynamic reality in a teeming, fractured and dangerously meaningless historical universe. The aspiration to find such meaning should be a jewel within Carlyle's critical heritage.

NOTES

1. T. Carlyle, *The French Revolution: A History*, ed. K. J. Fielding and David Sorensen (Oxford University Press, 1989), hereafter referred to as *FR*, with page references given in the text.
2. T. Carlyle, 'On History', in *Critical and Miscellaneous Essays* (London: Chapman & Hall, 1870) vol. II, p. 173, hereafter referred to as *CME*, with essay titles and volume and page references given in the text.
3. For example, M. H. Abrams, *Natural Supernaturalism, Tradition and Revolution in Romantic Literature* (London: Oxford University Press, 1971); Harold Bloom (ed.), *Thomas Carlyle* (New York: Chelsea House, 1986). See also John P. Farrell, *Revolution as Tragedy: The Dilemma of the Moderate from Scott to Arnold* (Ithaca and London: Cornell University Press, 1980) for Carlyle's contribution to a nineteenth-century tragic vision of the Revolution.

4. See Albert Lavalley, *Carlyle and the Idea of the Modern* (New Haven, Conn.: Yale University Press, 1968); John Clubbe, 'Epic Heroes in *The French Revolution*', in Horst W. Drescher (ed.), *Thomas Carlyle, 1981* (Frankfurt: Peter Lang, 1983); John Clubbe, 'Carlyle as Epic Historian', in J. R. Kincaid and A. J. Kuhn (eds), *Victorian Literature and Society: Essays Presented to Richard D. Altick* (Columbus, Ohio: Ohio State University Press, 1985); John D. Rosenberg, *Carlyle and the Burden of History* (Oxford: Clarendon Press, 1985).

5. The epitome of this view can be found in Jean-François Lyotard, *La Condition postmoderne: Rapport sur le savoir* (Paris: Minuit, 1979); (published in translation as *The Postmodern Condition: A Report on Knowledge* (Manchester: Manchester University Press, 1984). Useful commentary appears in Steven Connor, *Postmodernist Culture: An Introduction to Theories of the Contemporary* (Oxford: Basil Blackwell, 1989), esp. ch. 1. For an accessible overview of the philosophical and political strategy of anti-foundationalism, see 'Lyotard and the Politics of Antifoundationalism', *Radical Philosophy*, no. 44 (1986) pp. 8–13.

6. Such an approach has distinguished antecedents. Harold Bloom, pursuing a similar line, cites Nietzsche's claim (in *Twilight of the Gods*) that Carlyle was an unacknowledged atheist (Bloom (ed.), *Thomas Carlyle*, p. 8).

7. John Holloway, *The Victorian Sage: Studies in Argument* (London: Macmillan, 1953); G. B. Tennyson, *'Sartor' called 'Resartus': The Genesis, Structure, and Style of Thomas Carlyle's First Major Work* (Princeton: Princeton University Press, 1965); Gerry H. Brookes, *The Rhetorical Form of Carlyle's 'Sartor Resartus'* (Los Angeles: University of California, 1972).

8. Fraser, the magazine's editor, to Carlyle, *Letters of Thomas Carlyle: 1826–1836* (London: Macmillan, 1888) vol. 2, p. 128.

9. T. Carlyle, *Sartor Resartus* (London: Chapman & Hall, 1891) book 1, ch. IV, pp. 21 and 22; hereafter referred to as *SR*, with book, chapter and page references given in the text.

10. Gerry H. Brookes, *The Rhetorical Form*: 'We see for a moment the consequences of belief and assess them for ourselves, for the speaker, and perhaps for all men' (pp. 181–2).

11. J. Derrida, *De La Grammatologie* (Paris: Minuit, 1967) ch. 2, esp. pp. 231–2.

12. Peter Allan Dale, *The Victorian Critic and the Idea of History: Carlyle, Arnold, Pater* (Cambridge, Mass.: Harvard University Press, 1977) p. 45 and see ch. 1.

13. The religious Carlyle also mistrusts man not to be obsessed by himself if freed from mystical wonder and obligation to a world that belongs to God. Hence his avoidance of humanistic prognoses after the manner of the Saint-Simonians (Tennyson, *'Sartor' called 'Resartus'*, pp. 319–26).

14. M. H. Abrams (*Natural Supernaturalism*) takes Carlyle's notion of natural supernaturalism as a cosmic vision providing a romantic solution to the problem of loss of religious faith. Harold Bloom (*Thomas Carlyle*, pp. 7–8) disputes that, historically speaking, it could in any case be a solution to the problem Abrams describe. However that may be, my own view is that the way the idea appears in *Sartor* means that – whatever Carlyle may wish – it cannot function as much more than a

safety net for the more significant apprehension about symbols in the philosophy of clothes.

15. J. Holloway, *The Victorian Sage*, ch. 2, esp. pp. 26–7.
16. C. F. Harrold, 'Carlyle's General Method in the *French Revolution*', *Proceedings of the Modern Language Association*, vol. 43 (1928), pp. 1150–69.
17. H. M. Leicester, 'The Dialectic of Romantic Historiography: Prospect and Retrospect in *The French Revolution*', *Victorian Studies*, vol. xv (September 1971) No. 1, pp. 5–17.
18. Following a somewhat similar analysis of Carlyle's style of history writing, Jonathan Arac has shown how Carlyle's synecdochic technique of social description and plotting influenced nineteenth-century novelists trying to encapsulate their complex new social world (*Commissioned Spirits: The Shaping of Social Motion in Dickens, Carlyle, Melville and Hawthorne* (New Brunswick, New Jersey: Rutgers University Press, 1979).
19. As Albert Lavally has argued (*Idea of the Modern*), not the least reason why Carlyle's epic history is so modern is that, this time around, it is the elemental titans, in the form of the Sansculottes, who win the battle with the gods.
20. This must not be taken to license open season for just any imaginative and metaphorical interpretation of historical actions that a historian might be moved to toss in. There are severe and subtle constraints upon our interpretations of human actions present and past – though they are hard to apply in a clear-cut authoritative fashion. The tendency to project one's own emotional state onto others, a common phenomenon in psychotherapy, is, if anything, greater with historical subjects, who are unable to disabuse us. I am grateful to Ludmilla Jordanova for this point.
21. The lectures appeared in T. Carlyle, *Heroes, Hero Worship and the Heroic in History* (London: Chapman & Hall, 1841 and 1904); hereafter referred to as H, with page references given in the text. Philip Rosenberg in *The Seventh Hero: Thomas Carlyle and the Theory of Radical Activism* (Cambridge, Mass.: Harvard University Press, 1974) has suggestively reinterpreted the theory Carlyle expounded in these lectures. According to Rosenberg, Carlyle holds men to be heroes only where they speak for a unstated, wished-for hero: the people. Hence, notwithstanding the rightist political posture Carlyle apparently adopted, 'the heroic readiness of the masses makes the existence of the hero, as authoritative leader of others, in an important sense irrelevant' (p. 202).

3

Matthew Arnold: The Discourse of Criticism

GRAHAM HOLDERNESS

In the history of criticism Matthew Arnold stands as a central and substantial figure, largely responsible for the establishing of that discipline of 'English', the transformation of which is contemporary literary theory's acknowledged mission. Prior to this identification of Arnold as a master-strategist in the formation of a hegemonic cultural discourse, his critical work had been acknowledged and celebrated as a seminal influence by another architect of modern criticism, F. R. Leavis. Leavis' key statement, published in 1938, took the form of a polemical response to T. S. Eliot's evaluation of Arnold as a precursor of 1890s Aestheticism. The changing fortunes of Matthew Arnold's reputation, visibly mutating as it passes through the hands of so many key figures in 'the British Critical Tradition', clearly deserves a more sustained examination.

What provoked Leavis's intervention was Eliot's essay 'Arnold and Pater', published in 1930.[1] The linking of these two critics in a single title will probably seem to a contemporary reader something of an eccentricity. What connection could there be between Matthew Arnold, the critic who defined art as a 'criticism of life'[2] and Walter Pater, the aesthete who valued 'art for its own sake'?[3] Expressing a magisterial condescension for the intellectual powers of both critics, Eliot's comparative evaluation consisted mainly of an anti-rationalist, anti-humanist polemic against Arnold, from which Pater emerges as, if anything, more consistent and honest in his pursuit of virtually the same cause. Arnold's partially covert attempt to substitute something called Culture for religion was, in Eliot's view, precisely paralleled by Pater's Aestheticism, which openly proposed to replace Christianity with a secular religion of 'art for its own sake'.

The twinning of Arnold and Pater was however strenuously challenged by Eliot's much more influential disciple F. R. Leavis. Leavis' essay 'Arnold as Critic' (1938)[4] set out to rescue Arnold from this damning association. Here Arnold is reconstructed as a seminal figure in the evolution of a modern humanist criticism, a model instance of that strategic combination of moral fervour, intense sensibility and analytical power espoused by Leavis and his followers. Pater, on the other hand, is dismissed by Leavis as scarcely worth consideration, as the exponent of a deviant trend away from the true purposes of criticism's normative mission.

Eliot's case was not simply that Arnold espoused all the wrong ideas (the right ideas being of course, by implication, those of a modern right-wing Anglo-Catholic Royalist), but that he was not in the true sense of the vocation really a critic. Arnold was, Eliot asserted, 'rather a propagandist for criticism than a critic':[5] an influential ideologue rather than an interpreter whose critical practice could assist criticism with its various tasks and responsibilities. Leavis took exception to this latter charge, arguing (albeit extremely weakly) that Arnold's critical method was as important as his ideological stance. Arnold, in Leavis' view, accompanied an espousal of the correct ideas (a rational humanism based on a secularised winning of Christian ethics from Christian theology) with evidence of 'taste' and 'sensitivity' thus so leading to the successful practice of an effective critical method.

In contemporary post-structuralist criticism Arnold is recognised as a key figure in the establishment of 'Literature' as an academic discipline and as a pedagogic practice, and he is seen as a continuing influence over its enormous cultural and ethical pretensions. In Terry Eagleton's *The Function of Criticism*,[6] Arnold appears as a key figure in the later nineteenth-century attempt to negotiate, through the role of 'man of letters', the destructive contradiction between a residual confidence in the classical 'public sphere' established in the Augustan period, and the new forces of intellectual specialisation, the free-market commodification of culture and the growth and relative rise of the proletariat.

Eliot's doubts about the relations between theory and practice in Arnold's criticism have not, despite the intensity and power of this debate, been resolved. The question seems to me of more than historical interest to modern criticism, since it parallels the ambiguous relations between 'ideological' and 'formalist' critical practices visible in such theoretical controversies as the struggles of the 1920s between Marxism and Formalism in the USSR, the clash of historical and sociological forms of analysis with the New Criticism in the

1950s, and contemporary debates – both within progressive criticism itself, and between an embattled body of traditionalist criticism angrily counter-attacking a newly-confident and strongly professionalised array of feminist, new historicist and psychoanalytic critical methodologies.

Arnold's importance as a 'propagandist for criticism' is unquestionable. Many key terms of modern theoretical debate – the organisation of 'Literature' as an academic discipline, the existence of literary criticism and theory as a separate branch of that discipline, the relations within the discipline between different levels of the educational system, the relations between academic scholarship and various projects for popularising culture outwards from an academic centre are all foreshadowed in Arnold's work. If there is a 'British Critical Tradition', rather than a discontinuous series of ideological interventions into an uneven and contradictory process of socio-cultural development, then Arnold is obviously central to it.

His mark is visibly inscribed on such important cultural/educational interventions as the 1921 *Report on the Teaching of English in England* (the 'Newbolt Report'),[7] and on no less an organ of critical politics than *Scrutiny* itself. These two examples in some ways typify the Arnoldian influence in their attempt to mediate between upperclass scholarship and academic criticism, the mission of civilising the middle classes through university teaching, and the project of incorporating the proletarian masses by 'Literature' teaching in schools. This characteristic strategy of mediating elite academic possession with popular incorporation can be traced back to the fact that Arnold's own critical and theoretical essays co-exist with his reports on elementary schooling; the Newbolt Committee's aim was explicitly propounded as that of connecting different levels of class and culture by means of literature in education; and at times *Scrutiny* gave as much attention to educational practice as to textual criticism and literary theory (and indeed it was in schools that the Leavisite influence proved strongest and most enduring).

Throughout Arnold's writings we can find this concatenation of literary polemic, cultural theory, and the concept of literary training as a means of civilising the uneducated and promoting solidarity between social classes.

> Literature . . . is a powerful agency for benefiting the world and for civilising it . . . Civilisation is the humanisation of man in society.[8]

I am sure that the study of portions of the best English authors, and composition, might with advantage be made a part of their regular course of instruction to a much greater degree than it is at present. Such a training would tend to elevate and humanise a number of young men, who at present, notwithstanding the vast amount of raw information which they have amassed, are wholly uncultivated; and it would have the great social advantage of tending to bring them into intellectual sympathy with the educated of the upper classes.[9]

'Literature' then consists of 'the best English authors'. The purpose of teaching literature is to 'elevate' and 'humanise' those who read it. The effects of the process should be visible in the form of a new climate of social sympathy between classes. The inter-dependence between the various terms of the project clarifies the ultimately *political* significance of Arnold's literary theory and cultural philosophy. Is 'Literature' an agreed, self-evident totality of works and authors; or was the totality created to serve the specific ideological purpose of their mobilisation? By what means is this apparently consensual body of culture, defined elsewhere as 'the best that has been thought and said in the world'[10] to be transmitted to the 'uncultivated': by a process of democratic exchange, or simply by imposing a given product upon the passive sensibilities of the uneducated, so that the process of 'elevating' and 'humanising' is a one-way process of raising the uncivilised to the standard of the educated elite?

In Arnold's theory literature is given a new centrality, ranking in importance higher than the philosophy and ethics which also constituted, for him, the staple necessities of a humane education. The centrality of literature (here redefined as 'poetry') is connected with the decline of religion, which requires a new body of humane belief to replace its erstwhile functions:

The future of poetry is immense, because in poetry, where it is worthy of its high destinies, our race, as time goes on, will find an ever surer and surer stay. There is not a creed which is not shaken, not an accredited dogma which is not shown to be questionable, not a received tradition which does not threaten to dissolve. Our religion has materialised itself in the fact; it has attached its emotion to the fact, and now the fact is failing it. But for poetry the idea is everything; the rest is a world of illusion, of divine illusion.

Poetry attaches its emotion to the idea; the idea *is* the fact.   (*SP*, p. 238)

This concern with a perceived need on the part of 'our race' to find some substitute for its decaying religion – a body of cultural practice which will provide both an ethical system, a philosophical attitude, and an emotional consolation – is central to Arnold's theory of literature. 'More and more mankind will discover that we have to turn to poetry to interpret life for us, to console us, to sustain us' (*SP*, p. 238). Within the given cultural conditions of a Britain confronting severe internal tensions in its push towards imperial dominance, such a body of 'poetry' would of course have to be a *national* literature. The essay in which these propositions were offered first appeared in 1880 as a preface to T. H. Ward's edition of *The English Poets*. 'Literature' for Arnold offered the possibility of an ethical system which could be shared as a common property like a national religion or a standard national language; a system which could disseminate its values through an educational system, as Christianity had disseminated its values through the state church; a system which would operate, like religion, emotionally as well as intellectually, requiring complete acceptance, administering total conviction, to the communicant subject.

What though were the possibilities for constructing a coherent ethical system out of that diversified body of writings known as 'Literature'? For a start Arnold narrows down the focus of the concept literature to exclude an enormous amount of what it even now contains, such as the novel (Arnold found in Tolstoy's *Anna Karenina* no art, only a bare 'criticism of life')[11] and modern stage drama. Even with the general concept itself has been narrowed down to 'poetry', the diversified nature of the texts contained even within this selective definition seem to problematise the construction of an ethical system; poetry can, after all, be immoral (Burns), politically tendentious or radical (Milton), or even just dirty (Chaucer).

'Poetry' says Arnold in this central text 'is a criticism of life under the conditions fixed for such a criticism by the laws of poetic truth and poetic beauty' (*SP*, p. 240). That phrase, with its attempt to relate the moralistic function of criticism to the formal methods of its operation, is a crucial strategic move in Arnold's critical practice. While gesturing towards aesthetic considerations, it clears the way for a further narrowing of the canon to exclude inappropriate material on formal as well as ethical grounds. In general, the construction of a body of 'poetry' appropriate to the purposes of this theoretical project involved rigorous procedures of selection, conducted by the most arbitrary criteria ever employed in any theory of literature, Arnold's notorious 'touchstones' (*SP*, p. 242). Short passages, a few lines in length, abstracted from their contexts in Homer, Dante, Shakespeare, Milton, are quoted and offered to the reader as self-evidently, in aesthetic and moral terms, valuable. In each touchstone 'we' (an unspecified constituency of like-minded readers) are obliged to recognise an 'accent' of beauty and 'high seriousness'. Only the best literature can be effective as an agency of general moral improvement and 'civilisation': the evaluation of 'touchstones' is the means by which 'we' recognise what is 'the best'.

The 'touchstones' offered by Arnold, being single lines or de-contextualised short passages of verse, display in quotation their formal properties of style, manner, diction, rhythm more obviously than they convey any intelligible 'criticism of life'. Precisely what body of moral, philosophical or intellectual wisdom is conveyed by juxtaposing a line from Dante which embodies a central meta-physical statement, a description of sleep from Shakespeare's *Henry IV*, a line from Hamlet's dying speech to Horatio, and a defiant speech of Milton's Satan? If these passages do not demonstrate what Arnold calls 'criticism of life', then they must demonstrate 'poetic truth and poetic beauty' (*SP*, p. 243). But the relation between poetic form and ideological power remains undemonstrated. This lacuna of argument is confirmed by Arnold's discussion of Chaucer. Chaucer displays a 'sound representation of things', which has 'truth of substance'; and his verse has formal qualities that may be celebrated: the 'divine liquidness of diction', 'divine fluidity of movement' (characteristics Arnold also finds in Spenser, Shakespeare, Milton and Keats) (*SP*, pp. 243–4). But he is not up there with the true greats: he cannot stand comparison with Dante, Shakespeare, Milton. What he lacks is a new term introduced into the argument at this point: he lacks the 'accent of high seriousness' (*SP*, p. 245). Again Arnold attempts in a single phrase to reconcile the diverse theoretical elements of his critical polemic: 'high seriousness', the quality of a moralistic 'criticism of life', is known through the 'accent' of the poetry, a matter of linguistic organisation.

Leavis seized on this passage to defend Arnold against Eliot's accusation that he had no method of 'critical practice', that he was a critical propagandist rather than a practising critic. Arnold's assertion that the qualities of the 'best' literature could be known and identified by a sensitive reading of poetic 'accent' was of course exactly Leavis's own critical theory: "Absolute sincerity", a quality belonging to the "inmost soul" and manifested in an accent, an "accent that we feel if our sense is quick" – this phrasing, in the context, seems to be suggestive in a wholly creditable and profitable way."[12] Leavis defends even the 'touchstone' method as a useful critical 'tip': a 'tip for mobilising our sensibility; for focusing our relevant experience in a sensitive point; for reminding us vividly of what the best is like'.[13] In the context of a counter-polemic against Eliot, such a defence is intelligible: and certainly the theoretical vocabulary deployed here by Arnold – cultural standards, poetic 'sincerity' manifested in a poetic accent recognisable by the 'sensitive' reader – became in turn that of Leavis himself. The element of the comparison that is lacking from Arnold can be suggested by Leavis's use of terms such as 'mobilising' and 'focusing', the quasi-scientific language of analytical method inherited from I. A. Richards, which made the practice of strenuous, detailed textual explication an essential cornerstone of the *Scrutiny* critical method. In Arnold there is no evidence of such verbal analysis: in the practice of his criticism the terms denoting the moral and formal elements of poetry which he struggled so hard to unite – 'criticism of life' and 'laws of poetic truth and poetic beauty'; the quality of 'high seriousness' and its poetic 'accent' – separate and confront one another virtually as antinomies. The assertion of particular judgements through persuasive tone and constructed consensus ('we' men of 'taste') stands unsupported by any demonstration from the formal properties of literary texts. In formalistic terms, Arnold never advanced beyond the circular aestheticism of Keats' Grecian urn: that which is true is also beautiful; that which is beautiful must needs be true.

Eliot's case against Arnold can thus be seen to contain substantial elements of truth, obscured by the stridently ideological cast of Eliot's own perspective and the restoration job on Arnold's reputation ably performed by Leavis. Arnold clearly was a 'high theoretician' of literature rather than a practising critic. He had (unlike Johnson or Coleridge) no critical method. His particular judgements are underpinned by nothing more substantial than an attenuated legacy of Romantic sentiment, approaching very close to a bland appreciation of 'the beautiful'. Since his judgements could not be demonstrated by textual analysis in the methodological manner of later criticism (including the instances of Eliot and Leavis) they could only be enforced by a coercive rhetoric of 'standards', 'sensibility' and 'taste'.

Both the procedures of selection and their implicit rationale conceal themselves admirably in the feline rhetoric of Arnold's persuasive discourse. Selection masquerades as an activity in which the sensitive and intelligent reader empirically 'recognises' the internal qualities of certain passages of literature as manifesting 'criticism of life' conducted at an appropriate level of 'high seriousness'. In practice of course such a method would, if seriously followed, produce an utter anarchy of competing valuations, an extreme arbitrariness of 'judgement' and 'taste'. But Arnold is not expounding a scientific method; rather he is composing a mode of discourse with a particular persuasive and coercive purpose. The urbane, civilised tone of his prose invites complicity, assent; to dissent would be somehow bad-mannered, or worse, would display the vulgarity of one's own deficiencies of taste. Judgements of value such as those contained in Arnold's criticism are persuasive, not demonstrative; they plead for acceptance, and find their way into literature courses constructed by those who aspire towards Arnold's civilised urbanity.

In *Culture and Anarchy* (1867) Arnold displayed clearly how he conceived the directly *political* bearing of his cultural interventions: 'culture' was the only alternative he could see to unacceptable social change ('anarchy'). The enormous social responsibility being conferred by this theory on literature seems bizarre until this project is located within the specific ideological conjuncture of this historical 'moment'. The task addressed by *Culture and Anarchy* was nothing less than that undertaken in other European nations by the growth of secular social sciences. As Perry Anderson has demonstrated,[14] Britain experienced a peculiar cultural deformation in the late nineteenth century in that it failed to produce a classical sociology as an intellectual counter to Marxism, and to the radical and revolutionary movements analysed in, and inspired by Marxism. Without a native Marxist or bourgeois science of society, British culture experienced an unusual absence which various intellectual disciplines attempted to fill. The theory that 'Literature' as constituted by these ideological operations could effectively stand at the centre of a 'civilisation', however strange such an idea may now seem, took shape in these conditions, and was transmitted to the twentieth century as a potent ideological force.

NOTES

1. T. S. Eliot, 'Arnold and Pater', in *Selected Essays* (London: Faber and Faber, 1951) pp. 431–43.
2. M. Arnold, 'The Study of Poetry', in *Essays in Criticism First and Second Series* (London: Dent, 1964); hereafter referred to as *SP*, with page references given in the text.
3. W. Pater, *The Renaissance* (London: Collins, 1961) p. 224.
4. F. R. Leavis, 'Arnold as Critic', in F. R. Leavis (ed.), *A Selection from Scrutiny.* (Cambridge: Cambridge University Press, 1968) vol. 1, pp. 258–67.
5. T. S. Eliot, *The Sacred Wood* (London: Methuen, 1920) p. 1.
6. T. Eagleton, *The Function of Criticism* (London: Verso, 1984) pp. 60–7.
7. *The Teaching of English in England: Report of the Departmental Committee Appointed by the Board of Education to Enquire into the Position of English in the Educational System of England* (London: HMSO, 1921).
8. M. Arnold, 'Preface' to *Mixed Essays* (London: Smith, Elder, 1879) p. vi.
9. M. Arnold, 'General Report for the year 1852', in Sir F. Sanford (ed.), *Reports on Elementary Schools* (1852–82) (London: Macmillan, 1889) pp. 19-20.
10. M. Arnold, 'The Function of Criticism at the Present Time', in P. Keating (ed.), *The Victorian Prophets: A Reader from Carlyle to Wells* (London: Fontana, 1981) p. 196.
11. M. Arnold, 'Count Leo Tolstoi', *Essays in Criticism*, p. 362.
12. Leavis, 'Arnold as Critic', pp. 264–5.
13. Ibid., p. 265.
14. P. Anderson, 'Components of the National Culture', *New Left Review*, 56 (1968) pp. 50–6.

4

Samuel Butler: The First Post-Structuralist?

ROSS STEWART

It is curious how contemporary Samuel Butler (1835–1902) has become, how post-modern he now seems, not only in his autobiographical fiction, *Erewhon* and *The Way of All Flesh*,[1] but also in his homely theorising about the authorship of the *Odyssey* and Shakespeare's sonnets and his polemics contra Darwin, especially the first, *Life and Habit*.[2] Butler had boldly prophesied his literary immortality as his just reward for contumely and neglect, private and public. Indeed, he devoted the last two decades of his life to crafting his literary personality for posterity, touching up his memoirs and notebooks, adopting eccentric opinions and affecting conspicuously regular habits, and hiring Henry Festing Jones to keep a record of his sayings and doings. Jones it was who launched Butler towards immortality with the posthumous publication of *The Way of All Flesh* (1903), followed by his memoir of Butler (1919) and *The Notebooks* (1925).[3]

That Butler should have come to life beyond the grave whilst his more eminent contemporaries sink into ever deeper oblivion derives only in part from the calculated simplicity of his prose style, Augustan in its clarity and epigrammatic balance, antithetical to Victorian grandiloquence. He also gave Victorian public spiritedness short shrift, seeking to subvert rather than improve society, flaunting his own waywardness and egoism. His self-obsession in *The Notebooks* is monstrous – nothing that touches him in any way is too insignificant for him to record and annotate at length. The high-minded ideals of self-transcendence, which the Victorians pursued, have faded into obscurity as Butler's inquiry into the problematic relation between one's conflicting selves and reality has not. Butler's pretensions were on the grand scale of the giants of his age but by setting himself against the current of the times and riding his own hobby horses he never acquired the voice, the decision, the portentousness required by fame. An eminent Victorian had to sound confident of the reality of the self and the world, assured of the greatness of empire, and mindful of the gravity of merely parochial issues. Butler, though bumptious and overbearing of manner, grew less and less certain of anything. His religious faith survived Cambridge but died in London soon after he came down. Next he doubted reason, which 'betrays men into drawing hard and fast lines and to the defining by language, which rears and then scorches' (*E*, pp. 163–5). Like Hume and the sceptics who came before him, and Derrida and the post-structuralists who have come after, Butler wrote in order to question whether language ever can refer to anything other than itself. Concluding that 'contradiction in terms is the natural end of all propositions',[4] he devoted himself to disclosing the aporia or blind spots in the discourses of others and himself.[5] Writing with a beleagured uncertainty and bewildering indeterminacy, he resorted to subtle irony which constantly undermines whatever the ideology of his age compelled him to affirm.

Labelled 'man of one book' – *Erewhon* (1872) or 'Erewhon' Butler, as distinct from 'Hudibras' Butler (no relation), he squirmed: the collected works run to twenty volumes and are sufficiently varied that he should have escaped any single label. During his lifetime doubt was even cast on his authorship of *Erewhon*. His closest friend in the decade it took him to write the novel had been Charles Pauli, one of whose friends declared that he must have written it. This Pauli denied. 'You talked to him', the friend persisted, to which Pauli retorted, 'I have been a great deal with you, but you never wrote *Erewhon*'.[6] Droll, facetious, impudent, Pauli's wit was identical to Butler's; even if he didn't write *Erewhon*, he did make recommendations for chapters. In the dedication to *Life and Habit* of 1877 Butler thanked Pauli for his friendship and his 'invaluable criticism'. 'Pauli shaped me more than any man I have ever known',[7] he acknowledged, praising him as 'the only honest schoolmaster' for teaching him to see through the cant of the age.[8] Butler used to borrow or impersonate the identities of his friends and his method of composition was collaborative: 'I note what they say, think it over, adapt it and give it permanent form' (*NSB*, p. 364). In *Life and Habit* Butler has disclosed, under the guide of evolutionary theory, how he would come under the sway of another will, live vicariously through the other, and through successful mimicry emerge eventually as a replica of the original. Thus Pauli's friend was half right: as author of

Erewhon, Butler was decentred. The book's charm lies in its 'giddying uncertainty', in its open plurality in which a free play of signs could take place 'without fault, without truth, without origin'.[9]

It is ironic, therefore, that when the Edwardians exhumed Butler, they should have trumpeted him as the London superman and champion of the will. Ignoring deeper uncertainties, they took at face value the airtight personality he had fabricated from words in his later works. When Butler wrote, 'my books are me much more than anything else' (*FE*, p. 171), the Edwardians perceived an admirable authority and strength of personality. In fact, as when he asserted that 'the true life of anyone . . . is the life they live in the hearts of others' (*FE*, p. 306), Butler was trying to imply both that we adopt different personalities in each of our relationships with others and that the stable image we thus project is a necessary compensation for the fragmentation, dispersal or lack of identity we feel. He opposed the phonocentric tradition of western thought: his self was a purely linguistic construction; like Foucault, he detained the reader at the surface of his text so that he should not seek an origin or transcendental subject. In his manners, Butler imitated the swell, or elegant Victorian gentleman, whose 'good breeding, health, looks, temper and fortune' (*NSB*, p. 26) guaranteed a mechanical perfection and consigned the question of essence or inner life to obsolescence. In the 1860s Butler referred to the swell and *Origin of Species* as his gospels, ironically, as both were purely materialistic. Insofar as he rejected the romantic idealisation of the ego – a 'person' being 'nothing but a persona or mask' (*FE*, p. 64), 'capable of being created anew and directed according to the pleasure of the possessor' (*E*, p. 106) – he was existentialist. In contending that 'everything both is and is not, there is no such thing as a strict identity between any two things in any two consecutive seconds',[10] Butler, like Lacan, represents the self as a matrix of subject positions, the locus of a series of random and discontinuous attitudes. For Butler, as for Derrida, the integrity of the present moment is an illusion, since it is a structure dependent upon the past and future and thus as much absent as present. And yet, in his declining years, Butler, like Sartre's inauthentic waiter, lived for an image of himself. In *The Way of all Flesh*, Ernest Pontifex, like an existentialist, throws off 'the self of which you are conscious, your reasoning and reflecting self' (*WF*, p. 131) in order to act freely in response to his impulses. However, when a legacy makes him independent, he becomes a slave to his wardrobe and lives for the admiration and envy of society. One may account for his inconsistency by referring to Butler's panegyric on 'that crowning glory of human invention whereby we can be blind and see at one and the same moment' and 'not believe or mean things' which we 'profess to regard as indisputable' (*E*, p. 103). As de Man suggested, critics' moments of greatest insight are paradoxically their moments of greatest blindness. By contradicting himself, Butler reminds us that no author is perfect master of his language, that he is aware of the gulf between the enunciating 'I' and the 'I' as subject of the enunciation, and that he in his discourse is merely a grammatical construct written by the mind of the reader.

Quietist and vitalist, sceptic and pantheist, egoist and nihilist, solipsist and altruist, Dr Jekyl and Mr Hyde, Butler was a battle-ground where the psychomachia of late Victorian ideologies was fought. In his world, since 'our highest "is" is still only a very strong "may be" ' (*FE*, p. 84) and nothing is ever absolutely anything (*FE*, p. 277), opposites change places, merge and cancel each other out. His meaning is the spin-off of a potentially endless play of signifiers, with each signifier having many signifieds, where there is a constant sliding of the signified beneath the signifier and meaning constantly fades and evaporates. In *Erewhon*, by playing off opposites against one another, Butler suspends himself in the web of language and achieves a sceptical imperturbability. In his notebooks, chiasmus enabled him to qualify whatever he proposed in such a way that his statements contain a purely linguistic value, without external reference.[11] For him, 'ideas and feelings were expedient' and 'bore no necessary relation to the reality of things'.[12] 'Nothing,' he argued 'can be more unlike a stone than the idea of stones that exists in our minds . . . we know nothing whatever about the thing itself apart from our ideas about it'.[13] Writing was not mimetic but pathological, a struggle for equanimity through the adjustment of pressures and the release of energy within the mind. Language does not reach beyond itself.

Nevertheless, Butler did take on the orthodoxies of his age – Darwin, the church, Mrs Grundy and Oxbridge boasting that he was the *enfant terrible* of Literature and Science. Edmund Wilson accuses Butler of having failed to 'outgrow' being the 'bad boy' of pious parents, his 'father's rages and his mother's prayers' having inhibited his 'mental processes', causing him always to write with 'something of the sulkiness of the adolescent child'.[14] Butler's memoir of his parents is a morass of violent and contradictory feelings – constant 'fear and mistrust' of his father, the better man who had 'ambushed and wounded' him, while he himself was 'an unknown irrepressible force' striking terror into his father and every other authority figure (*B*, pp. 42 and 43). Barthes, in a discussion of the French symbolists applicable to Butler, suggests that when objects and events in the real world become lifeless and alienated, it is possible to put history 'into brackets', 'suspend the referent', and take on words as objects and events instead.[15] Writing turns in on itself narcissistically but remains troubled by the social guilt of its own uselessness. When history becomes 'terroristic' and the writer an outcast, writing becomes a way in which the tyranny of structural meaning could be momentarily ruptured and dislocated by a free play of language; and the writing/reading subject could be released from the straitjacket of a single identity into an ecstatically diffused self. The text, Barthes announces, 'is that uninhibited person who shows his behind to the Political Father' and thus suspends his guilt.[16] So Butler's polemics are alternately belligerent and defensive, cranky and pedantic, iconoclastic and conservative.

Having read *Origin of Species* shortly after publication (1859), Butler wrote admiringly to Darwin and submitted brilliant articles on the implications of the theory of evolution to *The Press* in Christchurch. Butler had emigrated to New Zealand under a cloud after refusing to take holy orders. Darwin's theory helped him to justify his apostasy and mitigated his guilt; he looked in Darwin for a surrogate father. *The Fair Haven*[17] (1875), Butler's second novel, an over-elaborated Swiftian satire, reveals how thoroughly Butler had rationalised his upbringing in order to explain and justify his conduct. It imputes blame to his father for beating him and thus alienating him from his true nature, destroying his respect for any figure of authority and rendering him incapable of faith. In an evocative scene, his hero in his boyhood shares a bedroom with a hypocritical, evangelical woman guest to his home. Feigning sleep, he watches her undress, and the discrepancy between her naked body and her pretty clothes is a revelation of hypocrisy which convinces him that the world 'was hollow, made up of sham and delusions, full of sound and fury, signifying nothing' (*FH*, p. 7). Butler adopts multiple narrators, the primary one unreliable, and exposes the discontinuities in their points of view, to dramatise the shattering effect upon the personality of such a shocking disillusionment. 'I had to steal my birthright' he complained elsewhere, 'I stole it and was bitterly punished. But I saved my soul alive' (*NSB*, p. 181). The savageness of that struggle is manifest in his crude attacks on Christianity. He incorporates into *The Fair Haven* a pamphlet he had published in 1865. In it he had argued cynically that Christ had survived the crucifixion but that unscrupulous priests had faked a miracle in order to exploit the timorousness and credulity of a backward people and thus establish a new religion and secure their own futures materially. He repeated that argument in his last work, *Erewhon Revisited*.[18] Once disillusioned, Butler had to point out in every book that there is no transcendental signifier and that representation is always a fallacy. Wittgenstein suggests that all sceptics begin like Butler by making the mistake of expecting language to relate directly to objects and ideas and then losing faith in everything when they learn it does not. However, to identify the common origins of scepticism is not to deny the creativity of its deconstruction of systems of thought.

Inevitably Butler lost faith in Darwin and from 1877 onward he attacked his theories and character. He came to resent the 'fulsome adulation lavished on Darwin'[19] by a 'powerful coterie' and 'unscrupulous and self-seeking clique' whom he accused of plagiarism and vilification (*NSB*, p. 369). Beneath Darwin's alleged mask of modesty and self-effacing simplicity, he detected ambition, aggression, bullying. When evolution became dogma as blindly accepted as religion, Butler was outraged: 'With everyone except men of science the fact that we have no certain absolute knowledge *va sans dire*' ('Life and Habit: II', *CE*, 1, p. 116). He argued that 'everything addressed to human minds at all must be more or less a compromise', such as the dot and the line, 'which we cannot conceive and which can have no existence', although with them we can draw up 'the laws whereby the earth can alone by measured and the orbits of the planets determined' (*FH*, p. 49). 'All classification,' he added in another context, 'is found to be arbitrary – to depend on our sense of our own convenience, and not on any inherent distinction in the nature of things themselves. Strictly speaking, there is only one thing and one action. The universe or God, and the action of the universe itself'.[20] Butler distrusted empiricism: 'Facts remain even now much at the mercy of the imagination' (*FE*, p. 281); since we see what we want to see, objectivity is impossible: 'Nothing is at all, except in so far as thinking has made it so' (*FE*, p. 281). He never worked inductively; he trusted intuition and supported his arguments allusively and analogically. Deconstruction follows a similar procedure to the same end. Nietzsche argues that philosophers establish their truth about the world by effacing their metaphors, or figurative discourse, which brought it into being, while Derrida tries to 'undo the idea that reason can somehow dispense with language and arrive at a pure, self-authenticating truth or method'.[21] Butler shares these doubts about language and truth, but Derrida's terms are more specialised and precise: 'writing is the endless displacement of meaning which both governs language and places it forever beyond the reach of stable, self-authenticating knowledge'.[22] What Butler calls the universe is, for the deconstructionist, language – 'a sprawling limitless web where none of the elements is absolutely definable'.[23]

Life and Habit, a satiric, witty and self-parodic book ostensibly about science, opens with an onslaught on empiricism – 'we have no really profound knowledge upon any subject . . . till we have left off feeling conscious of the possession of such knowledge' – personal identity – 'from the moment we become conscious of existing, it is an easy matter to begin doubting whether we exist at all' (*LH*, p. 18) – and belief – 'from the attempt to prove the existence of God to the denial of that existence altogether, the path is easy' (*LH*, p. 19)..All that one actually knows is incapable of 'logical treatment'; it is unconscious, manifested in 'instinctive actions' (*LH*, p. 25). Through a series of gigantic illogical leaps Butler hits upon the theory of instinct as unconscious memory to explain the immanence of will as the agent of evolution. Faith, need and desire are the trinity of drives necessary for the evolution of the amoeba, for example, into the elephant. We can only know or do what we want, need and believe we can do. How seriously Butler intended his theory to be taken, other than as a critique of Darwinism, cannot be determined. Certainly, his trinity is ironic, poking fun at Christianity and himself. Perhaps like Buffon, whose subtle irony he so admired, Butler was winking at the discerning reader who would be aware that our ideas are metaphoric and arbitrary, rather than representational.

Butler flirted with pantheism, panpsychism, the protoplasmic theory and vitalism. He did not shy away from the term 'God':

> As to what God is, beyond the fact that he is the Spirit and the Life which creates, governs, and upholds all living things, I can say nothing. I cannot pretend that I can show any more than others have done in what the Spirit and the Life consists. . . . I cannot show the connection between the consciousness and the will, and the organ, much less can I tear away the veil from the face of God, to show wherein will and consciousness consist. ('God the Known and God the Unknown', *CE*, vol. 1, pp. 11–12)

Whenever he preaches, Butler generates an ironic undercurrent of doubt as to whether he is in jest or earnest. Note above how the initial affirmation collapses under qualifications and reservations. From the pulpit Butler invariably undermines the known with the unknowable:

> we are only component atoms of a single compound creature, LIFE, which . . . has only come to be what it is, by the same sort of process as that by which any human art or manufacture is developed, i.e. through constantly doing the same thing over and over again, beginning from something which is barely recognizable as faith . . . and growing till it is first conscious of effort . . . and finally so powerful and so charged with memory as to be without all self-consciousness. . . . No conjecture can be made as to how the smallest particle of matter became so imbued with faith that it must be considered as the beginning of LIFE, or as to what such faith is, except that it is the very essence of all things and has no foundation.   (*LH*, p. 43)

Humanity is a bud on the tree of life, and there are bodies within bodies, trees upon trees, and worlds within and upon worlds: 'What we call life is part of the universal life of the deity – which is literally made manifest to us in flesh that can be seen and handled – ever changing, but the same yesterday, and today, and forever.'[24] The precious tone and the transparent anthropomorphic metaphors make the reader wonder whether Butler might not be deconstructing his own argument.

The source of Butler's knowledge is the impressionism of the stoics:

> Shall we see God . . . embodied in all living forms; as dwelling in them; as being that power in them whereby they have learnt to fashion themselves . . . to make itself not only a microcosm . . . but a little written history of the universe . . . into the bargain. From everlasting . . . invisible . . . imperishable . . . omniscient and omnipotent   (*EON*, pp. 27–8)

The bargain metaphor injects a note of bathos to deflate the rhetoric in the passage above. Here, incense and organ music create an ironic smokescreen: 'When the note of life is struck, the harmonics of death are sounded, and so, again, to strike death is to arouse the infinite harmonics of life that rise forthwith as incense curling upwards from a censer' (*LC*, pp. 58–9). Butler is not conjuring up a vision of the afterlife, but quibbling and blurring distinctions between life and death. In a lecture on 'How to Make the Best of Life' (1895), he declared the question unanswerable and then proceeded to explain how to make the best of death. In his sermons, he raises religious issues only to sidestep or scoff at them. A master of the *reductio ad absurdum*, he even set out to prove, by systematically depreciating consciousness, that inorganic matter is no less alive than the organic and fully awake. One must conclude, therefore, that his god was a juggle with words, a metaphor for the unknowable and inexplicable. 'Perfect invulnerable truth is beyond the grasp of reason or the expression in language' ('Life and Habit: II', *CE*, vol. 1, p. 139).

The extreme conservatism underlying avant garde deconstruction is well documented.[25] This deconstructionist theory, with its denial of a reality outside language, excludes itself from politics and justifies a single-minded pursuit of paradox. Butler was also compromised, the pettiness and regularity of his habits and the mercenary basis of his relations with others contradicting the far-reaching and liberal implications of his writing. At times he seemed to indulge in power worship and he certainly defended in bad faith positions he had demolished dialectically in his youth: having despised his grandfather and exposed him as a bully and hypocrite, he recanted and composed a memoir that is hagiographic. Butler's work on the *Odyssey* is more hopeful: he tries to subvert orthodox criticism by reducing the epic to his own homely scale, thus implying that all criticism is inherently subjective. Similarly, in theorising about the story behind and within Shakespeare's sonnets, he writes about the development of his own friendship with Pauli. Like a post-structuralist, he lets his discourse take precedence over the text he is supposedly investigating and again suggests that language is self-enclosed. In *Ex Voto* he celebrates the 'robust unconsciousness'[26] of Tabachetti and the neglected and anonymous artists who decorated the churches of northern Italy with their statues and paintings. This was Butler's way of debunking Victorian hero worship. Obscure himself, he resented the suggestion that certain 'geniuses' had access to a metaphysical presence denied ordinary mortals.

From a synchronic perspective, Butler's scepticism about the self and the referentiality of language differs little from the postmodernists. Historically, however, his hopes and fears, his obsessions and his idiom identify Butler as a Victorian undergoing the crisis of faith and experiencing the spiritual anguish peculiar to the age. Religious doubt tends not to bother the post-modernist; his anxieties are apt to be social and economic in origin, rather than existential or spiritual; brought up on Freud and Lacan, he can accommodate the plurality of his selves and possibly even enjoy the conflict of his competing identities. What may be fundamental and energising for the post-modern proved sadly harrowing and stultifying, in the end, for Butler. Having started by claiming Butler as a contemporary, I must conclude by accepting and admitting his difference as a Victorian.

NOTES

1. S. Butler, *Erewhon or Over the Range* (London and New York: Shrewsbury Edition, 1923); hereafter referred to as *E*, with page references given in the text. *The Way of All Flesh* (London and New York: Shrewsbury Edition, 1925); hereafter referred to as *WF*, with page references given in the text.
2. S. Butler, *Life and Habit* (London and New York: Shrewsbury Edition, 1923); hereafter referred to as *LH*, with page references given in the text.
3. H. F. Jones, *Samuel Butler, The Author of Erewhon*, 1835–1902: A Memoir (London: Macmillan, 1919) 2 vols. *The Notebooks of Samuel Butler*, with a new introduction by P. N. Furbank (London: Hogarth Press, 1985); hereafter referred to as *NSB*, with page references given in the text.
4. S. Butler, 'Life and Habit: ɪɪ', in *Collected Essays, 1* (London and New York: Shrewsbury Edition, 1925) pp. 104–86; hereafter referred to as *CE*, with volume number, essay-title and page references given in the text.
5. J. Culler discusses aporia in his account of 'Jacques Derrida', in J. Sturrock (ed.), *Structuralism and Since* (Oxford and New York: Oxford University Press, 1979) pp. 154–80.
6. A. T. Bartholomew (ed.), *Butleriana* (London: Nonesuch Press, 1932) p. 75; hereafter referred to as *B*, with page references given in the text.
7. G. Keynes and B. Hill (eds.), *Samuel Butler's Notebooks* (London: Jonathan Cape, 1951) p. 109.
8. A. T. Bartholomew, *Further Extracts from the Notebooks of Samuel Butler* (London: Jonathan Cape, 1934) p. 116; hereafter referred to as *FE*, with page references given in the text.
9. C. Norris, *Deconstruction: Theory and Practice* (London and New York: Methuen, 1982) pp. 114 and 59.
10. S. Butler, 'The Deadlock in Darwinism', in R. A. Stretfield (ed.), *The Humour of Homer and Other Essays* (London: Fifield, 1913) p. 291.
11. See R. Norrman, *Samuel Butler and the Meaning of Chiasmus* (London: Macmillan, 1986).

12. E. H. Turner, *Between Science and Religion* (New Haven and London: Yale University Press, 1974) pp. 164 and 200.
13. S. Butler, 'On the Genesis of Feeling', in *Collected Essays, 1* (London and New York: Shrewsbury Edition, 1925) pp. 187–217 and p. 202.
14. E. Wilson, *The Triple Thinkers* (New York, 1952) pp. 210–11.
15. R. Barthes cited in T. Eagleton, *Literary Theory: An Introduction* (Oxford: Basil Blackwell, 1983) p. 140.
16. Ibid., pp. 140–1.
17. S. Butler, *The Fair Haven* (London and New York: Shrewsbury Edition, 1923); hereafter referred to as *FH*, with page references given in the text.
18. S. Butler, *Erewhon Revisited* (London and New York: Shrewsbury Edition, 1925).
19. S. Butler, *Luck or Cunning as the Main Means of Organic Modification* (London: Jonathan Cape, 1922) p 224; hereafter referred to as *LC*, with page references given in text.
20. S. Butler, *Unconscious Memory* (London: Fifield, 1920) p. 181.
21. C. Norris, *Deconstruction*, p. 19.
22. Ibid., p. 29.
23. Eagleton, *Literary Theory*, p. 129.
24. S. Butler, *Evolution Old and New; or The Theories of Buffon, Dr Erasmus Darwin, and Lamarck, as Compared with that of Charles Darwin* (London: Fifield, 1911) p. 404; hereafter referred to as *EON*, with page references given in the text.
25. See, for example, Eagleton, *Literary Theory*, p. 145.
26. S. Butler, *Ex Voto* (London and New York: Shrewsbury Edition, 1923) p. 5.

5

Oscar Wilde and Reader-Response Criticism

B. J. MOORE-GILBERT

While his reputation as a dramatist has been steady, and interest in his life and personality has grown, Wilde the aesthetic theorist has remained a marginal figure within literary criticism. The dominant figures of the mainstream tradition have usually paid the critical positions generated by 'aestheticism' only grudging attention. In an essay on Baudelaire Eliot recognised that it was 'a doctrine which did affect criticism and appreciation',[1] and in *The Use of Poetry and the Use of Criticism*, he admitted that at least it contained 'a recognition of the error of the poet's trying to do other people's work'.[2] But Eliot's more typical disapproval of his 'aestheticist' forebears is registered in 'The Function of Criticism' which evidently alludes to Wilde's 'The Critic as Artist' in arguing that 'you cannot fuse creation with criticism as you can fuse criticism with creation'.[3] *The Use of Poetry* counterbalanced its faint praise for 'art for art's sake' by constructing it as a confusion of literature with mysticism and rejecting its separation of art and the world as 'a hopeless admission of irresponsibility'.[4]

As so often, when Eliot sneezed other critics caught a cold and the later mainstream tradition constituted itself as such partly by continuing to deny much validity to the aesthetic theory of figures like Wilde and Pater. In a series of essays from the 1930s to the 1950s, including 'Arnold as Critic', 'Arnold and Pater' and 'James as Critic', F. R. Leavis decried its effects and implications. In America, the New Criticism was equally hostile. Of particular relevance is Wimsatt and Beardsley's seminal essay of 1949, 'The Affective Fallacy, which denigrated the preoccupation of critics like Wilde along with the subjective response in reading:

> The Affective Fallacy is a confusion between the poem and its *results*. . . . It begins by trying to derive the standard of criticism from the psychological effects of the poem and ends in impressionism and relativism. The outcome . . . is that the poem itself, as an object of specifically critical judgement, tends to disappear.[5]

Not enough has been done in more recent times, especially within Britain, to reappraise Wilde's status as a critic. The MLA bibliography since 1963 includes barely a handful of articles on Wilde's criticism by British writers and recent overviews of the history of 'English Studies', such as Chris Baldick's *The Social Mission of English Criticism* (1983) or Brian Doyle's *English and Englishness* (1989), which between them contain four citations of Wilde, confirm the continuing marginalisation of his critical work.

Wilde's rehabilitation would be difficult to accomplish from within the traditional discourse of British criticism, quite apart from the problem that the body of his work may not be substantial enough, in the eyes of many, to qualify him for the status of a major critic. Firstly there seems good reason why traditional criticism, with its commitment to defining a role for itself as a social institution, should have been suspicious of Wilde. Wilde lampooned Arnold's project for an Academy, contending that criticism's social function is confined to refining the sensibilities of 'the elect', who are encouraged, according to *The Picture of Dorian Gray*, to cultivate 'the great aristocratic art of doing absolutely nothing'.[6] His claim that art should not involve itself in political and social questions (while obviously in itself a political position) means that a vast range of literature, most notably the Victorian novel, should not be considered as achievement of the first rank. At worst, Wilde's essays substantiate Eliot's charge of irresponsibility, as when Gilbert, in 'The Critic as Artist', celebrates art as a means to 'shield ourselves from the sordid perils of actual existence'.[7] Clearly, it is not in these aspects of Wilde's aesthetic theory that his 'radical potential' is to be sought.

But precisely because 'English Studies', as traditionally conceived, has come under such pressure from continental criticism since the 1960s, Wilde is now able to re-emerge as a critic worthy of serious attention. At the same time, this revolutionary body of theory has tended to be ignorant of the degree to which its ideas are adumbrated in the suppressed voices of the British tradition. While there are important analogies between some of Wilde's arguments and those of both deconstruction and contemporary psychoanalytic criticism, this essay will concentrate on the substantial links between Wilde and those critics in both Europe and America responsible for the emergence of 'reader-response' or 'reception' theory.

These labels are, of course, for the convenience of literary historians and the critics involved are sufficiently diverse to make detailed elaboration of the variety of their interests and approaches impossible in an essay of this length. Instead, Wilde will be reconsidered in terms of the summary provided by Elizabeth Freund in her recent overview of the development these theories, *The Return of the Reader.*

> In one mode or another, the swerve to the reader assumes that our relationship to reality (and the art object) is not a positive knowledge but a hermeneutic construct, that all perception is already an act of interpretation, that the notion of a 'text-in-itself' is empty, that a poem cannot be understood in isolation from its results, and that subject and object are indivisibly bound. By refocusing attention on the reader, reader-response criticism attempts to grapple with questions generally ignored by schools of criticism which teach us how to read; questions such as *why* do we read and what are the deepest sources of our engagement with literature? What does reading have to do with the life of the psyche, or the imagination, or our linguistic habits? What happens - consciously or unconsciously, cognitively or psychologically – during the reading process? Reader-response criticism probes the practical or theoretical consequences of the event of reading by further asking what the relationship is between the private and the public, or how and where meaning is made, authenticated and authorised, or why readers agree or disagree about their interpretations. In doing so it ventures to reconceptualize the terms of the text-reader interaction.[8]

Wilde, oddly, has been completely ignored by historians of 'reader-response' theory. Both Freund and Jane Tompkins, in *Reader-Response Criticism*, locate the origins of this critical tendency in the work of I. A. Richards. Freund finds in Richards 'an astonishing juncture of germinal (but also aborted) lines of inquiry' which later theories of reading have attempted to pursue.[9] If the same can be shown to be true of Wilde, it will help establish that he has a more important role in the history of British criticism than that merely of *provocateur* and that his criticism perhaps has a radical potential obscured by the misleading account of Wilde provided by the mainstream British critical tradition.

Like many later 'reader-response' theorists, Wilde initially manoeuvres the 'swerve to the reader' by reassessing a number of contexts through which art has traditionally been understood and valued and which have been responsible for underestimating the part played by the reader in constructing the meaning of the text. In order to 'liberate' the reader, Wilde sets himself the task of undermining successively the instrumental, mimetic and expressive theories of art. It is further important to consider Wilde's revaluation of these three theories because of the analogies his dialogues construct between the critical and creative acts. 'The Critic as Artist' argues thus: 'The critic occupies the same relation to the work of art that he criticises as the artist does to the visible world of form and colour, or the unseen world of passion and of thought (*CW*, p. 871).

In one sense, of course, concern for the reader is as old as aesthetic theory itself, as the discussion of Plato in 'The Critic as Artist' acknowledges. But the long tradition of criticism, which asserts the instrumental potential of the arts (to change society or 'improve' the reader), usually constructs the reader as something to be acted upon, rather than acting, in the process of reading. Wilde constantly attempts to challenge the secondary position this places the reader in *vis-à-vis* author and text. 'The Critic as Artist' flatly rejects the subordination of aesthetic values to pragmatic moral and political concerns and condemns 'those baser forms of sensual or didactic art that seek to excite to action of evil or of good' (*CW*, p. 884). The conviction that aesthetics 'are higher than ethics' (*CW*, p. 897) underlies the famous epigram in *Dorian Gray*: 'There is no such thing as a moral or an immoral book. Books are well written or badly written. That is all' (*DG*, p. 5).

Gilbert's argument involves a reversal of the traditional hierarchy of form and content proposed by critics like Arnold, whose view of the beneficial role to be played by culture rested ultimately upon a belief that it embodied the values to facilitate social renewal. If aesthetics are higher than ethics, artist and critic must be far more alive to questions of form than content. In 'The Decay of Lying', Vivian asserts that 'those who do not love Beauty more than Truth never know the inmost shrine of Art' (*CW*, p. 842). He adduces a number of cases to support his thesis. Dickens, Charles Reade and

George Eliot are all attacked for their efforts to present accurate pictures of contemporary society. This is dismissed as a 'foolish attempt to be modern, to draw public attention to the state of our convict prisons and the management of our private lunatic asylums' (*CW*, p. 830). Realism, for Wilde, continually subordinates form to content for moral or political ends. Instead, Vivian declares: 'To art's subject matter we should be more or less indifferent' (*CW*, p. 830). By liberating literature from the duty to instruct, Wilde also liberates the reader from limiting him/herself to absorbing the 'message' of art, thus broadening the range of response which can legitimately be brought to the text.

Wilde's assault on the mimetic theory of art is partly motivated by its limited focus upon the relationship between the text and the world, an equation which usually ignores the reader, or limits his/her role to appreciating the art-work in terms of its approximation to an external world. Wilde begins by rejecting mainstream conceptions of the nature of language. Whereas one often has the impression in Arnold's writing that the poet first has ideas and subsequently finds words suitable to express those ideas, Gilbert insists, in 'The Critic as Artist', that language is 'the parent, and not the child, of thought (*CW*, p. 868). Content is, therefore, necessarily dependent upon expression rather than being prior to it. Art, then, is constructive and productive, not simply imitative. Gilbert argues thus at the end of the essay:

> Form is everything. It is the secret of life. Find expression for a sorrow, and it will become dear to you. Find expression for a joy, and you intensify its ecstasy. Do you wish to love? Use Love's Litany and the words will create the yearning from which the world fancies they spring. (*CW*, p. 893)

Far from art having to imitate reality and thus be in some sense secondary to it, the world created by art is in fact prior to the natural one. What one sees and values in nature, according to 'The Decay of Lying' is dependent upon cultural conditioning in which exposure to art plays a crucial part: 'Nature is no great mother who has borne us. She is our creation. It is in our brain that she quickens to life. Things are because we see them, and what we see and how we see it, depends on the Arts that have influenced us' (*CW*, p. 838). Culture therefore determines how we see nature and form embodies conventions which make knowledge of the world possible.

This textualisation of Nature – 'The Critic as Artist' refers to it as a 'Book' (*CW*, p. 898) – exposes the 'natural' as a cultural construct, a point elaborated upon in the discussion of a number of 'nature' artists. Cyril's discussion of Wordsworth rejects the common belief that the poet was inspired by the natural world: 'Wordsworth went to the lakes, but he was never a lake poet. He found in stones the sermons he had already hidden there. He went moralising about the district, but his good work was produced when he returned, not to Nature but to poetry' (*CW*, p. 831). The painter Whistler made the fogs on the Thames visible by constructing them out of artistic forms and convention. 'At present, people see fogs, not because there are fogs, but because poets and painters have taught them the mysterious loveliness of such effects' (*CW*, p. 838).

Art is not only prior, but superior to Nature. Its superiority lies partly in its greater capacity for creativity and synthesis than nature: 'She has flowers that no forest knows of, birds that no woodland possesses' (*CW*, p. 835). Moreover, according to Vivian, the perfection realisable in art reveals all of Nature's defects, 'her curious crudities, her extraordinary monotony, her absolutely unfinished condition' (*CW*, p. 825). It is this defectiveness which underlies the apparently outrageous claim that 'Nature, no less than life, is an imitation of art' (*CW*, p. 838). Wilde demonstrates this through the way that culture (including elements like fashion) shapes those exposed to it. Victorian women thus began to imitate the image of women constructed by the Pre-Raphaelites and Dorian Gray's admirers aped his style. According to Vivian, art cannot develop by attempting a faithful reproduction of external reality: 'All bad art comes from returning to Life and Nature and elevating them to ideals' (*CW*, p. 843). Rather, the artist progresses 'by the imitation of the best models' (*CW*, p. 827).

The third element in Wilde's 'swerve to the reader' involves an attack upon expressive theories of art, and is designed to undermine the traditional inferiority of the reader in the author-reader hierarchy. Wilde begins by rejecting the theory that reading is a re-creation of the opinions or sensibility of a being superior in depth and range of feeling and perception to the reader, versions of which are to be found in the work of mainstream critics as diverse as Arnold and Richards. As Lord Henry waspishly remarks in *Dorian Gray*, 'a man can paint like Velasquez and yet be as dull as possible' (*DG*, p. 235).

Instead, art impersonalises the author's subjective feeling by giving it forms (for instance rhyme and rhythm), which derive from and

return to the public domain, and mediate it through the *social* institution of language. Basil Hallward learns of the essential impersonality of art in *Dorian Gray*. Initially fearful of allowing his portrait of
Dorian to be publicly displayed because he feels it reveals too much
of himself as a private individual, Basil comes to accept Lord Henry's argument that there is no danger of this. He explains his change
of heart to Dorian: 'Art is always more abstract than we fancy. Form
and colour tell us of form and colour – that is all. It often seems to me
that art conceals the artist far more completely than it ever reveals
him' (*DG*, p. 129). While in inception Hamlet and Romeo may have
expressed elements of Shakespeare's nature, once given concrete
form they are independent of their creator. There is thus 'no such
thing as Shakespeare's Hamlet' (*CW*, p. 878). 'The Decay of Lying'
argues that Hamlet's theory of mimesis 'no more represents Shakespeare's real views upon art than the speeches of Iago represent his
real views upon morals' (*CW*, p. 835). Part of Wilde's hostility to
nineteenth-century art derives from his sense that it tries to promote
a cult of the artist's personality. As Basil complains in *Dorian Gray*:
'We live in an age when men treat art as if it were meant to be a mode
of autobiography' (*DG*, p. 182).

But the argument of 'The Critic as Artist' that the 'opinions, the
character, the achievements of the man, matter very little' in estimat-
ing his work (*CW*, p. 857), involves a more fundamental attack on the
traditions of biographical criticism emanating from the Romantic
period. Gilbert's assertion that criticism 'does not confine itself . . . to
discovering the real intention of the artist and accepting that as final'
(*CW*, p. 873), is premised upon the argument that the finished work
has 'an independent life of its own, and may deliver a message far
other than that which was put into its lips to say' (*CW*, p. 874). This
desire to liberate the reader from simply reconstructing the author's
intention as a means to understand and evaluate the work of art is
perhaps the first articulation of the modern period's perception of
the damaging results of 'the intentional fallacy'.

The next stage of Wilde's attempt to free the reader from the
subordinate position in which s/he is placed by traditional theories
of art proceeds through an insistence upon the crucial role of criticism in cultural life. Wilde concurs with several mainstream arguments in this respect. 'The Critic as Artist' cites the authority of
Arnold for its proposition that criticism is an essential precondition
of creativity (*CW*, p. 895). According to Gilbert, 'no one who does not
possess this critical faculty can create anything at all in art' (*CW*,

p. 866). The essay cogently argues that it is the critical faculty which recognises when a particular style has outlived its usefulness and which then invents fresh forms. The preservation and transmission of culture, moreover, 'can be made by the critical spirit alone, and indeed may be said to be one with it' (*CW*, p. 884).

But far from seeing the critical faculty as inferior to the creative one, as Arnold finally does, Gilbert argues that 'Criticism is really creative in the highest sense of the word' (*CW*, p. 871). Indeed it is in some respects 'more creative than creation' (*CW*, p. 898). Gilbert sees the nineteenth century as a watershed in civilisation not because of its artistic achievements, but because of its critical advances. In particular, he specifies the work of Darwin and Renan, 'the one the critic of the Book of Nature, the other the critic of the books of God' (*CW*, p. 898). It is criticism, then, which is responsible for the contemporary revolution in human thought and Gilbert concludes thus: 'Creation is always behind the age. It is criticism that leads it' (*CW*, p. 898).

'The Critic as Artist' suggests three principal ways in which criticism can be seen as creative. Firstly, it argues that since the work of art cannot speak about itself, it is reliant upon criticism to speak for it. Thus criticism 'reveals to us a secret of which, in truth, [the work of art] knows nothing' (*CW*, p. 873). The work of art, furthermore, 'whispers of a thousand different things which were not present in the mind of the artist' (*CW*, p. 874). Moreover, the very qualities which enable artists to create, according to Gilbert, disable them from understanding their work in a critical sense. He cites the mutual misunderstandings of the Romantic poets to substantiate his claim that the 'very concentration of vision that makes a man an artist, limits by its sheer intensity his faculty of appreciation' (*CW*, p. 894).

Secondly, as has been seen, criticism stands in the same relation to the art-work as the art-work to the world. Criticism, then, 'works with materials, and puts them into a form that is at once new and delightful. What more can one say of poetry?' (*CW*, p. 872). Contemporary art-criticism is one example adduced by Wilde to argue his case. 'Pen, Pencil and Poison' praises Wainewright as 'one of the first to develop what has been called the art-literature of the nineteenth century, that form of literature which has found in Mr Ruskin and Mr Browning its two most perfect exponents' (*CW*, p. 848). 'The Critic as Artist' cites the work of Pater, which according to Gilbert 'treats the work of art simply as a starting-point for a new creation' and by 'its equal beauty' comes to stand as a new work of art in its own right (*CW*, p. 873). Indeed, Gilbert estimates Ruskin's criticism as being, in certain respects, greater than the painting of Turner which inspired it.

Wilde's own practice bears out his argument that criticism should be as creative as art itself. Following Pater, who theorised under 'the fanciful guise of fiction' (*CW*, p. 888), his ideas are aestheticised in the form of a novel, *Dorian Gray* and in pieces like 'The Decay of Lying', which are as close to drama as the essay form. In his blurring of the distinction between creative and critical discourse, Wilde anticipates certain tendencies in post-structuralist thinking. Gilbert's suggestion that criticism will escape its traditionally subordinate, secondary role to creative writing prefigures the euphoric claim of Josué Harari's anthology *Textual Strategies*, which asserts that 'criticism has reached a state of maturity where it is now openly challenging the primacy of literature. Criticism has become an independent operation that is primary in the production of texts.'[10]

Thirdly, and perhaps most radically, Gilbert insists on the 'incompleteness' (*CW*, p. 875) of the text prior to the reader's response to it. Criticism, in his opinion, 'fills with wonder a form which the artist may have left void, or not understood, or understood incompletely' (*CW*, p. 874). The choice of Aristotle's *Treatise on Poetry* to illustrate his thesis is particularly apposite since it consists of 'notes dotted down for an art lecture, or of isolated fragments destined for some larger book' (*CW*, p. 864). Gilbert's critique synthetically draws the fragments into a 'richer unity' (*CW*, p. 875) than exists in the original, by expanding the 'notes' into something more coherent. Wilde consistently conceives of the text as essentially fragmentary. Thus Pater's work is represented as a 'mosaic' and Browning has the 'incompleteness of the Titan' (*CW*, p. 859). It is in the act of criticism 'that Art becomes complete' (*CW*, p. 875). In this respect, Wilde anticipates the continental 'reader-response' theory associated with figures like Ingarden and Iser, who see the author's text as interrupted by 'spots of indeterminacy', 'gaps' and 'blanks', which must be resolved, filled in or 'concretised' by the reader before the text has meaning.

But while Wilde insists that criticism can create a 'richer unity' in the work of art, there is no suggestion that the reader can complete it in the sense of imposing some final coherence. In this respect only 'music is the perfect type of art. Music can never reveal its ultimate secret' (*CW*, p. 875). Wilde's perception of the polysemic nature of art divides him sharply from mainstream critics like Arnold and further anticipates recent continental theory. But Wilde's sense of the irreducibly plural, contradictory and diffuse meaning of the text takes him further than some contemporary 'reader-response' theorists who suppose that an organic whole will emerge once the process of 'concretisation' has taken place. Thus Gilbert alludes to the 'thousand different things' that *Tannhauser* speaks to him of and concludes: 'Beauty has as many meanings as man has moods' (*CW*, p. 874). Understanding is a literally endless process because of the intertextual nature of art. For example, to appreciate the literature of the nineteenth century, 'one must realise every century that has preceded it and that has contributed to its making' (*CW*, p. 883).

Nor can the hermeneutic circle be completed by reference to a coherent, self-contained subjectivity in the reader which is capable of a complete response to the text. Like Dorian Gray, Wilde seems to 'wonder at the shallow psychology of those who conceive the Ego in man as a thing simple, permanent, reliable, and of one essence. To him, man was a being with myriad lives and myriad sensations, a complex, multiform creature that bore within itself strange legacies of thought and passion' (*DG*, p. 159). Wilde's textualisation of the reader explodes the idea of a unifying subjectivity in a manner which anticipates the argument of Roland Barthes in *S/Z*: 'This "I" which approaches the text is already itself a plurality of other texts, of codes which are infinite or, more precisely whose origins are lost.'[11]

Given these premises, it is inevitable that Wilde's conception of critical practice differs radically from the mainstream, particularly as represented by Arnold. In the dialogues, Arnold's normative critical values and procedures are seen as essentially moral and 'the critic should be able to recognise that the sphere of Art and the sphere of Ethics are absolutely distinct and separate' (*CW*, p. 889). Wilde is particularly hostile to the supreme virtue of disinterestedness favoured by Arnold, which involves an attempt to suppress the subjective response which the dialogues see as crucial to the critical act: '[The] more strongly this personality enters into the interpretation, the more real the interpretation becomes, the more satisfying, the more convincing, and the more true' (*CW*, p. 877). Gilbert is convinced that it is a fallacy to expect the reader, as Arnold does, to be able to approach the text with an 'open' mind which is truly objective or innocent. In this respect, 'The Critic as Artist' foreshadows Gadamer's rehabilitation of prejudice in *Truth and Method* (1975), where it is seen as a crucial precondition of understanding and, indeed, a primary means of articulating critical response.

The critical dialogues proceed to demolish the secondary critical virtues proposed by Arnold to ensure criticism's 'disinterestedness'. The Wildean critic has no reason to be sincere, at least according to Lord Henry in *Dorian Gray*. He argues that 'the probabilities are that the more insincere the man is, the more purely intellectual will the idea be' (*DG*, p. 15). In order to achieve a genuinely free play of the mind, the critic needs constantly to find 'fresh points of view' (*CW*, p. 889), a process best encouraged by adopting positions one does not necessarily believe in. 'The Critic as Artist' derides, both as critical value and discursive voice, the 'sweet reasonableness' promoted by Arnold: 'For Art, as Plato saw . . . creates in listener and spectator a form of divine madness' (*CW*, p. 889). With criticism and art liberated from the duty to instruct, 'high seriousness' ceases to be a major priority. One of the delights of Wilde's essays is their witty, teasing tone, as in Gilbert's comment that 'Meredith is a prose Browning and so is Browning' (*CW*, p. 860), or Vivian's barb that *Robert Elsmere* 'is simply Arnold's *Literature and Dogma* with the literature left out' (*CW*, p. 829).

In both form and argument, the dialogues also reject the univocal, self-consistent discourse of mainstream criticism. 'The Truth of Masks' concludes thus: 'Not that I agree with everything that I have said in this essay. There is much with which I entirely disagree. The essay simply represents an artistic standpoint, and in aesthetic criticism attitude is everything' (*CW*, p. 913). In 'The Decay of Lying', Vivian is equally teasing: 'Like Emerson, I write over the door of my library the word "Whim"' (*CW*, p. 826). The deconstructive tendency embodied in the form of dialogues is also celebrated in *Dorian Gray*, where Erskine advances paradox as 'the way of truth. To test Reality, we must see it on the tight-rope. When the Verities become acrobats, we can judge them' (*DG*, p. 48).

But perhaps the most radical aspect of Wilde's rejection of mainstream practice is his argument for the necessity of critical misreading, which foreshadows the contemporary theory of 'misprision', most powerfully argued in Harold Bloom's *The Anxiety of Influence* (1973). Far from trying to see the object as in itself it really is, as critics from Arnold to Leavis have insisted is the critic's duty, 'The Critic as Artist' claims that criticism 'need not necessarily bear any obvious resemblance to the thing it criticises' (*CW*, p. 874).

Instead, Gilbert encourages the reader to recreate the object and put it into 'a form that is at once new and delightful . . . No ignoble considerations of probability . . . affect it ever' (*CW*, p. 872). Gilbert rejects the basic premises of orthodox criticism when he goes on to argue that it is not incumbent upon the critic to help his audience understand a given work of art, but 'rather to deepen its mystery, to raise round it and round its maker, that mist of wonder which is dear to both gods and worshippers alike' (*CW*, p. 876). In a sense, Wilde seems to be ascribing to good criticism the quality of 'ostranenie' which the Russian formalists valued in literature – the capacity to estrange the onlooker from the object being represented, in order to allow it to be seen anew.

The pre-eminent place given to the reader's involvement in constructing the meaning of the text governs Wilde's system of hierarchies in evaluating the arts. Within this scheme, those art-forms which limit the reader's imaginative response are valued least. As has been seen, music is ranked high because its meaning is always indefinite. But 'the ultimate art is literature, and the finest and fullest medium that of words' (*CW*, p. 888). The more 'realistic' an art-form is, the lower it is placed in the scale. Literary realists, for instance, are 'far too intelligible . . . they do not stir the imagination, but set definite bounds to it' (*CW*, pp. 874–5).

By contrast, Wilde privileges 'decorative' art forms which tend to both foreground their status as art and engage the reader more deeply in constructing their meaning. 'Decorative' works possess 'the subtle quality of suggestion, and seem to tell one that even from them there is an escape into a wider world'. (*CW*, p. 875). Poetry is thus preferred to prose and within prose, romance and fantasy are set over the novel. In discriminating between art which invites the reader's active participation from that which constrains the reader, Wilde anticipates Barthes' distinction in *S/Z* between 'readerly' and 'writerly' texts. Like Wilde, Barthes gives the highest status to literature which subverts the author's traditional authority over the reader in order to emphasise the latter's crucial role in producing the text.

TO CRITICISE THE CRITIC

As has been seen, traditional British criticism has found ample reasons for suspicion of Wilde, some of which must also be shared by those with a materialist perspective. But of more immediate concern to this essay is an evaluation of the degree to which Wilde resolves the problems engendered by 'reader-response' criticism, the most pressing of which is where, if at all, the limits of the reader's freedom are to be drawn. The tendency of 'reader-response' theory, in Freund's view, is progressively to enfranchise the reader until the irksome dichotomy of reader/text is abolished by the assimilation of the text into the reader or the reader into the text: 'The outcome of this turn of events is to undermine the reader-response project, for when the discrete concepts of "reader" and "text" lose their specific difference the *raison d'être* for both a *text*-centred and a *reader-* or *self*-centred criticism is undone'.[12]

Many 'reader-response' theorists have sought to prevent their project collapsing by counterbalancing the freedom they seek on the reader's behalf with a variety of normative models of literary competence. Richards' ideal of 'Good Sense', Culler's 'ideal reader', Ingarden's distinction between 'adequate' and 'inadequate' concretisations, Fish's model of 'interpretive communities' – all are designed to avoid the critical anarchy inherent in totally enfranchising the reader. At times, Wilde appears to reject any such constraints, offering the reader complete licence to both interpret and misinterpret the work of art. 'The Critic as Artist', for instance, claims that the 'one characteristic of a beautiful form is that one can put into it whatever one wishes, and see in it whatever one chooses to see' (*CW*, p. 874). Elsewhere, Gilbert bluntly asserts that criticism is 'the purest form of personal impression' (*CW*, p. 872) and 'is in its essence purely subjective' (*CW*, p. 873). But, in fact, Wilde seems well aware that this argument threatens the project of criticism itself. Since, in the end, criticism must always be of something, or it ceases to be criticism, the dialogues backtrack, readmitting constraints on interpretation which they ostensibly aim to abolish.

At one level, *Dorian Gray* can be understood as an allegory of the disastrous effects of misinterpretation which arise from over-indulgence of the subjective response. Because Gothic – to which the novel self-consciously affiliates itself as a mode – characteristically refuses to resolve the indeterminacies it constructs, the question of whether Basil's portrait really changes cannot be definitively answered. But there is certainly plenty of evidence that the change is 'read into' the painting by Dorian. The novel stresses Dorian's tendency to paranoia after the death of Sybil Vane. This causes him to construct his servant Victor as a spy, a 'misreading' which leads ultimately to the latter's dismissal. Later on, in a moment of intense stress at his country house, Dorian has a vision of Sybil's vengeful brother at the window. As he calms down, he realises that 'perhaps it had been only his fancy that had called vengeance out of the night, and set the hideous shapes of punishment before him' (*DG*, p. 221). Dorian's tendency to project his anxieties could thus explain the 'change' in the portrait. After all, at the end of the novel, when the portrait is returned to public view, it shows no evidence of the deterioration which has terrified Dorian. Once Dorian accepts his friend's gift, it remains unseen until the evening of Basil's murder, even by the frame-maker Hubbard. Dorian first senses a 'change' in the painting while experiencing severe guilt about jilting Sybil Vane. After receiving news of her death, Dorian is still uncertain that the painting has degenerated: 'Had the portrait really changed? Or had it been simply his own imagination . . . Surely a painted canvas could not alter' (*DG*, p. 107). As a precaution, Dorian takes every step to keep the portrait concealed. But in his calmer moments, he is confident that he has nothing to fear from an unauthorised view of the work: 'He was quite conscious that this would tell them nothing' (*DG*, p. 157).

Basil Hallward's visit to Dorian on the evening of his death ostensibly provides corroboration for Dorian's conviction that the portrait really has changed. But the artist's response to his work is actually quite ambiguous: 'The surface seemed to be quite undisturbed, and as he had left it' (*DG*, p. 175). For Basil, it is essentially the 'expression' which has 'altered' (*DG*, p. 173). But the alteration in the expression of the painting could be explained in terms of Basil's own 'altered' view of Dorian. Convinced that Dorian has become the monstrously depraved figure of current gossip, Basil has come to plead with his friend to change his ways. Thus Basil could be said to find within the portrait the prior change in his own attitude towards his sitter. At one point, Dorian describes the painting as a text which he invites Basil to read (*DG*, p. 171). The tragic irony is that his 'misreading' provides Dorian with the motive to murder him. Later, Dorian appears to acknowledge that his extreme reaction was provoked by his own 'misreading': 'As the thought crept through his brain, he grew pale with terror, and the air seemed to him to have become suddenly colder. Oh! in what a wild hour of madness he had killed his friend!' (*DG*, p. 222). The possibility that Basil and Dorian have projected their own anxieties onto the painting, rather than perceiving any 'objective' change, is further supported by the authorial voice: 'Nay, without thought or conscious desire, might not things external to ourselves vibrate in unison with our moods and passions, atom calling to atom in secret love of strange affinity? (*DG*, p. 120).

In order to prevent the misreading of which *Dorian Gray*, on one level, provides an extreme example, Wilde's dialogues end by paradoxically readmitting constraints upon the reader derived from the instrumental, mimetic and expressive theories of art. Thus having in a sense abolished Beethoven and Shakespeare as standards by which to interpret their work, Gilbert reinstates them, at least to some degree, as guides to the critic. Since 'art springs from personality, so it is only to personality that it can be revealed, and from the meeting of the two comes right interpretative criticism' (*CW*, p. 878). Later in the essay, Gilbert advances the positively Arnoldian view that one of the purposes of criticism is 'to realise the experiences of those who are greater than we are. The pain of Leopardi crying out against life becomes our pain' (*CW*, p. 883). Similarly, having just insisted that criticism 'is no more to be judged by any low standard of imitation or resemblance than is the work of the poet or sculptor' (p. 871), Gilbert withdraws: 'Some resemblance, no doubt, the creative work of the critic will have to the work that has stirred him to creation' (*CW*, p. 875).

It could be argued that Wilde sidesteps many of the problems of 'reader-response' theory by talking not of readers but of critics, which implies some sense of conformity to agreed practices and norms. But the competence this implies is not, for Wilde, the product of an 'interpretive community' understood in the narrow sense of the academic institution. In the formation of the critical sensibility, 'the dullness of tutors and professors matters very little' (*CW*, p. 891). Nonetheless, his frequent allusions to the 'elect' implies the existence of an undefined community whose norms provide a framework for the interpretive process. For the 'elect', critical competence begins with exposure from an early age to the beautiful in all its forms and is, according to 'Pen, Pencil and Poison', 'made perfect by frequent contact with the best work' (*CW*, p. 847). The crucial result of this is internalisation of the principles of aesthetic form: 'The harmony that resides in the delicate proportions of lines and masses becomes mirrored in the mind. The repetitions of pattern give us rest. The marvels of design stir the imagination. In the mere loveliness of the materials employed there are latent elements of culture' (*CW*, p. 892).

Such an education, according to Gilbert, will develop 'that unerring instinct that reveals to one all things under their condition of beauty' (*CW*, p. 893). But instinct must be complemented by a formidable amount of contextual knowledge relating to the historical and aesthetic affiliations of the work of art. 'The Critic as Artist' draws a distinction between 'synthetic' and 'analytic' criticism. If, as 'Pen, Pencil and Poison' argues, 'the first step in aesthetic criticism is to realise one's own impressions' (*CW*, p. 847), the second involves something much more conventional. Thus in 'The Portrait of Mr W. H.', we find Cyril Graham attempting to complete his 'synthetic' impression of the true identity of W. H. by corroboration from the sonnets themselves, with all the subordination to textual evidence that this implies. 'The Critic as Artist' sets exacting standards for 'analytic' criticism:

> And he who desires to understand Shakespeare truly must understand the relations in which Shakespeare stood to the Renaissance and the Reformation, to the age of Elizabeth and the age of James; he must be familiar with the history of the struggle for supremacy between the old classical forms and the new spirit of romance, between the school of Sidney, and Daniel, and Johnson, and the school of Marlowe and Marlowe's greater son; he must know the materials that were at Shakespeare's disposal and the method in which he used them, and the conditions of theatrical presentation in the sixteenth and seventeenth century, their limitations and their opportunities for freedom, and the literary criticism of Shakespeare's day, its aims and modes and canons; he must study the English language in its progress, and blank or rhymed verse in its various developments; he must study the Greek drama, and the connection between the art of the creator of the Agamemnon and the art of the creator of Macbeth; in a word, he must be able to bind Elizabethan London to the Athens of Pericles, and to learn Shakespeare's true position in the history of European drama and the drama of the world. (*CW*, pp. 886–7).

Gilbert's elaboration of the prerequisites of 'analytic' critical response indicates the degree to which Wilde takes back from the reader with one hand what he has given with the other. Far from being totally free, the reader is now constituted as a series of 'pre-understandings' which are the preconditions of adequate response. Moreover, the reader's subjectivity is actually constituted by discourses which are socially determined and produced. Thus 'the soul that dwells within us is no single spiritual entity, making us personal and individual, created for our service' (*CW*, p. 883). In this light, the reader can now be seen to embody a whole series of cultural codes which are called into play by the text, so that while the text was formerly seen as something constituted by the reader, the reader now appears to be 'produced' by the text. In this respect, Gilbert's comments on creative imagination seem equally applicable to the critical act. The former, he suggests, far from being the self-expression of individual genius, is structured and produced by conventions which are social and historical in genesis. While 'synthetic' criticism 'deals with art . . . as impressive purely' (*CW*, p. 876), 'analytic' criticism realises 'the collective life of the race' (*CW*, p. 883). The sensibility produced by criticism is, to a large degree, 'the result of heredity. It is simply concentrated race-experience' (*CW*, p. 884).

By following the 'swerve' to the reader right to the end of its curve. Wilde in a sense returns to the position from which he started. His trajectory anticipates the essential aporia into which much contemporary 'reader-response' theory issues. In Freund's view this body of theory constitutes 'a complex and interminable dialectic which persists in trying – but repeatedly fails – to negotiate the question whether reading is a transitive or intransitive verb: does the reader control the text or does the text control the reader?'[13] But if Wilde is no more successful than many of his successors in resolving the problems which he articulates – and one must note that such a desire for coherence derives from the orthodox critical discourse to which Wilde was so antagonistic – his exploration of the critical possibilities inherent in turning the focus away from the text's relationship with the author and the world to that with the reader remains one of the most productive in the history of 'reader-response' theory.

NOTES

1. T. S. Eliot, 'Baudelaire', in *Selected Essays* (London: Faber & Faber, 1976) p. 420.
2. T. S. Eliot, *The Use of Poetry and the Use of Criticism* (London: Faber & Faber, 1933) p. 152.
3. T. S. Eliot, 'The Function of Criticism', in *Selected Essays*, pp. 23–34, pp. 30–1.
4. T. S. Eliot, *The Use of Poetry*, p. 26.
5. W. Wimsatt and M. Beardsley, 'The Affective Fallacy', in W. Wimsatt, *The Verbal Icon: Studies in the Meaning of Poetry* (London: Methuen, 1974), pp. 21–39, p. 21.

6. O. Wilde, *The Picture of Dorian Gray* (Harmondsworth: Penguin, 1973) p. 39; hereafter referred to as *DG*, with page references given in the text.

7. O. Wilde, 'The Critic as Artist', in *The Complete Works of Oscar Wilde* (London: Hamlyn, 1963) p. 881; hereafter referred to as *CW*, with essay-titles and page references given in the text.

8. E. Freund, *The Return of the Reader* (London & New York: Methuen, 1987) pp. 5–6. As well as Freund, a good introduction to the field that stresses the continental origins of 'reader-response' theory is provided by R. Holub, *Reception Theory* (London & New York: Methuen, 1984). In addition, there are two useful anthologies of primary critical material with critical introductions. These are J. P. Tompkins (ed.), *Reader-Response Criticism* (London: Johns Hopkins University Press, 1980) and S. Suleiman and I. Crosman (eds.), *The Reader in the Text* (Guildford: Princeton University Press, 1980).

9. Freund, *The Return of the Reader*, p. 25.

10. J. Harari, 'Critical Factions/Critical Fictions', in J. Harari (ed.), *Textual Strategies: Perspectives in Post-Structuralist Criticism* (Ithaca: Cornell University Press, 1979) p. 70.

11. R. Barthes, *S/Z*, tr. R. Miller (London: Cape, 1975) p. 154.

12. Freund, *The Return of the Reader*, p. 10.

13. Ibid., p. 104.

6

Is There a Method in his Theory? A. C. Bradley and Contemporary Criticism

ADRIAN PAGE

Coleridge once wrote that until he understood a man's ignorance he 'presumed himself ignorant of his understanding'.[1] The twentieth century has seen generations of literary critics who are convinced that Bradley made a relatively simple error when composing *Shakespearean Tragedy*[2] which has invalidated the greater part of what he has to say. On re-reading Bradley, however, it becomes clear that the fallacy which he is presumed to be guilty of is explicitly rejected. There are undoubtedly inconsistencies and occasional lapses in Bradley's criticism, yet the actual limits of his critical vision are much harder to determine than academic folklore would make us believe.

Bradley is generally thought of as operating with a nineteenth-century notion of character as a fixed set of propensities which an individual is born with and never loses. Hence drama is reduced to psychology, tragedy to fate, and Shakespearean poetry to the delineation of a character study. Furthermore there is a culprit who is responsible for these distortions: Bradley's fascination with Hegel is ultimately to blame and neatly explains the weak foundations of his argument in idealism.[3]

It is true that the theoretical position outlined above can be found in Hegel's theory of tragedy; it is used to describe Greek tragedy: 'It is just the strength of the great characters that they do not choose but throughout, from start to finish, *are* what they will and accomplish.'[4] In a play where the characters represent particular roles within a philosophical design, each is bound closely to one function. In this sense their character is both action and destiny, since they are subordinated to the playwright's allegorical structure.

Even Hegel does not entirely subscribe to his view, however. The trend he describes was towards a more fully-developed characterisation so that the explanation of tragedy had to focus on the subjectivity of the tragic hero. For Hegel the cause of tragedy lies in the presumptuous hero who acts in defiance of the ethical structure of the universe. Certain presumptuous acts are doomed to fail because of the eternal supremacy of goodness; since the ethical structure remains the same, any tragic action is brought about by an individual who attempts to usurp it. The psychology of the would-be miscreant therefore holds the key to the nature and outcome of any rebellion against the natural order. Daring to defy the gods is both dangerous and appealing. For Hegel, however, the hamartia within the tragic figure's soul is a bad feature which is eventually defeated by goodness; it is an imbalance in the 'ethical substance': the mixture of good and bad within the self.

Bradley, however, objects to precisely this point. Hegel's remarks are a 'rationalisation of fate' which is 'not satisfactory'[5] Bradley cites the example of *Antigone* where he argues that, 'we can hardly say that it [the tragedy] depends solely on the characters of Creon and Antigone' (*OLP*, p. 82). In *Othello* also the element of chance is so great according to Bradley, that only an 'extraordinary fatality' could be responsible. He continues by asserting that it is inconsistent to argue that 'the order is responsible for the good in Desdemona, but Iago for the evil in Iago' (*ST*, p. 27). The moral order is constituted by the characters themselves: 'they are within it and a part of it' (*ST*, p. 27). The 'moral order' is therefore a social order which exists only within the play. The balance of good and evil is a function of the characters' interactions rather than a metaphysical ethical structure which is transcendent.

Bradley's rejection of the extreme idealism of Hegel marks the beginning of an approach to character which is more in keeping with contemporary materialist theories: there are no immutable characters whose behaviour only reveals what was present from the outset. Instead it is action which constitutes character, and to grasp a dramatic character is to grasp the complex of social relations in which he or she participates rather than to infer a set of unchanging characteristics which somehow explain all their behaviour. The famous dictum that plot is character in action need not be read as meaning that the plot is predetermined by an equally pre-established mentality. Bradley envisages a dialectical relationship between these two elements of a drama: 'the centre of a tragedy, therefore, may be said to

lie in action issuing from character, or in character issuing in action
. . . to say that it lay in *mere* character, or was a psychological interest,
would be a great mistake' (*ST*, p. 7). Soliloquies, for example, are not
always regarded by Bradley as cases of the character giving us a
privileged insight into their mind by expounding on motives. In the
case of Hamlet's repetitions (*ST*, pp. 119–20) it is the fact that he
repeats himself so often that is significant, not the matter of what he
repeats. The repetition is a functional device rather than a direct
expression of 'character'. Such a remark calls to mind Marx's views
on self-consciousness: 'Whilst in ordinary life every shopkeeper is
very well able to distinguish between what somebody professes to
be and what he really is, our historians have not won even this trivial
insight.'[6]

The materialist view of character, later developed by Althusser in
his theory of ideology as material practice, is that character is in-
ferred from behaviour. If character is an intellectual construct derived from human action, and all we know of certain characters such
as Hamlet is contained in the play of the same name, then there is a
sense in which the study of the character of Hamlet *is* synonymous
with a study of the action of the play. All we can possibly discover
about the character of Hamlet is contained in what he does. When
Bradley says that 'The dictum that, with Shakespeare, "character is
destiny" is no doubt an exaggeration . . . but it is the exaggeration of
a vital truth' (*ST*, pp. 7–8) he is not therefore stating a belief in
extreme idealism.[7] Character, according to the materialist theory, is
action, and it is our actions which commit us to certain paths which
lead to destruction. By a roundabout logic it might therefore be said
that destiny is the inevitable outcome of character, but this does not
imply that character is rigidly determined. Seen from one angle the
statement Bradley considers only expresses a logical relationship
between action and fate. The quotation is in fact abbreviated by
Terence Hawkes and omits a crucial parenthetical statement. Bradley
points out that certain characters could be imagined as avoiding
their fate in different circumstances (*ST*, p. 7). It must therefore
follow that Bradley believed that fate was not dependent on character but contingent on both character and circumstances.

It would have been unacceptable to Bradley to maintain that
character determined the course of a drama from the outset, since his
theory of tragedy is formulated in opposition to Hegel's. Hegel
suggests that the tragic character is morally responsible for the catastrophe, whereas Bradley argues that a peculiar combination of cir-

cumstances make the good which we admire in a character 'reinforce' the evil which opposes them (*OLP*, p. 89). Tragedy, for Bradley,
is the cruel irony which makes goodness rebound on itself.

Morris Weitz reminds us that Bradley is more of a modern critic
in that, 'as a critic of *Hamlet* [he] engages in poetics when he offers a
definition of tragedy'.[8] Questions as to what literature *is* precede the
issue of defining literary method. In Todorov's words, poetics 'does
not seek to name meaning, but aims at a knowledge of the general
laws which preside over the birth of each work. But, in contradistinc-
tion to such sciences as psychology, sociology, etc., it seeks these
laws within literature itself'.[9] Bradley's essay on Hegel's theory of
tragedy is just such a practice. Literary criticism is no longer a
perfectly 'natural' activity which can be carried on by exercising
one's intuitive judgement.

In Hegel's account of tragedy, the subjectivity of the central figure
is the cause of the action, and must therefore precede it. The business
of the literary critic was often seen as attempting to grasp the subjectivity of the main protagonist with sufficient clarity to see how the
rest of the play followed from this. This, however, is a strategy which
Bradley flatly rejects: 'The only way, if there is any way, in which a
conception of Hamlet's character could be proved true, would be to
show that it, and it alone, explains all the relevant facts presented by
the text of the drama. To attempt such a demonstration here would
obviously be impossible, even if I felt certain of the interpretation of
the facts' (*ST*, pp. 102–3). It would be overstating the case to represent Bradley as a thoroughgoing materialist, yet he does point the
way out of the idealist paradoxes to which Hegel is prey. The non-
Hegelian theory of tragedy is illustrated clearly in the remarks on
Macbeth. Bradley compares this play with *The Iliad* (*ST*, p. 291). When
Achilles is divided between wreaking revenge on Agamemnon for
stealing the woman Briseis from him, and remaining faithful to his
people and their ruler, he illustrates Bradley's belief that tragedy is
caused by the clash of good with good. The ethical substance is not
divided against itself, but has to contend with the fact that 'the
inward powers of the mind answer in their essence to vaster powers
without' (*ST*, p. 292). In the case of Achilles this is demonstrated by
the intervention of the goddess Athene who prevents him from
making any rash decision. The individual is not autonomous but
always remains subject to external forces which can cause conflict
within the self. Thus it is tragic, in Bradley's view, that ordinary
personal ties can come into conflict with obligations towards the

state (*OLP*, p. 75). The moral powers which may conflict within tragic characters are not ideal entities, but the social formations of the day. If the mind of the central character has to acknowledge that it is subject to external forces, then the solution to his or her problems does not lie in a simple change of heart. The tragic circumstances are not simply ideal mental phenomena but material facts.

Hegel's notion of tragedy laid the blame squarely on the tragic heroes, and he also suggests that it is within their power to alter the situation. As Marx said of the 'young Hegelians', they behaved as if oppressive conditions could be thrown off 'by a radical effort of thought alone'.[10] Hamlet, in Bradleian terms, is both full of 'godlike "apprehension"' and yet 'powerless in his petty sphere of action' (*ST*, p. 102). Raymond Williams criticised the theoretical stance of Lukács on the grounds that he neglects the social structure which ensures that the individual lives and suffers its contradictions. In Williams' opinion, Lukács is a post-Hegelian rather than a Marxist critic. Later, however, in his discussion of Brecht's *Mother Courage*, Williams speaks of the 'dramatisation of conflicting instincts, conflicting illusions, and commanding insights.'[11] As the example of *Mother Courage* shows, to take the mind of a tragic figure as the site of the contradictions which derive from material circumstances is not necessarily to commit the idealist fallacy of supposing that the contradictions can be analysed away. The explanation of Mother Courage's circumstances lies in the society which she inhabited, yet the drama is played out by making us acquainted with the limited choices which pass before her mind. To describe the focus of the drama is one thing, and to account for the situation within which it takes place, is another.

Hence, when Bradley remarks that 'Hamlet's difficulties are not practical, "external" ones; *almost* the whole of his difficulty was internal' (*ST*, 76; my italics), he is not committing himself to a neo-Hegelian reading of the play in which subjectivity can be made a heaven or a hell at will. The chapter on *Hamlet* begins by refuting various theories which explain the action in psychological terms, on the grounds that they are 'reductive'. The best description of Hamlet's state which Bradley can give is that he is suffering from 'melancholy', yet the temptation to characterise Hamlet in Medieval terms is scrupulously avoided. The humours do not account for the action of the play: 'The psychological point of view is not equivalent to the tragic' (*ST*, p. 102).

The contradiction that Hamlet is 'powerless from the very divinity of his thought' leads us to the reading of the play which Brecht suggests in *A Short Organum for the Theatre*.[12] Bradley, in pointing out that Hamlet is capable of indifference to the feelings and fate of those he loves, also remarks that he is prone to outbursts of uncontrolled emotion. In Bradleian terms, Hamlet is divided against himself in that the competing claims of reason and emotion both have good on their side. Brecht is able to supply the historicist reading which explains this situation: 'These events show the young man, already somewhat stout making the most ineffective use of the new approach to Reason which he has picked up at the University of Wittenberg. In the feudal business to which he returns it simply hampers him. Faced with irrational practices, his reason is utterly impractical. He falls a tragic victim to the discrepancy between such reasoning and such action.'[13]

Despite the fact that Bradley does not recognise the source of this confusion in Hamlet's mind, his reading of the play is consistent with this Brechtian thesis which situates the play in history. The scene where Hamlet spares Claudius at prayer is crucial for Bradley and he argues that all the disasters results from it. He maintains, however, that 'the feeling of intense hatred which Hamlet expresses is not the cause of his sparing the King, and in his heart he knows this; but it does not follow that this feeling is unreal' (*ST*, pp. 108–9). At this stage of the play, Bradley regards the confrontation between reason and emotion to be at its height. The desire for revenge is strong but conflicts with the moral revulsion at the thought of murdering a man like a paid assassin. Hamlet's moral sensibility should, according to the doctrines of the new Renaissance humanism, find itself sanctioned by the natural feelings within, yet in Hamlet's case there is a contradiction. Reason here does not seem to be the highest expression of the essential nobility of mankind. In terms of Bradley's theory of tragedy, Hamlet is caught on the horns of a dilemma, and the fatal move is to 'assert the right' of one power over the other (*OLP*, p. 73). What Hamlet does is to resort to reasoning rather than recognising that he is torn between the rational and the irrational. Once again Bradley's reading of this scene demonstrates that we should not take each speech by Hamlet as a direct expression of his internal state: here the reasoning is significant structurally rather than for what is said. Although he postpones the decision, this is not an advantageous move; like Achilles in *The Iliad*, he discovers that delay can be just as fatal as the wrong action. In a similar manner to the classical epic, *Hamlet* portrays the social determination of subjectivity as unavoidable. Bradley makes the point that the 'speculative habit', as he describes Hamlet's penchant for reason, is both a partial cause of his morbid state and a symptom of it (*ST*, p. 93).

Complete autonomy, however, seems to be the ideal of the rational man who would be king. Hamlet knows that in contrast to the corrupt family about him, he must 'rule' himself before he would dictate to others. A further contradiction observed by Bradley is that Hamlet believes to be 'ruled' by passion and praises Horatio as 'a man who is not passion's slave ' (*ST*, p. 99). In speaking to his father's ghost, Hamlet nonetheless describes himself as 'lapsed in passion' and therefore unable to fulfil his promises. Ideally the future king should be independent of such influences and confident that he is able to act freely. Those characters who, as Bradley puts it, 'possess in abundance' the qualities which Hamlet seems to lack, are shown to be subject to the desires of others. Although Laertes acts with decisive vengeance in mind, he responds positively to Claudius when asked, 'Will you be rul'd by me? (IV, vii, 57). The result of such a willingness is ultimately that the character in question is manipulated. In contrast, when Hamlet sees the ghost for a second time, Horatio attempts to stop him with the words, 'Be rul'd; you shall not go' (I, v, 81) and is unsuccessful. The agony Hamlet suffers is that of being unable to discover an entirely free course of action in a world where the social determination of action becomes increasingly apparent.

The Brechtian reading proposes that we see Hamlet as someone in the grip of an illusion; the necessity for revenge is merely an obligation which others would make us believe to be a compelling moral imperative. It is therefore possible for the victim of this illusion to deny the apparent inevitability of the situation by a mental effort. Bradley also enables the reader of the play to reject the notion of tragic inevitability by reminding us that Hamlet could have murdered Claudius at prayer without necessarily suffering terrible consequences. 'He would certainly have had the people on his side who loved him and despised Claudius' (*ST*, p. 108). Brecht's criticism of Shakespearean drama is that 'Shakespeare's great solitary figures, bearing on their breast the star of their fate, carry through with irresistible force their futile and deadly outbursts . . . the catastrophe is beyond criticism.'[14] The treatment of Hamlet in *Shakespearean Tragedy* concludes with the statement that 'the apparent failure of Hamlet's life is not the ultimate truth about him' (*ST*, p. 141). In criticising Hegel, Bradley was especially careful to deny that tragedies ended with a 'reconciliation' whereby the ultimate justice of the cosmic moral order had to be acknowledged in the end. The preceding argument draws on Brecht's theory and Bradley's criticism to show how they are compatible and together indicate how a reading of the play which emphasises the historical contradictions is possible. This should come as no surprise if we consider Brecht's attitude towards the influence of Hegel on aesthetics: 'as Marx repeatedly insisted, this aesthetics (Kant and Hegel) stands head and shoulders above the aesthetic opinions of many supposed Marxists'.[15]

Terence Hawkes summarises Bradley's concerns as 'the reading of character; the inner nature of human beings which determines their deeds and their fate'.[16] There is undoubtedly a sense in which this is true, yet the same might be said of Brecht. A particular intellectual fixation might well account for a tragic life, yet this is not to say that it must do so. Character is only a synchronic abstraction from a continually developing sequence, and Bradley insists that it must be properly grasped as a process. 'Action' is a key term in the Bradleian concept of drama and character is only truly seen in a dynamic context.

Hawkes bases his essay on Bradley on the premise that he is a philosophical idealist. According to Hawkes, he sees the text of Shakespearean drama as the realisation of an idea in the mind of the writer. Criticism therefore seeks to rediscover this original conception by imaginative recreation of the archetypal text. The critical recreation, on this theory, becomes another ideal mental phenomenon which readers of Bradley may come to identify with the play itself. The difficulty of discriminating between two such intangible entities may lead to their confusion. Knowing Bradley's mind is virtually one and the same as knowing the play.

It is clear from the history of philosophy that it is very difficult indeed to rid any theory of the accusation of idealism, and it has to be conceded that Bradley is subject to its influence. He was originally a lecturer in philosophy and could not have failed to be influenced by his brother, the philosopher F. H. Bradley, whose famous work *Appearance and Reality* was published in 1893. The first section of this influential work claims that reality is of a different order altogether, and that we cannot therefore attain any knowledge of it. The argument is, of course, an extreme idealist position and Bradley seems to have accepted it in relation to the literary text as well: writing on *The Teaching of English Literature* in 1891, A. C. Bradley asserts, 'Our main object here is that the work should become to us what it was to the writer: an object unattainable, since *Macbeth* can be to us what it was to Shakespeare only on condition that our minds become Shakespeare's mind'.[17] The principal argument against idealist theories is clearly well known to him, yet Bradley continues to insist that the only way to achieve the kind of intense involvement in literature which bears fruit is to attempt the impossible.

An analogy with this position might be that of the theologian who maintains that God is entirely transcendent and cannot intervene in this world. Such a view might lead to a utilitarian approach to the promotion of the general good much more reminiscent of materialist theories. It has, however, to be assumed, as an act of faith, that the theologian's will coincides with that of God. The actual practices of such a believer might be indistinguishable from a materialist thinker. It does not follow that a mistaken theory must invalidate the method derived from it. Bradley, for example, often refers to the impossibility of knowing just how Shakespeare's plays were actually produced in his own day: 'The Othello of our stage can never be Shakespeare's Othello' (*ST*, p. 145). Perhaps it needs to be asked how similar this approach is to that of the new historicism, with its desire to 'recover the political dimension of Renaissance drama'.[18]

As Hawkes remarks, Bradley's *method* implies that there is no *hors texte*, as Derrida has it. Seymour Chatman has suggested that Bradley's work, 'remains something of a model of open trait-analysis and deserves reconsideration'.[19] Chatman compares Bradley's method to that of Barthes in *S/Z* where he produces a literary analysis of Balzac's story *Sarrasine*. Barthes refuses to accept that the proper name 'Sarrasine' signifies an identifiable collection of qualities which together partake of a unique identity: 'To state that Sarrasine is "active or passive by turns" is to attempt to locate something in his character "which doesn't take", to attempt to name that something'.[20] In identifying the properties or characteristics of one figure, we are merely dealing with fragments of the supposed character. Barthes describes the search for the identity of a fictional character as a 'metonymic slide'; each characteristic is only a part of the character and is soon made to relate to another metonym by finding similarities. A process of what Barthes calls 'thematics' begins in which the 'essence' of the character is overshadowed by the development of a tangential theme of the narrative. In logical terms, statements about the character are necessary conditions in that they are true of the character in question. They never amount to sufficient conditions, however, in that we can infer all the character's behaviour from the description alone. Any statement about a character, however true, can only succeed in achieving a partial description.

When Bradley says, 'Iago's plot is Iago's character in action' (*ST*, p. 145) this is a statement intended to capture the uniqueness of Iago. His 'intrigue' is unparalleled in Shakespearean drama yet this is not simply a detective story: Iago's character unfolds in the very nature of the plot he weaves. We know very little about his life prior to the events of the play, and it is from the plot that we learn just how devious and unprincipled he is. The statement can be taken, with a different emphasis, to mean that we learn about Iago's character only from his actions which compose the plot of the play – a remark which does not automatically suggest that his character determines his behaviour and therefore the play.

In Bradley's actual method, he acts in accordance with the principles outlined above in that he infers character retrospectively from action. He has discovered from his analysis of *Hamlet* that character may be fraught with contradictions, hence he does not assume in Aristotelean fashion that all characters act consistently from rational motives. In the chapters on Hamlet's character, he proceeds in such a way that he avoids the contradictions of the hermeneutic circle. Rather than assuming a reading of the play and approaching all Hamlet's actions as confirming this, he does seem to make a genuine effort to follow the patterns of characterisation without begging the question of the nature of that character. Finally he is driven to admit that 'the text admits of no sure interpretation' (*ST*, p. 128).

In the case of Iago, the method of 'open-trait analysis' is applied. Bradley distinguishes three highly significant features of the character which are closely related. They are, an extreme belief in the will-to-power; a thirst for danger and excitement, and an almost artistic desire to be the 'author' of a plot of his own construction (*ST*, pp. 186–9). It is easy to see how these three aspects seem to lead naturally to each other; each is a significant element of Iago, yet the pursuit of his personal characteristics leads to a theme of the play rather than a deeper understanding of Iago. Bradley points out that 'the very forces that moved him and made his fate are not evil things' (*ST*, p. 191). The characteristics just cited are not in themselves evil; they might equally well be applied to Hamlet; they fail to explain the appearance of 'motiveless malignity' and the perversity which seems to be so much a part of Iago. According to *Shakespearean Tragedy* neither Hamlet nor Iago understand the forces which move them (*ST*, p. 185). Another way of putting this might be that in their cases, self-consciousness and action are clearly at odds with each other .

Bradley's attempt to break out of the hermeneutic circle and ground his treatment of character on an unbiased account of the plays' action leaves us with a deepening sense of the mystery of character itself. Howard Felperin, in a much more recent essay on *The Winter's Tale*, argues that the play's discourse is continually centred on an absent figure or event. The vital elements of the discourse are, in fact, creations posited by the text which have no existence within it. In Felperin's opinion the radical difference between presence and reference entails 'the radical subjectivity of all interpretation'[21] In a similar vein, Iago becomes an eternal mystery because it is necessary to refer in criticism to emotions such as lust or envy to explain his behaviour, yet these are not manifested in the text. It is the lack of any recognisable emotions which creates 'the very horror of him' (*ST*, p. 183).

A. D. Nuttall is adamant that 'Of course Bradley never supposes for a moment that Hamlet was a real man'.[22] In his work on L. C. Knights' famous essay 'How Many Children Had Lady Macbeth?', where this accusation was made, Nuttall distinguishes between 'transparent' and 'opaque' criticism. The latter seeks to show that the text reveals things as they are, and the former sees the illusion of real life generated by the text to be no more than 'mimetic enchantment'.

At first sight Knights' position that *Macbeth* is a 'poem', in that it, 'calls into play, directs and integrates certain interests',[23] is a materialist response from a Marxist critic to a naive realist position with its heavy emphasis on biographical speculation. There are undoubtedly moments when Bradley is so saturated with a sense of the characters' identity that he speaks as if they were existing beings. One such time is when he asserts that 'Goneril would not have condescended to the lie which Regan so needlessly tells to Oswald' (*ST*, p. 249).

Even if we grant these lapses, however, the attitude of Knights remains ironically guilty of the fallacies which Bradley is accused of. By insisting on *Macbeth* as a poem, Knights is forced to argue that the pervading sense of evil, which captures the essence of the play, is immanent from the beginning and is gradually revealed. There is no development of the plot, only a slow unveiling: 'it is clear that the impulses which are awakened in Act I are part of the whole response'.[24] The picture accumulates until the evidence is overwhelming: 'it is not', according to Knights, 'something which happens in the last act, corresponding to the dénouement or unravelling of the plot'.[25] Significantly, Knights finds himself having to deny the notion of drama as narrative: in the synchronic vision of poetry a certain set of existing relations is articulated, whereas for Bradley *Macbeth* is a 'remarkable exhibition of the *development* of a character' (*ST*, p. 301; my italics). For Knights, *Macbeth* is a statement of evil; that evil is there at the beginning of the play and only gathers strength until Macbeth identifies with it towards the end. Knights is the critic who is guilty of supposing that plot is really only a pretext for elaborating a character whose moral worth is already decided. The question of Macbeth's children is, in fact, needed to enable a dramatic reading of certain lines in the text. Bradley's concern is with whether the text provides evidence for particular interpretations of those lines by the actors. Some textual issues are only finally laid to rest by the performers on stage.

NOTES

1. S. Coleridge, quoted in W. C. Booth, *Critical Understanding: The Powers and Limits of Pluralism* (Chicago & London: University of Chicago Press, 1979).
2. A. C. Bradley, *Shakespearian Tragedy* (London: Macmillan, 1969); hereafter referred to as *ST*, with page references given in the text.
3. See, for example, the introduction to John Drakakis (ed.), *Alternative Shakespeares* (London: Methuen, 1985) pp. 6–9. Drakais is, however, strictly incorrect to say that Bradley abstracts from Hegel what he believes to be the essence of a dramatic conflict. The passage which Drakakis quotes from A. C. Bradley's *Oxford Lectures on Poetry* (London: Macmillan, 1962) regarding the concept of 'ethical substance' (p. 6) is not a direct statement of belief but an attempt to summarise Hegel's theory in order to take issue with it. As he remarks on p. 73, 'such in outline is Hegel's view'.
4. G. W. F. Hegel, *Aesthetics: Lectures on Fine Art*, tr. T. M. Knor (Oxford: Oxford University Press, 1975) p. 1214.
5. A. C. Bradley, *Oxford Lectures on Poetry* (London: Macmillan, 1962) p. 83; hereafter referred to as *OLP*, with page references given in the text.
6. K. Marx and F. Engels, *The German Ideology* (London: Lawrence & Wishart, 1977) p. 67.
7. See, for example, T. Hawkes, *That Shakespeherian Rag: Essays on a Critical Process* (London: Methuen, 1986).
8. M. Weitz, *Hamlet and the Philosophy of Literary Criticism* (London: Faber & Faber, 1965) p. 15.
9. T. Todorov, *Introduction to Poetics* (Sussex: Harvester, 1981) p. 6.

10. K. Marx, *The German Ideology*, p. 41.
11. R. Williams, *Modern Tragedy* (London: Verso, 1966) p. 35.
12. Brecht, quoted in J. Willet (ed.), *Brecht on Theatre* (London: Methuen, 1964) p. 186.
13. Ibid., p. 202.
14. Ibid., p. 189.
15. Ibid., p. 163.
16. T. Hawkes, *That Shakespeherian Rag*, p. 34.
17. A. Bradley, quoted in K. Cooke, *A. C. Bradley & his Influence on Twentieth-Century Shakespeare Criticism* (Oxford: Clarendon, 1972) p. 36.
18. J. Dollimore & A. Sinfield (eds), *Political Shakespeare: New Essays in Cultural Materialism* (Manchester: Manchester University Press, 1985) p. 7.
19. S. Chatman, *Story and Discourse: Narrative Structure in Fiction and Film* (Cornell: Cornell University Press, 1978) p. 134.
20. R. Barthes, *S/Z*, tr. R. Miller (New York: Hill and Warey, 1974) p. 92.
21. H. Felperin, ' "Tongue Tied Our Queen": The Deconstruction of Presence in *The Winter's Tale*', in P. Parker and G. Hartman (eds.), *Shakespeare and the Question of Theory* (London: Methuen, 1985) p. 16. Felperin poses the question of whether Bradley 'went too far' (p. 4).
22. A. D. Nuttal, *A New Mimesis: Shakespeare and the Representation of Reality* (London: Methuen, 1985) p. 82.
23. L. C. Knights, 'How Many Children had Lady Macbeth?', in *Explorations*, p. 20.
24. Ibid., p. 20.
25. Ibid., p. 30.

7

E. M. Forster: The Isolation of the Reader

ANDREW SMITH

E. M. Forster's critical output was principally limited to *Aspects of the Novel* (1928)[1] and a selection of various journalistic articles and essays, *Abinger Harvest* (1967).[2] In these works Forster articulates a problematic attack on some of the modernist enterprises, in particular those of the avant-garde, by means of a criticism that is secured in a bourgeois-humanist approach towards literary evaluation. He employs vague terminology in his critical writings, praising a form of literature, which he sees as exemplified by Proust, which can ably discuss 'life'. Such a view would appear to privilege realism over other forms but, as will be discussed, the status of realism is a problematic area in Forster's critical idiom. Forster is not just an evaluator of literature, but is also an interpreter of the critical tradition, and it will be suggested here that it is possible to draw out a reading of Forster's 'The Machine Stops'[3] which re-defines that tradition in terms of a partially unresolvable dialectic; and that such a reading is possible by virtue of Forster's recognition of a dialectical antagonism between the processes of literature and the function of criticism. The effect of this is to suggest that Forster's radical contribution can be seen as an exposure of the discontinuous elements at play within the apparent coherence of the notion of the British critical Tradition: 'in the rather ramshackly course that lies ahead of us, we cannot consider fiction by periods, we must not contemplate the stream of time. Another image better suits our powers: that of all the novelists writing their novels at once' (*AN*, p. 8).

Here Forster makes two distinct qualitative statements which define his basic formulation of literary criticism; these are that criticism is somehow more than history can define, but paradoxically, also that criticism is less than history can express. Such an idea is grounded in an assumption about literary production which sees creativity constructed through intertextual relationships, meaning that: 'History develops, Art stands still' (*AN*, p. 13). Art is thus simultaneously larger than history because it deals in 'timeless' truths, but is also diminished by history by being static, culturally inert, in relation to these historical formations. As Forster puts it: 'Empires fall, votes are accorded, but to these people [novelists] writing in the Circular room it is the feel of the pen between their fingers that matters most' (*AN*, p. 13).

For Forster, writers; 'are approximated by the act of creation' (*AN*, p. 5), a theory which he attempts to exemplify through the juxtapositioning of Samuel Richardson with Henry James, H. G. Wells with Dickens and Sterne with Virginia Woolf (*AN*, pp. 13–15). The implication is that somehow these texts communicate with each other, absorb and reinforce each other, in such a fashion which makes it possible to 'refuse to have anything to do with chronology' (*AN*, p. 15). History is thus less than art precisely because it is inimical to the process of literary production. History shapes and informs in ways in which are resisted by literature which can both transcend history and stand in a superior relationship to it by being able to comment on its (dis)contents. Thus criticism and the literature it examines have for Forster a superior relationship to the historical than the historical has to itself.

Such a paradox, i.e. of a literature which is free from history, but which is somehow constrained to examine it, is brought into focus in his examination of the relationship between literature and verisimilitude, because 'the novel is sogged with humanity; there is no escaping the uplift or the downpour' (*AN*, p. 15).

'Good' literature is therefore defined by its ability to render 'life' comprehensible; in essence this is a call for as an invisible form of literature as possible which is able to provide access to social beings and social worlds without drawing attention to its own means of production: 'The novelist who betrays too much interest in his [*sic*] own method can never be more than interesting, he has given up the creation of character and summoned us to help analyse his own mind, and a heavy drop in the emotional thermometer results' (*AN*, p. 56).

Literature for Forster then, is 'sogged with [a] humanity', which can be elevated or not depending on its ability to reflect 'human nature'. There is again an obvious paradox here, in that if literature for Forster is closely allied to, if not overlapped by a notion of humanity, then it would necessarily follow that all literature will reflect on humanity in some fashion. However, for Forster humanity comes to be defined in terms of a liberal bourgeois-humanism which he seeks to inscribe within criticism as a literary standard in order that it can be read out of certain worthy ('humane') texts. His approach towards Modernism reflects these concerns and is exemplified in his differing treatment of Joyce and Proust.

Forster's general appraisal of Joyce is that 'in spite of all his internal looseness he is too tight, he is never vague except after due deliberation, it is talk, talk, never song' (*AN*, p. 94). More specifically he attacks *Ulysses* as 'a dogged attempt to cover the universe with mud, an inverted Victorianism, an attempt to make crossness and dirt succeed where sweetness and light failed, a simplification of the human character in the interests of Hell' (*AN*, p. 84). In the first quote it can be seen that Forster has raised the notion of humanity as a classificatory measure of literature into an aesthetic evaluation – 'it is talk, talk, never song'; in the appraisal of *Ulysses* he attacks Joyce on the grounds that if there is a humanity in his writing, it is an inverted one, replacing 'crossness' for 'sweetness', 'dirt' for 'light' in effect, 'Hell' for 'Goodness'.

It is because Joyce is seen to invert humanity by Forster, that his aesthetic is vilified here. It is Joyce's destructive urge which transgresses the law of humanity which Forster has introduced, not solely as means to define 'good' literature but also as an evaluation of an aesthetic which defines the appropriate ways in which the novelist should discuss the world. As a means of approach Forster approves of a less visible (less 'talk, talk') aesthetic which is more akin to the processes of perception: 'this power to expand and contract perception . . . this right to intermittent knowledge – I find it one of the great advantages of the novel form, and it has a parallel in our perception of life' (*AN*, p. 56). This is worth bearing in mind when looking at Forster's comments on *A la Recherche du temps perdu* in *Abinger Harvest*: 'It is an adventure in the modern mode where the nerves and brain as well as the blood take part, and the whole man moves to encounter he does not know what; certainly not to any goal' (*AN*, p. 111).

However it is this very formlessness, with one important social proviso, which supplies it with its verisimilitude: 'Ten times as long as an ordinary novel! And as baffling as life itself – life when apprehended by the modern cultivated man' (*AH*, p. 110). In *Aspects of the Novel* he writes: 'The book is chaotic, ill-constructed, it has and will have no external shape; and yet it hangs together because it is stitched internally, because it contains rhythms' (*AN*, p. 113).

Forster's formulation of humanity is thus grounded in a specific social context, i.e. that of the 'modern cultivated man'; and it is because of this cultivation that Proust is able to reflect 'life' in a more coherent fashion than Joyce who is perceived to be in some fashion anti-culture and therefore anti-life. Proust has 'rhythms', Joyce 'talk, talk, never song'.

Gertrude Stein, due to her interest in disrupting commonly held notions of time, comes in for similar vilification from Forster, because 'as soon as fiction is completely delivered from time it cannot express anything at all (*AN*, p. 28). This is because a conception of 'time' plays another prominent feature in Forster's critical lexicon which is closely tied to his formulation of a bourgeois humanity, he writes: 'The time-sequence cannot be destroyed without carrying in its ruin all that should have taken its place; the novel that would express values only becomes unintelligible and therefore valueless' (*AN*, p. 29).

Forster is essentially positing a recommendation for a coherent plot structure which can, through its narrative progression, reveal both the development of humanity and engage the similarily 'humane' reader with its development of social value, because 'we want to know what happens next', therefore meaning that 'the backbone of a novel has to be a story' (*AN*, p. 18) – by implication, a kind of story which would celebrate the aesthetics of realism (by heading towards a disclosure which is textual closure) against the aesthetics of the avant-garde, as it is represented for Forster by Joyce and Stein. The question this poses is where exactly does this leave Proust? A further dilemma for the theoretical coherence of *Aspects of the Novel* is posed when he writes that 'why has a novel to be planned? Cannot it grow? Why need it close, as a play closes? Cannot it open out?' (*AN*, p. 67). He then proceeds to analyse Gide's *Les Faux-Monnayeurs*, praising it for its intertextuality, its inclusion of the diary Gide kept whilst writing the novel, which prompts Forster to view a 'future perfect' synthesis of Gide's novel in which 'the diary, the novel and his impressions of both will interact' (*AN*, pp. 66–7). Shortly afterwards he writes that 'All that is pre-arranged is false' (*AN*, p. 71).

These oscillations in *Aspects of the Novel* are ones which are never coherently resolved. Realism appears to be favoured over the Modernist avant-garde, only for this avant-garde to redeem itself either

as an ultra-realism (Proust) or else as an exciting challenge to orthodox realist aesthetics (Gide). The only way in which these disparate
views are reconciled is in a formulation of humanity which perceives
literature as being somehow morally uplifting; expressing the morality of the 'modern cultivated man'.

Placing these views within the tradition of British criticism would,
on the surface, appear to pose few problems. In a sense, it fits in
somewhere between Mathew Arnold and F. R. Leavis; between the
view that literature would supply a flexible and subtle ideology for
the new emerging (mercantile) middle classes and that the con-
sumption of literature could be morally good in itself.[4]

Aspects of the Novel would appear to prop up a concept borrowed
from *Scrutiny*, namely that a rewarding reading was one which
entailed a close textual scrutiny, which in turn meant that elements
of the historical and the cultural could be suspended within the
quest for some kind of textual integrity which would enhance the
reader's perception and feeling about the world – as long as that
literature was able to express the world in some one to one (sign for
object) relationship. There is thus a possible, orthodox, reading of
Forster which is based in a perception of the British critical tradition
as a coherent movement; which can be described in terms of its
essential reificatory attitude towards class formation, (the education
of the middle classes, Arnold) and its suspension of the historical
context which has made such criticism possible in the first place
(F. R. and Q. D. Leavis).[5]

A motivating principle which resides behind any formulation of
the critical tradition will necessarily involve conceptualisations of
power, of how it introduces structures or forms of classification. This
is not to suggest that Forster's use of certain classificatory categories
is the most pertinent way in which to define his work, but rather that
it is possible in some way to deconstruct the notion of power as it is
reflected in the notion of a coherent, logically evolving British critical
tradition.

Michel Foucault writes: 'where there is power, there is resistance,
and yet, or rather consequently, this resistance is never in a position
of exteriority in relation to power.'[6] He goes on to say that 'there is a
plurality of resistances, each of them a special case: resistances that
are possible, necessary, improbable; others that are spontaneous,
savage, solitary, concerted, rampant, or violent'.[7] Resistance to power
in Foucault's scheme is thus ubiquitous, encompassing all forms of
possible rebellion; possible/impossible, solitary/concerted, which

still exist within the area traversed by a discourse. As suggested earlier, Forster would appear to be readily assimilable to a conceptualisation of British criticism, appearing to bridge the logical space between Arnold and Leavis. The problematic therefore becomes one of how is it possible to reclaim Forster for radical politics which reveals him to be resisting the post-priori (obvious) attempt to place him cogently within an 'already' existing critical tradition.

My suggestion here is that such a practice is possible due to two features which are bound up with an historical account of Modernism itself. James McFarlane in 'The Mind of Modernism' writes that 'the defining thing in the Modernist mode is not so much that things fall apart but that they fall together. . . . In Modernism, the centre is seen exerting not a centrifugal but a centripetal force; and the consequence is not disintegration but (as it were) superintegration.'[8] What McFarlane is implying here is that behind Modernism there is a theory of history (and of knowledge) which is dialectical in character (a 'superintegration' of opposites). In Hegel and Marx there were the disparate theories of an evolving world spirit and a developing revolutionary proletariat; with Darwin there was the theory of biology evolving to its necessarily perfect stage; in Freud's schemata there was a linking of Eros and Thanatos. The general historical context was thus one which defined knowledge, economics, biology and psychology as heading towards some state of perfection, of the act of becoming as a merging of opposites.

Such a grounding of Modernism within a theory of dialectics in turn helps explain Forster's comment in *Abinger Harvest* on the state of mind of the critic: 'Their state of mind is the exact antithesis of that of the author whom they propose to interpret' (*AH*, p. 129). The critic's view and the novelist's view are not just different they are an 'exact antithesis', together forming a dialectic, filling out each other's textual spaces. Together they exist in some symbiotic relationship, each reliant on the other for relays of communication – for the novelist to explain the world, for the critic to relocate that explanation in terms of a classificatory system based in a bourgeois-humanist cultural perspective.

Thus, there is both an historical grounding in assumptions about evolution (historical, social and psychological) which supplies Modernism with its own impetus, and there is also an explicit recognition of the idea of united antagonisms in Forster's view of the relationship between the critic and the novelist himself. For Forster then, criticism functions as a means through which to divide literature into systems of social credibility dependent upon some haphazard theory of verisimilitude. In effect the Forster of *Aspects of the Novel* and *Abinger Harvest* can be seen as a critic of Modernism, and as a product of Modernism's own epistemological uncertainties.

It is at this point, having focused on the idea of the collapsing of opposites, that it is possible to relocate Forster in terms of radical politics which frees him from a theory of British criticism as a sustained, expanding process. This is because, if Forster's criticism offers a broad analysis of Modernism itself, it follows that, in his fiction, there resides the possibility of attacking established critical assumptions. It will now be argued that a more cogent analysis of a theory of criticism resides in a reading of Forster's 'The Machine Stops' than it does in either *Aspects of the Novel* or *Abinger Harvest*. This is not, of course, an attempt to suggest that in Forster's fiction he is concerned principally with criticism, but rather that, in Forster's view of the critic and novelist as mutually reinforcing, he has opened up the relationship in such a fashion which enables him to articulate ideas about the tradition in a fictional format, and also to suggest that 'The Machine Stops' can be read in such a way that it offers a pertinent critique of the processes of literary assessment and reveals Forster's 'resistance' to the established power of the critical canon.

On one level 'The Machine Stops' appears to be an expression of a fear of what science can produce when divorced from moral codes. However, there is another possible reading which is inherent in the way structures of communication are defined in the story, in which Kuno says to his mother: 'The machine is much, but it is not everything. I see something like you in this plate, but I do not see you. I hear something like you through this telephone, but I do not hear you' (*MS*, p. 110). In effect the machine has regulated communication to such an extent that it can only offer an approximation of real social contact; it controls images by promoting them as if they were the thing which they really represent. Thus there is a sense in which there is a disruption in the notion of the relationship of the signifier being securely anchored to the signified, which Forster, as stated previously, had seen as the defining feature of what constituted a positive realist(ic) aesthetic, an invisible literature.

The problematisation of communication here is also implicit in the critical evaluation of texts. Forster called for a literature which was invisible, but criticism is unable to replicate this invisibility because it is implicated in systems of epistemology, rather than in systems of ontology. That is, criticism has become engaged with a knowledge that it sees as being somehow free from ideological issues, but it is a language which is distorted due to the constraint put upon it to be objective. In this sense it is a visible use of language which, paradoxically, has the effect of calling attention to its own process of production. In terms of this it is significant to see how knowledge is employed. Knowledge is disseminated in the machine by its lecturers. They, in effect, function as its guardians, regulating what is possible within the field of an episteme but, more than this, they adopt a particular strategy towards knowledge which asks the reader-in-the-machine (Kuno's mother for example) to eschew any notion of a point to point relationship between signifiers and signifieds: 'First-hand ideas do not really exist. They are but the physical impressions produced by love and fear, and on this gross foundation who could erect a philosophy? Let your ideas be second-hand, and if possible tenth-hand, for then they will be far removed from that disturbing element – direct observation' (*MS*, p. 135).

It is important to remember here that direct observation was the literary aesthetic elevated by Forster into a classificatory principle in *Aspects of the Novel*, because it provided direct access to a bourgeois social experience. Conversely, criticism employs a language about literature which is grounded in structures of epistemology, which have come into existence through the accumulation of certain knowledge-claims about texts – claims which may be second – or tenth-hand, here equated with second – or tenth-rate, as they lack the perceived originality of artistic achievement. Literature and criticism thus offer two different approaches which are inimical to each other, and which revolve around Forster's preoccupation with a humanity defined in terms of a liberal bourgeois-humanism; in effect what is 'in-humane' here is criticism, because although it is 'sogged with humanity', it is a humanity which is dialectically antagonistic to that of fiction.

In the world of 'The Machine Stops' the only book which still survives as a relic 'from the ages of litter' is the 'Book of the machine' (*MS*, p. 14). This is a modern secular Bible which is a manual of (dis)information concerning the processes of the machine. The irony here is that the only text which the machine permits to exist is a text which promotes anti-text propaganda, and through its policing of disinformation actually reveals the duplicitous fashion in which the written word can be used. A nostalgia for the written word is articulated through Kuno, and his attempts to reclaim arcadia as some kind of aesthetic experience mean that, in effect, Kuno becomes a metaphor for the bourgeois-humanist writer as he searches for an invisible form of communication which can avoid the apparently ambiguous quality of language as it is articulated in a critical idiom which is constructed in terms of a 'tenth-hand' kind of knowledge (and by implication, language).

As Kuno says to his mother after his visit to the surface: 'It was naked, humanity seemed naked, and all these tubes and buttons and machineries neither came into the world with us, nor will they follow us out' (*MS*, p. 127). Humanity was 'naked', invisible, immediately accessible, but screened off and unapproachable, as it is in the machine through its promotion of the image as reality. The machine can thus be read as a metaphor for the critical practice itself. This is because of the way in which it controls how images are used and interpreted by virtue of controlling communication systems; in effect it represents the process through which criticism controls reading positions – by the introduction of reading strategies inscribed through the process of classification. It is through such a regulation of knowledge that the critical tradition operates.

So far then, in this interpretation of 'The Machine Stops' it is possible to see parallels with Forster's overt criticism in *Aspects of the Novel*. Criticism and literature co-exist, but in an antagonistic relationship – the language which literature employs is not that of criticism. It is the function of criticism to promote uniformity by virtue of promoting specific reading practices; in the machine 'the hum of many workings clothed their thoughts in one garment of subserviency' (*MS*, p. 142). But it is a process of reading which is inevitably tied to the referent of literature itself, meaning, for Kuno, a model of the bourgeois-humanist writer: 'There was I, with a pneumatic stopper by my side and a respirator bobbing over my head, imprisoned, all three of us' (*MS*, p. 130). Criticism and the literature which it preys upon are thus co-mingled with each other, offering resistance to each other but, in Foucault's scheme of power, 'never in a position of exteriority' to each other. It is because of this that critical assumptions about criticism can leak over into fictional antagonisms, a collapsing of opposites into a dialectic which is never resolved. Criticism and literature in Forster's scheme thus face each other but address positions which neither really holds. Literature is not solely the bastion of bourgeois-humanism, and criticism is unable to employ a language grounded in empirical models.

The question which now arises, is how does this relocate Forster in terms of radical politics given that 'The Machine Stops' can be read as a reworking of the relationship between the novelist and the critical practice?

The role of the machine as critical discourse is to regulate knowledge by introducing classificatory procedures. In a sense, 'The Machine Stops' articulates fears about the effects of introducing such procedures. The reader-in-the-machine (i.e. Kuno's mother) is seen as isolated, and thus alienated from 'real' direct forms of communication. She is quite content to consume the images which the machine deals in (its interpretations) as if they were in fact real in their own right: 'The room, though it contained nothing, was in touch with all that she cared for in the world' (*MS*, p. 113). The machine, because it controls knowledge, necessarily defines forms of interpretation; but it is a knowledge which alienates, and its apparent disinterestedness – 'To it the darkness and the light are one' (*MS*, p. 142) – is revealed to have a disguised motivation.

In Forster there lies the implication that the critical practice is not only 'bad' for literature, but also bad, by extension, for its readership (i.e. the state of the alienated reader-in-the-machine). In this sense its (class-) interested use of knowledge is having the opposite effect of its apparent intent, that is instead of producing a 'sensitive' intelligent reader, it is in fact alienating the reader from certain forms of experience which lie outside of the scope (classificatory systems) of criticism. In this sense it is only a partial form of 'humanity' which the reader is put in touch with.[9] It is because of this that the reader is unable to comprehend a total conception of humanity and becomes alienated from him/herself as a reader.

The effect of this is to undermine some of the class premises of contemporary criticism, pointing out how its bourgeois philosophy is undermined through the actual act of its articulation. In this sense it reveals the tradition to be a self-defeating process of class promotion. It has achieved this by calling attention to the nebulous concept of bourgeois-humanism, and its inability to offer a systematic approach towards the analysis of literature. In this sense Forster in 'The Machine Stops' lampoons his own critical stance in *Aspects of the Novel*, but in another sense Forster is replying to some of the epistemological uncertainties which his overt critical position has prompted. In 'The Machine Stops' there is a critique of the 'field of problematization'[10] traversed by the critical discourse, because what is radical in the story is that it introduces the idea of deliberation as an achievement of reader orientation. It locates the reader in a position outside of the critical discourse in order to reveal to the reader how he/she is implicated in certain reading practices which places him/her as 'reader-in-the-machine'. In this sense it spatially opens up the relationship between the critical text and the fictional text and inserts the reader as the potential resolution of these opposing forces.

Forster thus relocates the notion of a close textual scrutiny in terms of a cultural position which reveals it to be a glossing over of certain political (class) differences. As such, it reveals this scrutiny to be a facile, abrupt and partial reading of the cultural formation of texts. 'The Machine Stops' achieves this by virtue of its location in a popular medium – the science fiction story – in opposition to the privileging of 'high' art which the critical canon appears to promote. It thus functions as a gesture of defiance towards practices of reading and it operates as a resistance to power, by both allying itself with its procedures (debating the function of the reader-in-the-machine) and by destabilising such procedures (debating the role of criticism in creating the reader-in-the machine).

Forster's critical approach can be defined in terms of a conceptualisation of humanity; in effect he never moves far beyond this. He sees a clear division between the aspirations of literature as a form to evaluate the world, and criticism which both explicates that literature but is antagonistic towards it. It is however in the tension of Forster's unresolved dialectic between literature and criticism that his radical worth resides. In 'The Machine Stops' he provides a parable on the relationship of reader to text as mediated by criticism, of reader-in-the-machine to life as mediated by the machine. In this he establishes the assumption, developed in *Aspects of the Novel*, that the truly creative act is an invisible form of literature, but that such definitions of what constitutes such a creative act are grounded in specific class practices which are ultimately self-contradictory. Criticism, in seeking to promote certain class positions, begins to erode those positions by denying to that class certain aspects of culture. The critical tradition in 'The Machine Stops' can thus be seen as relocated by virtue of a perceived contradiction within bourgeois-humanism.

What Forster has to offer, then, is a radical new appraisal of the contemporary critical climate, which sees the critical movement as one which is grounded in a necessary discontinuity, a discontinuity between public statements (critical judgements) and the effects that such statements were supposed to have on a private, isolated, readership.

NOTES

1. E. M. Forster, *Aspects of the Novel* (London: William Clowes, 1974); hereafter referred to as *AN*, with page references given in the text.
2. E. M. Forster, *Abinger Harvest* (London: Penguin, 1967); hereafter referred to as *AH*, with pages references given in the text.
3. E. M. Forster, 'The Machine Stops', in *Collected Short Stories* (London: Penguin, 1982); hereafter referred to as *MS*, with page references given in the text.
4. See T. Eagleton, *Literary Theory: An Introduction* (Oxford: Blackwell, 1983) pp. 17–53 for a brief but useful account of the historical development of critical perspectives.
5. Ibid., see specifically pp. 30–9.
6. M. Foucault, *The History of Sexuality*, vol. 1 (London: Penguin, 1984) p. 95.
7. Ibid., p. 96.
8. J. McFarlane, 'The Mind of Modernism', in M. Bradley and J. McFarlane (eds), *Modernism (1890–1950)* (London: Penguin, 1976) p. 91.
9. It should be noted that the idea of 'partial humanity' is only relevant within a context, which is defined by Forster's bourgeois-humanism.
10. M. Foucault, *The History of Sexuality*, vol. 2 (London: Penguin, 1985) p. 28.

8

The Moth and the Moth-Hunter: The Literary Criticism of Virginia Woolf

LAURA KRANZLER

There were no whirring wings this time, but here and there, dotted about on the veins of sweet stuff, were soft brown lumps. These lumps seemed unspeakably precious, too deeply attached to the liquid to be disturbed. Their probosces were deep plunged, and as they drew in the sweetness, their wings quivered slightly as if in ecstasy. Even when the light was full upon them they could not tear themselves away, but sat there, quivering a little more uneasily perhaps, but allowing us to examine the tracery on the upper wing, those stains, spots, and veinings by which we decided their fate.[1]

This passage occurs midway through an essay by Virginia Woolf entitled 'Reading'. Although the essay is ostensibly a review of books by Thomas Browne and Hakluyt, among others, there are several pages of description of the writer luring, capturing, and killing prize moth specimens. Moths are a consistently rich symbol for Woolf, both in her fiction and, as here, in her critical essays. The original title of *The Waves* was *The Moths*, and in Woolf's discussion of moth-hunting in 'Reading' and the essay 'The Death of the Moth', an image of the moth as light, energy, creativity, and the imaginative spirit is articulated and, curiously, destroyed. The aim of moth-hunting is not simply an exercise in nature-appreciation, but rather the risky and tantalising capture and killing of an alien species whose beauty must be preserved under glass. Woolf writes that the capture of the scarlet underwing seemed a kind of proof of 'our skill against the hostile and alien forces' ('Reading', *CE*, II, p. 25). Woolf's discussion of moth-hunting in 'Reading' thus reveals a deeply am-bivalent attitude towards criticism, creativity and the reading process. The description of the moths, their probosces 'deep plunged' in the rum-soaked flannel, their wings 'quivering' in ecstasy, suggests an erotic, almost sexual image of readers, their noses stuck in books, their intellects trembling with pleasure. This idea of creativity is borne out in 'The Death of the Moth', in which a dying moth represents 'little or nothing but life' ('The Death of the Moth', *CE*, I, p. 360). The essay 'Reading' is, however, not only concerned with readers and texts but, more specifically, with readers as *critics* of authors and texts. The moth is both creative writer and imaginative text, whereas the moth-hunter 'captures' and kills the creative process, imprisoning it under the threatening practice of evaluative criticism which impinges on imaginative freedom. The images of readers, moths and moth-hunters therefore suggest a relationship between creativity which is joyous and ecstatic, and a critical practice which pinions and destroys the imaginative spirit. Moreover, the moth is an androgynous being. Woolf refers to it with the masculine pronoun, which possesses a phallic proboscis that 'plunges' into wetness (the damp flannel), those quivering wings, on the other hand, convey an idea of feminine sexual *jouissance*. The above passage, then, encapsulates some of Woolf's most fundamental ambiguities and contradictions concerning gender, reading, writing, and critical practice.

Woolf, as is well known, began her literary career as reviewer and journalist for such papers as the *Guardian* and the *Times Literary Supplement*, having apprenticed herself as a child as chief correspondent for the *Hyde Park Gate News*. She wrote for money, and not always with pleasure, and often resented having to tailor her criticism to the needs of the publishing industry.[2] She writes bitterly of the reviewer's job and its damaging effect on the aspiring young writer, citing the need for fine discrimination and subtle evaluation. On the other hand, she warns that standards are finally only subjective, and subordinate to the demands of the market-place.

The review has become an expression of individual opinion, given without any attempt to refer to 'eternal standards' by a man who is in a hurry; who is pressed for space; who is expected to cater in that little space for many different interests; who is bothered by the knowledge that he is not fulfilling his task; who is doubtful what that task is; and who, finally, is forced to hedge. ('Reviewing', *CE*, II, pp. 208–9)

A reviewer such as Woolf hires herself out to a publisher, and therefore must review what she is given; often she is relegated to 'inferior' fiction. Of the reviewer Woolf writes, 'most of the books he reviews are not worth the scratch of a pen upon paper' ('Reviewing', *CE*, II, p. 211). (It is interesting, and provocative, that she continually refers to the critic, writer and reader as 'he'; presumably she is aligning herself with the masculine authoritative pronoun.) In fact, this essay on reviewing was so scathing that in *Collected Essays* Leonard Woolf had to provide a mitigating endnote to the piece stating his disagreement with Woolf's attacks. Virginia Woolf's answer to the problem of reviewing was for the reviewer to meet privately with the author on the same terms as doctor or consultant, so that 'the fear of affecting sales [caused by unfavourable reviews] and of hurting feelings would be removed' ('Reviewing', *CE*, II, p. 212). She repeats this proposal in *Three Guineas*, commenting on the fact that the present economic conditions required advertising (in the form of reviewing) in order that books could be sold. The recommendation for 'a panel of critics recruited from reviewers' occurs in a discussion of the degenerate state of 'literary prostitution', whereby writers and reviewers produce art and criticism not according to aesthetic standards, but according to what will sell.[3] Her essay, 'The Patron and the Crocus', in particular, castigates the system of writing reviews for pay in which the demands of the mass media determine journalistic production. Thus, many of Woolf's review essays often condemn the very act of reviewing in which they themselves are engaged, and here is a crucial contradiction in the mass of articles and critical reviews Woolf so painstakingly and so elegantly produced.

There is, then, a tension in much of Woolf's criticism which seems split between the consciousness of critic and that of novelist or artist. In 'Letter to a Young Poet' she cautions one such prospective writer against the damaging influence of the critic:

> if you publish, your freedom will be checked; you will be thinking what people will say; you will write for others when you ought only to be writing for yourself. And what point can there be in curbing the wild torrent of spontaneous nonsense which is now, for a few years only, your divine gift in order to publish prim little books of experimental verses? . . . your friends will pepper your manuscripts with far more serious and searching criticism than

any you will get from the reviewers. ('Letter to a Young Poet', *CE*, II, p. 194)

This passage is a curiously complex mixture of patronising encouragement and criticism: on the one hand, Woolf sides with the poet against the publishing forces which, like the moth-hunters, truncate and curtail the free imaginative spirit. On the other hand, as representative (if not agent) of those forces, Woolf-as-critic derides that 'divine gift' as 'spontaneous nonsense'; moreover, as published reviewer, she produces the very sort of criticism which would censor the poet's 'torrential' creativity. Many of Woolf's critical essays are saturated with evaluations of the writer's style, form, characterisation and language. From her testimonials of Shakespeare (upon whom only Coleridge is fit to comment[4]) to poor Eliza Haywood, 'the scribbling dame' who was a 'writer of no importance',[5] Woolf recommends this writer to our most favourable notice, and that to total disregard. On the one hand, then, Woolf suggests that ill-directed criticism will perpetually stifle an artist's burgeoning creativity. On the other hand, however, it may be worth speculating whether Woolf's determinedly evaluative practice as paid critic would encourage any but the most supremely self-confident writer to publish.

Certainly Woolf believes in the need for literary discrimination. Although she admits that critics have failed to recognize genius, or have commended sadly inadequate works (hence Leonard Woolf's cautionary footnote), she still upholds the requirement of certain aesthetic standards:

As for the critics whose task it is to pass judgment upon the books of the moment, whose work, let us admit, is difficult, dangerous, and often distasteful, let us ask them to be generous of encouragement, but sparing of those wreaths and coronets which are so apt to get awry, and fade, and make the wearers, in six months' time, look a little ridiculous. ('How It Strikes a Contemporary', *CE*, II, p. 161)

The standards Woolf would apply would seem to be the 'touchstones' of Matthew Arnold, as well as 'one's own instincts', which should be followed 'fearlessly . . . rather than submit[ting] them to the control of any critic or reviewer' ('How It Strikes a Contemporary', *CE*, II, p. 154). This appeal to an independently-determined canon of 'greats' therefore seems to work against the fearless following of one's instincts, since the very ideology of a canon presumably implies the presence of a collective critical consensus, the very essence of which demands conformity to a kind of tradition from which Woolf's own work attempts to break away. It seems unlikely, therefore, that there can be a reconciliation between artists writing for themselves, and the continual consideration that their work should be worthy of those sparingly-conferred coronets of literary greatness.

The writing which Woolf appears to admire most is, understandably, that which most closely approximates her own. Thus, in writing on Dorothy Richardson's work, she comments appreciatively that Richardson's characters' 'discoveries are concerned with the states of being and not with the states of doing. Miriam is a wave of "life itself", of the atmosphere of the table rather than of the table; of the silence rather than of the sound.'[6] This passage suggests Woolf's own novel *The Voyage Out*, where Terence Hewet dreams of writing a novel 'about Silence . . . the things people don't say'.[7] In Woolf's essay on Jane Austen, she speculates that had Austen lived longer she would have 'devised a method, clear and composed as ever, but deeper and more suggestive, for conveying not only what people say, but what they leave unsaid' ('Jane Austen', *CE*, I, p. 153). Again, this is a fair assessment of Woolf's own fictional project, perhaps most elegantly realised in the pregnantly empty conversations between Mrs and Mr Ramsay. In the famous essay 'Modern Fiction', Woolf evaluates the achievements of her contemporaries, from Wells, Bennett and Galsworthy to Turgenev, and she outlines evocatively and imagistically her oft-quoted conception of the artist's relation to the representation of 'life': 'Life is not a series of gig-lamps symmetrically arranged; life is a luminous halo, a semi-transparent envelope surrounding us from the beginning of consciousness to the end' ('Modern Fiction', *CE*, II, p. 106).

Woolf's evocation of the moth-like spirit of what it means to live, which she describes as 'unknown and uncircumscribed', is too delicate to withstand the heavy descriptive bent of a writer like Arnold Bennett. Woolf's well-known dispute with the 'Edwardians', 'Mr Bennett and Mrs Brown', is her most explicit defence of her break with the 'materialists' – Wells, Galsworthy and Bennett – in favour of the mysterious, elusive 'Mrs Brown', a character she impressionistically evokes more than describes.[8] This character, like the dying moth, 'is, of course, the spirit we live by, life itself', and this is too fragile to be grasped in the clumsy Edwardian paw ('Mr Bennett and Mrs Brown', *CE*, I, p. 337). In the same essay Woolf scolds the reader for accepting the 'professional airs and graces' of writers, with whom she aligns herself, arguing that to assume that writers 'know more of Mrs. Brown than you do' is a 'fatal mistake' ('Mr Bennett and Mrs Brown', *CE*, I, p. 336). Although Woolf is arguing that there is no transcendental 'Mrs Brown', and that character and consciousness can never be definitively pinned down by author or reader, she is privileging a reading based on her own modernist aesthetic that is at variance with those of a previous literary tradition.

There is, then, a curious tension between Woolf's valorisation of the kind of modernist poetry-prose which she practises, and the 'masterpieces' of the past which she had exhorted young writers to consult as Arnoldian touchstones against which to measure their talent. Woolf correlates her defiant break with tradition with the historical shift which occurred around 1910, when 'human relations ... shifted ... And when human relations change there is at the same time a change in religion, conduct, politics, and literature' ('Mr Bennett and Mrs Brown', *CE*, I, p. 321). Certainly Woolf is not arguing that pre-modernist writers are deficient in one way or another by virtue of their historical placement – in her essays she continues to uphold the 'greats'. Nevertheless, if the standards of the past no longer apply in the post-1910 world, then what is the young writer to consult when searching for guidance of her own?[9]

Although many of Woolf's own novels work against the reader's attempts to construct fictional people such as Jacob Flanders as identifiable characters, the project of 'Mr Bennett and Mrs Brown' is actually a defence of the character as conceived by the reader. In criticising the Edwardians, who attempt to place character without actually 'seeing' her, Woolf empathetically produces an image of Mrs Brown as she imagines her. In her essay 'On Re-reading Novels', Woolf confirms that 'we identify ourselves with this person or that. We fasten upon the character or the scene which is congenial. We swing our imaginations capriciously from spot to spot' ('On Re-reading Novels', *CE*, II, p. 124). This is not unambiguously the post-structuralist dream of letting the free play of signifiers work through the reader's consciousness, however; Woolf in this essay specifically directs the reader to correlate what is read with authorial intentions. 'We should read at arm's length from the distractions we have named. We must receive impressions but we must relate them to each other as the author intended' ('On Re-reading Novels', *CE*, II, p. 124). Much of Woolf's criticism is decidedly author-centered, almost arrogantly so, in that she can presume to read the character of the author as it is encoded in the literary text.

> The dominion which writers have over us is immediately personal; it is their actual voice that we hear in the rise and fall of the sentence; their shape and colour that we see in the page, so that even their old shoes have a way of being worn on this side rather than on that, which seems not gossip but revelation.   ('Flumina Amem Silvasque', *BP*, p. 190)

In this passage Woolf is clearly locating at least some of the charm of literature within the charm of the writers themselves. Thus, for example, in her essay on *Aurora Leigh* Woolf can claim 'through the voice of Aurora the character, the circumstances, the idiosyncracies of Elizabeth Barrett Browning ring in our ears' ('Aurora Leigh', *CE*, I, p. 212). Because Barrett Browning's persona is so indelibly inscribed, her poem is not a successful character study but rather a more general work about the lives of historical Victorian people ('Aurora Leigh', *CE*, I, p. 217). Curiously, however, in the same essay Woolf praises Barrett Browning for being 'one of those rare writers who risk themselves adventurously and disinterestedly in an imaginative life which is independent of their private lives and demands to be considered apart from personalities' ('Aurora Leigh', *CE*, I, p. 214). There is, quite clearly, a tension here in Woolf's consideration of the writer as individual and a valorisation of those who can transcend personal idiosyncracies in favour of a more disinterested art. (How this contradiction is resolved in the case of Barrett Browning is remarkably unclear.) Thus, in an essay on George Moore, Woolf writes appreciatively of 'the great novelist [who] feels, sees, believes with such intensity of conviction that he hurls his belief outside himself and it flies off and lives an independent life of its own' ('George Moore', *CE*, I, p. 338).

This tension between the artist-as-person and the impersonal writer, 'engaged upon some vast building', who is to be considered anonymous, is most clearly marked in Woolf's discussion of women writers and the material circumstances surrounding the literary producer ('How It Strikes a Contemporary', *CE*, II, p. 161). In her famous essay 'Women and Fiction', Woolf describes the woman writer who is so caught up in a polemical discourse about sex and gender that the aesthetic dimension of the work is obscured by the writer's insistence on what lies 'outside' the literary text.

> In *Middlemarch* and in *Jane Eyre* we are conscious . . . of a woman's presence – of someone resenting the treatment of her sex and pleading for its rights. . . . It introduces a distortion and is frequently the cause of weakness. The desire to plead some personal cause or to make a character the mouthpiece of some personal discontent or grievance always has a distressing effect, as if the spot at which the reader's attention is directed were suddenly twofold instead of single.   ('Women and Fiction', *CE*, II, p. 144)

In this passage Woolf is castigating the need of writers – particularly women writers – to make their gender known and to register complaints about gender inequality. Women who trumpet their sex on the page are either unnaturally self-assertive or unnaturally docile, rather than achieving the 'aloofness' which Woolf sees as the work of 'genius and originality' (Women and Fiction', *CE*, II, p. 145). Like American writers, who also have reason to react against a hegemonic tradition (the British empire),[10] women writers are so concerned with anticipating a potentially hostile audience that, as Woolf sees it, the 'meaning' of the literary enterprise gets buried under the onslaught of spleen or is muted by simpering feminine docility. Woolf's answer in her own work, particularly in *A Room of One's Own*, is to defuse anger through playfulness and wit. She eludes the 'Angel in the House,'[11] of Victorian ideology through irony and indirectness. Nevertheless, such 'light-fingered allusiveness' both reveals rage against a patriarchal structure that systematically excludes women, and is an attempt at placating the Angel of female submissiveness by secreting such anger under 'charm and conciliation'.[12] Certainly much of Woolf's fiction articulates anger through demonstration of the injustices committed against women, and the social and psychological crippling they undergo as a result. Curiously, as Hermione Lee points out, *Three Guineas*, the most openly polemical of Woolf's work, seeks to 'dissolve' feminist anger through a 'genderless dream of power, freedom and cooperation'.[13] Despite Woolf's 'genderless dream', however, it appears that much of women's writing, as she conceives it, is impoverished by its inability – or refusal – to reform anger, as she attempts to do, through irony and wit. Woolf's position on women writers reveals a conviction that gender – particularly the feminine – will always out, either due to material conditions or else to the structure of the 'woman's sentence'.

In 'Women and Fiction' Woolf theorises the construction of a kind of female writing that is produced by the necessity of women finding an alternative representational structure to a limiting patriarchal discourse.

> The very form of the sentence does not fit her. It is a sentence made by men; it is too loose, too heavy, too pompous for a woman's use. Yet in a novel, which covers so wide a stretch of ground, an ordinary and usual type of sentence has to be found to carry the reader on easily and naturally from one end of the book to the other. And this a woman must make for herself, altering and adapting the current sentence until she writes one that takes the natural shape of her thought without crushing or distorting it. ('Women and Fiction', *CE*, II, p. 148)

The female sentence as Woolf describes it is thus a conscious and deliberate aesthetic construction, not the psychological consequence of the gendered entrance into language posited by contemporary post-structuralists and psycho-linguists such as Julia Kristeva and Jacques Lacan.[14] Rather, the vocabulary Woolf employs – 'make', 'altering', 'adapting' – suggests that women must consciously produce an alternative structure of representation if they are to articulate experience which is not an empty mimicry of men's.[15] Dorothy Richardson is one writer who has invented the 'psychological sentence of the feminine gender. It is of a more elastic fibre than the old, capable of stretching to the extreme'.[16] Richardson's writing, in other words, explores the female unconscious in a language which seeks to go beyond any limited sense of *doing*, to represent the consciousness of *being*. Unfortunately, Woolf thinks her project lacks unity and substance, and is too much the 'helter-skelter of flying fragments' ('Dorothy Richardson', *WW*, p. 190). Yet Woolf is quick to affirm that Richardson's sentence is not *intrinsically* 'feminine', but is so by virtue of what she writes about based on her experience in society as a woman. 'It is a woman's sentence, but only in the sense that it is used to describe a woman's mind by a writer who is neither proud nor afraid of anything that she may discover in the psychology of her sex' ('Dorothy Richardson', *WW*, p. 190). Nevertheless, form and content converge, as in Woolf's own work, where the linear structure is broken up by means of alliteration, indirection, interception, and the pervasive sense of a poetic rhythm, all of which 'enacts a commitment to the heterogeneity of female experience'.[17] In much of Woolf's writing she celebrates the ability of women to free themselves from a rigidifying, oppressive linearity which compresses the 'semi-transparent envelope' into static and reified concepts and categories. Whereas men like Mr Ramsay can only conceptualise thought along a linear alphabetical plan in a teleological project that privileges experience which moves from point to point, these women, and women's writing more generally, can express the said and the not-said, can articulate the fluid moth-wings of experience without crushing them.

Of course, men's writing can participate in this representational strategy as well. Moreover, although some of Woolf's own writing approximates to the semiotic 'writing of the body' of French feminist thought,[18] men have a certain freedom in conveying a more direct expression of sexuality and the body than is accessible to women – at least, those writing before and during Woolf's lifetime. In 'Professions for Women' Woolf speaks of the painful experience of the woman writer who is 'fishing' in the unconscious imagination but comes up hard against the block which forbids her to articulate, with any specificity, the female experience of the sexual body. 'She had thought of something, something about the body, about the passions which it was unfitting for her as a woman to say' ('Professions for Women', *CE*, II, p. 288). Outdated Victorian prudery made it difficult, if not impossible, for women in Woolf's day to speak frankly and openly about the sexual body. The woman writer, therefore, had to invent, as Woolf did, an alternative system of describing the sexual body because the direct routes were blocked and circumscribed by patriarchal discourse. Thus Woolf's theory of women's writing acknowledges the power of a 'female sentence' which realises in form and in content the reality of what it is to be a woman living in patriarchal society, and she has a great deal to say about the ways in which the material circumstances influence and shape the creative process itself.

Much has already been written about that vastly influential work, *A Room of One's Own*, in which Woolf boldly and baldly states, 'a woman must have money and a room of her own if she is to write fiction'.[19] This is the work in which she most clearly articulates the connection between writing and the material conditions of social and sexual history, arguing that women's writing is relegated to an inferior position in history because women inhabit an inferior position in the material world. Woolf argues that potential 'Judith Shakespeares' are forbidden to earn a living by writing, and have been silenced by a society which suppresses female expression because these women lack access to the resources which would allow them to proclaim their 'trivial' interests as valuable and part of the dominant culture (*RO*, p. 74). It is worth noting, however, that Woolf applies the same criteria to women writers as she did to make ones in her reviews, thus involving them in all the contradictions discussed earlier. Although Woolf argues that women write out of anger or deferral because they are responding to a particular kind of critical reception, she herself is part of that (sometimes hostile) reception. True, she locates the motivation for the 'unaesthetic' response within a patriarchal culture which oppresses women, but it could be proposed that her very aesthetic standards are part of a patriarchal literary tradition. Of course, as 'Mr Bennett and Mrs Brown' shows, she seeks to break with a tradition which perpetuates certain representational strategies which ignore or devalue the 'feminine': Mrs Brown is, of course, a female character. Nevertheless, Woolf finds fault with a practice of women writing consciously *as* women (and men writing as men), and so it seems as though there is a kind of impasse from which the gendered writer cannot extricate herself: she is exhorted to write like a woman, but without deference to a patriarchal culture which has, after all, helped to produce and define gender differentiation.

There is a similar impasse for the writer of class as well as gender. In 'The Niece of an Earl', Woolf suggests that class – particularly in England – marks the writer as indelibly as the stamp of gender. She argues that the English writer cannot escape the enclosure and myopia produced by hierarchical class distinctions: 'His work is influenced by his birth. He is fated to know intimately, and so to describe with understanding, only those who are of his own social rank. He cannot escape from the box in which he has been bred' ('The Niece of an Earl', *CE*, I, p. 221). Woolf mourns the inability of the middle-class writer to penetrate the domains of the lower class: 'The rising novelist is never pestered to come to gin and winkles with the plumber and his wife' ('The Niece of an Earl', *CE*, I, p. 222). In fact Woolf's own work demonstrates this class-bound limitation. While Woolf acknowledges that writers – particularly of the middle class – must transcend their boundaries based on money and status, much of the representation of the working class in her work is shadowy and vague. Certainly she protests against this alienating hierarchy:

Mrs Dalloway is a brilliantly ironic castigation of privilege and power. It is, however, an ambiguous critique of the social classes, by virtue of the fact that its heroine is both victimised by, and proudly defensive of, the culture which has produced her.[20] Thus, Woolf argues that writers cannot move away from their assigned social rank in the same way that women writers in particular cannot escape gender, but she exhibits an uneasy tension between representing class as a prison, and rejecting any conscious egalitarian moves to rupture class boundaries.

'The Leaning Tower' is probably Woolf's best-known defence of her position, in which she attacks writers who turn against the society that sheltered and helped them prosper, particularly the post-World War I poets. In this essay she scorns those writers who have achieved success largely due to a privileged education, and who then turn on their families and their money, writing works of 'discord and bitterness . . . confusion and . . . compromise' ('The Leaning Tower', *CE*, II, p. 172). Like women writers whose work is 'distorted' by their protests against, or deference to, partriarchal authority, Day Lewis, Auden, Spender, Isherwood and others preach in shrill and discordant tones against a bourgeois society from which (as Woolf sees it) they have only benefited. She regards their writings as the egotistical assuagement of guilt bred in luxury and privilege, and she argues that their self-propagandising is better suited to autobiography, not art. Thus she advises the Workers Educational Association (with whom she aligns herself as 'we') to begin to write for themselves, rather than allowing self-conscious middle-class writers to speak for them. 'We must become critics because in future we are not going to leave writing to be done for us by a small class of well-to-do young men who have only a pinch, a thimbleful of experience to give us. We are going to add our own experience, to make our own contribution' ('The Leaning Tower', *CE*, II, p. 181). It is worth wondering, however, how a class structured by oppression could possibly free itself sufficiently to write without the same 'bitterness and discord' of the post-war poets. Since the class system is structured by exploitation, to write about the lower class *is* to write about the experience of that exploitation.

Woolf's theory, that the material circumstances produce the artist, is, then, compromised by her appeal to an aesthetic practice which is, if not removed, at least effectively distanced from social and historical considerations. Her approval of Emily Brontë's work, for example, is based on Brontë's romantic otherworldliness, her ability in

Wuthering Heights to 'tear up all that we know human beings by, and fill these unrecognizable transparencies with such a gust of life that they transcend reality' ('*Jane Eyre* and *Wuthering Heights*', CE, I, p. 190). It is as though Woolf can find in the work of art an aesthetic experience which reveals 'life's meaning' (whatever that may be) in some kind of universal and transcendental truth which goes deeper and is more profound than argument based on social and political reality. She looks to a time when 'the greater impersonality of women's lives will encourage the poetic spirit . . . [women writers] will look beyond the personal and political relationships to the wider questions which the poet tries to solve – of our destiny and the meaning of life' ('Women and Fiction', CE, II, p. 147). In 'The Narrow Bridge of Art', she describes the novel of the future that comes closest to poetry not because it conveys a sense of what it means to live in the social and historical world, but because it will explore 'the relations of man to nature, to fate; his imagination; his dreams' ('The Narrow Bridge of Art', CE, II, p. 226). Of course, she adds that the novel-poem 'will also give the sneer, the contrast, the question, the closeness and complexity of life', but the meaning of that 'life' is not related to the gritty realities of class, gender, and other experiences which make 'life' different for each individual ('The Narrow Bridge of Art', CE, II, p. 226). It is true *The Years* was Woolf's attempt to relate art to history, but she abandoned the first draft, *The Pargiters*, which explicitly related each fictional chapter to polemical essays, in favour of fiction alone. It is also true, of course, that her fictional works often make reference to such structuring elements as the social strata and World War I, and she writes hopefully of a time when women's writing will be less 'personal' and will 'become more critical of society' ('Women and Fiction', CE, II, p. 147). Nevertheless, in *Three Guineas*, the text which speaks most openly about the political world, she finds greatest truth not 'in the bark of the guns and the bray of the gramophones' but urges the reader instead to listen 'to the voice of the poets, answering each other' (*TG*, p. 163). Woolf suggests that the goals of freedom and peace have 'haunted the human mind since the beginning of time', reading the desire for peace as some kind of trans-historical 'dream' even as she peppers her argument with facts, quotations, and the scholarly appeal of footnotes (*TG*, p. 163). Thus it appears as though once ideal material conditions can be achieved – peace, money, space, education – the artist or writer may then transcend those conditions and find refuge in a literary practice which promotes 'egolessness', androgyny, and the self-less creative spirit.[21]

Woolf looks forward to a time, then, when cultural conditions will shift, allowing the 'butterfly' to triumph over the 'gadfly', when the artist in the writer will be more successful than the reformer ('Women and Fiction', *CE*, II, p. 147). The pressure of 'granite' against 'rainbow', or the conflict between political rhetoric and the artistic temperament, will be resolved. The androgynous writer will be able to transcend the obligations of gender because, as Woolf describes in *A Room of One's Own*, the 'man' and 'woman' parts of the brain will be able to 'live in harmony together, spiritually cooperating' (*RO*, p. 98). Shakespeare is her ideal example of the androgynous writer who can fuse consciousness in a heterosexual unity, a mental wholeness composed not of monolithic sameness, but a harmony of different perceptions and experiences which culture apportions out and labels 'feminine' and 'masculine'. The word 'feminist', for example, which she dreams of burning in *Three Guineas*, will no longer be relevant in a world in which women and men can work together in a cooperative spirit, and it will no longer be necessary to write consciously of gender and the self because difference will no longer be seen as discordant or problematical. This is not to suggest that sexual and personal differences will be subsumed under some mass monolith which will smooth out all contradictions, but rather that heterogeneity can be embraced in a harmonious unity of composition, not conflict. Nevertheless, the contradictions in Woolf's own work do appear to be in uneasy juxtaposition; there is still the impression that gender is less important – even in its still-embattled condition – or inferior to the heightened aesthetic response. Thus she commends women writers like Austen who are able to disregard the very conditions which produced them as women, somehow seeming to transcend the culture in which they live. In praise of these writers Woolf says 'to take no more thought of their sex when they wrote than of the colour of their eyes was one of their conspicuous distinctions, and of itself a proof that they wrote at the bidding of a profound and imperious instinct' ('Women Novelists', *WW*, p. 70).

We return, then, to the moths in Woolf's essay 'Reading', where feminine and masculine are androgynously fused in the quivering wings and phallic probosces, fluttering intellect and readerly rapture. At the same time, however, the moth-hunter is an image of the pinioning and truncating of the creative spirit, which Woolf sees as endemic to the critical and reading process. Woolf's own critical practice – evaluative, contradictory – encourages while striving to contain certain narrative experiences, always aiming for the aestheticised response, sometimes at the expense of the historical and material self which produced it. Her ambivalence toward the critical, writing and reading self is thus clearly expressed in the tension in her essays which encourage the independent creative artist while embedding that encouragement in the very critical practice which censures and discriminates among forms of imaginative expression. It is as though Woolf is commenting upon her own self-divisions as author and critic when she writes, 'it is only by knowing how to write that you can make use in literature of your self; that self which, while it is essential to literature, is also its most dangerous antagonist. Never to be yourself and yet always – that is the problem' ('The Modern Essay', *CE*, ɪɪ, p. 46).

NOTES

1. V. Woolf, 'Reading', in L. Woolf (ed.), *Collected Essays*, 4 vols (London: Hogarth, 1966–1967) vol. ɪɪ, pp. 12–33; p. 23; hereafter referred to as *CE*, with volume and page numbers given in the text.
2. See A. Zwerdling, *Virginia Woolf and the Real World* (London: University of California Press, 1979) pp. 38–61, for a discussion of Woolf as 'the reluctant satirist'. See also Q. Bell, *Virginia Woolf: A Biography* (London: Triad/Paladin, 1987) vol. ɪ, pp. 28–30, for a discussion of Woolf's childhood journalism.
3. V. Woolf, *Three Guineas* (London: Hogarth Press, 1986) p. 195, n. 18; hereafter referred to as *TG* in the text.
4. V. Woolf, 'Coleridge as Critic', in M. Lyon (ed.), *Books and Portraits* (London: Triad Grafton, 1986) p. 47; hereafter referred to as *BP* in the text.
5. V. Woolf, 'A Scribbling Dame', in Lyon, *Books and Portraits*, p. 151.
6. V. Woolf, 'Dorothy Richardson', in M. Barrett (ed.), *Women and Writing* (London: Women's Press, 1988) p. 192; hereafter referred to as *WW* in the text.
7. V. Woolf, *The Voyage Out* (London: Triad Grafton, 1988) p. 220.
8. For two articles which argue that Woolf was responding in 'Mr Bennett and Mrs Brown' to personal attacks from Bennett see S. Hynes, 'The Whole Contention between Mr Bennett and Mrs Woolf', *Novel: A Forum on Fiction*, vol. I (Autumn 1967) no. 1, pp. 34–44; and Irving Kreutz, 'Mr Bennett and Mrs Woolf', *Modern Fiction Studies*, vol. 8 (1962–63), pp. 103–15.
9. Woolf argues that it is the *form* of a literary work which survives and

'endures, however mood or fashion may change' ('On Re-reading Novels', *Collected Essays*, II, p. 124).

10. See 'American Fiction', *Collected Essays*, II, pp. 111–21, for Woolf's discussion of the 'handicapped' American writer.
11. 'Killing the Angel in the House was part of the occupation of a woman writer' ('Professions for Women', *Collected Essays*, II, p. 286).
12. H. Lee, Introduction to *Three Guineas* (London: Hogarth, 1990) p. x.
13. Ibid., p. xvii.
14. Similarly, Woolf argues that American writers coin new words in the same way some women writers construct new sentences, in an effort to overcome the limitations of a representational structure produced by a different cultural group (in this case, the British). See 'American Fiction', *Collected Essays*, II, p. 120.
15. Lee, *Three Guineas*, p. x.
16. Woolf, 'Dorothy Richardson', in *Women and Writing*, p. 191.
17. M. Minow-Pinkney, *Virginia Woolf and the Problem of the Subject: Feminine Writing in the Major Novels* (London: Harvester, 1987) p. 104.
18. See T. Moi, *Sexual/Textual Politics* (London: Methuen, 1985) for the clearest and most explicitly argued account of the theoretical writings of Hélène Cixous, Julia Kristeva and Luce Irigaray.
19. V. Woolf, *A Room of One's Own* (London: Harcourt Brace Jovanovich, 1981) p. 4; hereafter referred to as *RO* in the text.
20. For a discussion of *Mrs Dalloway*'s relation to class, see Zwerdling, *Virginia Woolf* pp. 120–43.
21. The argument of this essay is not to de-historicise Woolf; certainly, as Barrett points out, Woolf's view of the 'pure work of art . . . was, of course, far more common in Woolf's time that it is now. (Barrett, Introduction, in *Women and Writing*, p. 23). Nevertheless, Woolf herself is responding to writers working at the same time as herself who see literature as fundamentally rooted in historical reality, and part of her aesthetic project is to mark herself off as distinct from them.

9

D. H. Lawrence: Cliques and Consciousness

JIM REILLY

I

I am following Lawrence's example and taking a broad conception of what constitutes 'criticism' and quoting novels alongside essays, studies and reviews. The barrier between critical and fictional forms is for Lawrence a thoroughly permeable one. F. R. Leavis called his seminal study *D. H. Lawrence: Novelist*[1] to counter the view that his subject was primarily a thinker and critic indiscriminately using genres – lyric, drama, fiction, essay, travel writing, criticism – for consistent polemical purposes. But one of the attitudes he was countering is perhaps Lawrence's own. Lawrence's fiction sometimes chafes against his own formulation 'Never trust the artist. Trust the tale.'[2] *Kangaroo* suspends tale altogether for two chapters as the artist, speaking through his protagonist, delivers another version of the anti-democratic diatribe Lawrence is everywhere rehearsing. The suspension of 'tale' is freely acknowledged – 'Chapter follows chapter and nothing doing'[3] – and the soliloquising artist dismisses, with an ironic pretence of defending, the work's own novelistic status and reliance on that fictional staple, dialogue, 'I hope, dear reader, you like plenty of *conversation* in a novel: it makes it so much lighter and brisker' (*K*, p. 311). The reader's impatience is acknowledged by being dismissed: 'If you don't like the novel, don't read it' (*K*, p. 313). *Kangaroo* momentarily becomes all artist – or rather critic – and no tale, with little or no interest in soliciting trust from a reader it can do without. It is an extreme illustration of the fact that Lawrence is everywhere a critic and, like Gudrun Brangwen, 'critical of everything'. Even his own life with its restless migrations between class positions and, in later years, various illusory heartlands, was another form, perhaps his ultimate one, of critical statement.

My particular subject from within the ubiquity of Lawrentian criticism is his fraught and contradictory conception of individuality, with particular reference to his relation to and commentary on nineteenth-century and Edwardian fiction. The choice of individualism as an issue is less selective a reading than one might think since Lawrence's typical and apparently disparate concerns – political, sexual, religious, literary – are continually resolving themselves into variants of this troublesome Ur-issue. The politics of *Kangaroo* protest the claim of the individualistic 'aristocratic principle' in the face of the pernicious 'merging' of democracy. What is anathematised is contemporary sex seen as poisonously individualised, alienated and masturbatory, *Apocalypse* reads *The Book of Revelation* as a pivotal moment in the instituting of that persistent archetype 'the individual, the Christian, the democrat'.[4] Lawrence's literary criticism – praising Hardy's independent and 'aristocratic' characters, maligning Galsworthy's worldly and 'social' ones – scrutinises fiction for the realisation of an individualistic ideal.

Lawrence famously declared to Edward Garnett apropos of *Women in Love* 'You mustn't look in my novel for the old stable ego of the character'.[5] Leaving aside the question of whether that novel in particular does break the mould of the stable ego, we can say that it seems that everywhere else in Lawrence's writings we are continually confronted with something that looks very like that ego in full-throated self-justification. We don't have to go looking for it. Lawrentian voices – whether of characters, narrators or his own, whether lyric, dramatic or discursive – exist in a constant flurry, formulating and broadcasting their beleaguered individuality. Lawrentian texts unleash a fantastic iteration of egotistical energy; here are a few examples:

> The central law of all organic life is that each organism is intrinsically isolate and single in itself. (*SCAL*, p. 71)

> At the solar plexus, the dynamic knowledge is this, that *I am I* . . . I am I, in vital centrality. I am I, the vital centre of all things.[6]

> The purest lesson our era has taught is that man, at his highest, is an individual, single, isolate, alone, in direct communication with the unknown God, which prompts within him, (*K*, p. 332)

> Each soul *should* be alone. And in the end the desire for a 'perfect

relationship' is just a vicious, unmanly craving. 'Tous nos malheurs viennent de ne pouvoir être seuls'.   (*SCAL*, p. 151)

Life is individual, always was individual and always will be. Life consists of living individuals, and always did so consist, in the beginning of everything. There never was any universe, any cosmos, of which the first reality was anything but living, incorporate individuals.   (*FU*, p. 150)

She only knew that it was not limited mechanical energy, nor mere purpose of self-preservation and self-assertion. It was a consummation, a being infinite. Self was a oneness with the infinite. To be oneself was a supreme, gleaming triumph of infinity.[7]

'Now', thought Richard to himself, waving his front paws with gratification: 'I must sound the muezzin and summon all men back to their central, isolate selves'.   (*K*, p. 309)

II

In his criticism of the characterisation in the novels of John Galsworthy Lawrence sets out the terms of his typically urgent and contradictory formulations about identity. He asks why we feel an instinctive refusal to identify the Forsythes with our own humanity, why they appear so inferior. They seem to have 'lost caste as human beings', having sunk to the level of the 'social being'. His argument drifts from a commentary on Galsworthy to a lament over the supposed historical demise of individualism.

The human individual is a queer animal, always changing. But the fatal change to-day is the collapse from the psychology of the free human individual into the psychology of the social being, just as the fatal change in the past was a collapse from the freeman's psyche to the psyche of the slave. The free moral and the slave moral, the human moral and the social moral: these are the abiding antitheses.

While a man remains a man, a true human individual, there is at the core of him a certain innocence or naïveté which defies all analysis, and which you cannot bargain with, you can only deal with in good faith from your own corresponding innocence or naïveté. This does not mean that the human being is nothing but naïve or innocent. He is Mr Worldly Wiseman also in his own degree. But in his essential core he is naïve, and money does not touch him. Money, of course, with every man living goes a long way. With the alive human being it may go as far as his penultimate feeling. But in the last naked him it does not enter.

With the social being it goes right through the centre and is the controlling principle no matter how much he may pretend, nor how much bluff he may put up. He may give away all he has to the poor and still reveal himself as a social being swayed finally and helplessly by the money-sway, and by the social moral, which is inhuman.

It seems to me that when the human being becomes too much divided between his subjective and objective consciousness, at last something splits in him and he becomes a social being. When he becomes too much aware of objective reality, and of his own isolation in the face of a universe of objective reality, the core of his identity splits, his nucleus collapses, his innocence or his naïveté perishes, and he becomes only a subjective-objective reality, a divided thing hinged together but not strictly individual.[8]

This is tellingly contorted. An attack on Galsworthy's characterisation for its depiction of aberrant 'social beings' slides into Lawrence's own characterisation of contemporary society under the same lights. Should Lawrence rather not be praising Galsworthy for the psychological veracity of all his men and women of property? Is it Galsworthy's characters, or us, who have 'lost caste as human beings'? Is the problem timeless or historical – 'abiding antitheses' or 'the fatal change of to-day'? While apparently denying their relation, Lawrence in fact illuminates the intimacy of the connection between identity and 'the money-sway'. He struggles here against the intuitions of his own characterisation. Connie Chatterley refutes her author's belief that money only touches the 'penultimate feeling' and his assertion of the possibility of a man remaining a man. She is certain that 'Once you are alive, money is a necessity, and the only absolute necessity' and that 'There was only one class nowadays: moneyboys. The moneyboy and the moneygirl, the only difference was how much you'd got, and how much you wanted.'[9] Lawrence's striking definition of contemporary identity – 'a subjective – objective reality, a divided thing hinged together but not strictly indi-

vidual' – is recalled in Ursula Brangwen's self-depiction, or rather
self-interrogation, in *The Rainbow*.

> How to act, that was the question? Whither to go, how to become
> oneself? One was not oneself, one was merely a half-stated ques-
> tion. How to become oneself, how to know the question and
> answer of oneself, when one was merely an unfixed something –
> nothing, blowing about like the winds of heaven, undefined,
> unstated.   (*R*, p. 284)

The form of identity Lawrence evokes and criticises in 'John
Galsworthy' with its perverse contradictoriness and incoherence, 'a
subjective-objective reality . . . hinged together but not strictly individual', can be read as historically specific, its emergence being 'the
fatal change' not of 'to-day' but of the preceeding century. Marx and
Engels argue that contemporary identity is thoroughly ideological
and class-bound. What is designated by that apparently ahistorical
and classless abstraction, the 'individual', is in fact 'no other person
than the bourgeois, than the middle-class owner of property', a
person who must be 'swept out of the way, and made impossible'.[10]
That such an argument exercises Lawrence is evident from Charlie
May's re-iteration of it in *Lady Chatterley's Lover*: 'then the individual,
especially the *personal* man, is bourgeois: so he must be suppressed'
(*LCL*, p. 40). Nineteenth-century identity is the 'something-nothing'
torn between the utterly contradictory accounts of individuality offered by Engels and J. S. Mill. For Engels the nineteenth century is
characterised by competition and universal struggle, most graphic-
ally expressed in the city's unprecedented massing of competitive
identities. 'Individuality' is indeed merely conjectural within a culture where, with a crushing perversity, identities are, on the one
hand, physically and socially amassed and, on the other, mentally
and ideologically atomised.

> The brutal indifference, the unfeeling isolation of each in his
> private interest becomes the most repellent and offensive, the
> more these individuals are crowded together, within a limited
> space. And, however much one may be aware that this isolation
> of the individual, this narrow self-seeking, is the fundamental
> principle of our society everywhere, it is nowhere so shamelessly
> barefaced, so self-conscious as just here in the crowding of the
> great city. The dissolution of mankind into monads, of which each

one has a separate purpose, the world of atoms, is here carried out to its utmost extreme.[11]

Meanwhile the existential oppression of 'isolation', 'self-seeking', and 'competition' Engels condemns have their bourgeois ideologues. Under that near-numinous term 'individuality' these conditions are transmuted into the most highly valued of bourgeois ideological constructions and the innermost presupposition of its discourse. A paradigmatic instance is the famous chapter of Mill's *On Liberty*, 'On Individuality as One of the Elements of Well-Being'. Mill echoes the dilemma Engels identifies but argues for the further promulgation, rather than eradication, of 'private interest':

> It is not by watering down into uniformity all that is individual in themselves, but by cultivating and calling it forth, within the limits imposed by the rights and interests of others, that human beings become a noble and beautiful object of contemplation. . . . In proportion to the development of his individuality, each person becomes more valuable to himself, and is, therefore, capable of being more valuable to others. There is a greater fullness of life about his own existence, and when there is more life in the units there is more in the mass which is composed of them.[12]

If Somers in *Kangaroo* regards himself as a 'muezzin summoning men to their central, isolate selves' then Mill was a prior prophet of the same doctrinaire individualism. Both the Engels and the Mill passages pivot on essentially the same oxymoronic hinging of social and individual identities that Lawrence evokes when talking of the 'subjective-objective reality . . . hinged together but not strictly individual' and the 'unfixed something-nothing' of Ursula's self-imaging – Engels' crowded dissolution, Mill's massed units.

Victorian culture pulls people taut between the poles identified by Engels and Mill. Under capitalism, the subject is caught in a rush towards an 'individualism' variously anathematised and eulogised. This movement is perversely countered by the emergence of historically unprecedented huge human groupings, physical and ideological, in cities with their polarising factions of bourgeoisie and proletariat. The nineteenth-century novel had been the site of criticism, but also construction, of these, to use a term of Dickens, 'impossible existences'.[13] Characterisation in nineteenth-century fiction can be seen as a continual negotiation between these contradictions

– sometimes even evoking the oxymoronic 'hinged' terms like Lawrence's. In the first sentence of the novel the 'something-nothing' Ursula is bought by her lover, Skrebensky; *Wuthering Heights* has Heathcliff introduced, with a perhaps comparable oxymoronic version of identity, as a 'solitary neighbour'. This term encapsulates the impossible collision of social and isolate definitions of identity which that novel is, in characterisation and narrative form, continually re-invoking. It everywhere dramatises the conflict between opposed versions of identity, one being the older Catherine's inarticulate intimation of an ideal form of being beyond individualism and claustrophobic containment within the monadic self, 'I cannot express it; but surely you and everybody have a notion that there is, or should be, an existence of yours beyond you. What were the use of my creation if I were entirely contained here?'. Her refusal of a privatised identity confronts Nelly Dean's insistence upon the universality of private interest, which, being entirely consistent with the nineteeth-century's dominant discourse, can be voiced without comparable hesitancy of expression, 'Well, we *must* be for ourselves in the long run; the mild and generous are only more justly selfish than the domineering.'[14]

Egoism and altruism become perversely confounded as social and individual impulses and identities contend and merge. It is extraordinary how often characterisation in Victorian fiction re-states the felt contradiction of conflated isolate and communal identities as people live out the ontological impossibility of the 'solitary neighbour'. Dickens' Pip puzzles over whether he is common or uncommon. Hardy describes Tess as 'an almost standard woman' where we don't know which term to stress or value, the communality or her degree of independence from it, her neighbourliness or her solitude. Walter Benjamin in his great study of Baudelaire's representation of the new forms of identity, at once secretive and conspiratorial, bred by teeming, labyrinthine and politically turbulent nineteenth-century Paris, concludes 'Baudelaire loved solitude, but he wanted it in a crowd'.[15] Benjamin's characterisation of Baudelaire is echoed by David Musselwhite's of Dickens. He finds in the letters 'the titanic and never resolved struggle' between 'intense psychological stress and the dispersal of self in the anonymity and volatility of the crowd'.[16] Dickens himself articulated the same perception of new massed yet irredeemably private and secretive urban identities of which Musselwhite argues he was an illustration. The narrator of *A Tale of Two Cities* ponders the 'solemn consideration' that in 'a great city . . . every beating heart in the hundreds of thousands of breasts is . . . a secret to the heart nearest it'.[17] Wherever was that 'old stable ego of the character'?

Evidence can be found that Lawrence himself makes a comparable analysis of the nineteenth-century inheritance of fraught and contradictory identities. He suggests that the growth of pornography is an outcome of a new immanence of, using the term Dickens stresses, 'secrecy'. Nineteenth-century fiction – *Jane Eyre*, *The Mill on the Floss* and *Anna Karenina* are his instances – is a more pornographic form than its literary predecessors because it is essentially predicated upon secrecy. The obscenity he identifies is the ubiquity of neurotically enclosed, onanistic identities. He first provides an ahistorical version of the dilemma I have identified as peculiarly nineteenth-century, 'there are two great categories of meaning, for ever separate. There is mob-meaning, and there is individual meaning' ('Pornography and Obscenity', *SLC*, p. 33). But he goes on to argue that 'The real masturbation of Englishmen began only in the nineteenth century'. This modern 'masturbation' is none other than individuality become self-consuming secrecy, 'Enclosed within the vicious circle of the self, with no vital contacts outside, the self becomes emptier and emptier, till it is almost a nullus, a nothingness' (*SLC*, p. 43). (So we can choose our Lawrentian definitions of the 'self' – 'a supreme, gleaming triumph of infinity' or 'a nullus, a nothingness'.)

But in his extended reading of nineteenth-century fiction Lawrence is less willing to acknowledge the problematic nature of 'individual meaning'. In *Study of Thomas Hardy* he argues that Hardy, like all great artists, has an inborn taste for aristocrats – both actual aristocrats and those who, like Tess and Jude in Lawrence's reading, are aristocrats of the spirit. Aristocratism is here largely a synonym for individualism. Aristocrats are traditionally privileged in being able to give exclusive attention to the Lawrentian imperative of hatching the one-and-only phoenix of themselves, while everyone else is occupied making, not themselves, but money and products. Indeed the spiritual and emotional aristocracy Lawrence admires is always shading into the more literal and political. When Somers in *Kangaroo* reiterates the argument of the *Study* – 'You've got to have an awakening of the old recognition of the old aristocratic principle, the *innate* difference between people' (*K*, p. 305) – it is in the overtly politicised context of his sympathy for the anti-democratic ravings of self-appointed leader Kangaroo and his quasi-fascist movement, the Diggers. For Lawrence to read his own 'aristocratic principle' into Hardy, and *Tess* and *Jude* in particular, is wilful. Aristocracy is primarily a hoax in Hardy, faked signifier of an irrecoverable or never-existent historical and personal authenticity. Tess's misery is precipitated by dilusions of aristocratic origin and authority at once irrecoverable and already re-appropriated by that living historical hoax, Alec 'D'Urberville'. Sue Bridehead seems to suggest that the whole tragedy of Jude and herself stems from their finding that Mill's individualistic ideal is unrealisable.

The alienation Lawrence dubs 'aristocratism' and 'individuality' adjacent fictional traditions have dubbed egoism, loneliness, solitude, secrecy. 'I know no speck so troublesome as self' complains our guide to a Midlands town apparently suffering an epidemic of egoism, trying with difficulty not to exhaust the vocabulary of self-ishness – 'the immense need of being something important and predominating', 'The miserable isolation of egotistic fears', 'habitual self-cherishing anxiety', 'a very distinct and intense vision of his chief good', 'passionate egoism', 'our supreme selves', and, in a phrase whose connotations Lawrence would have turned to the positive, 'the sense of a stupendous self'.[18] The alienation Eliot moralises as 'egoism', Conrad fears as 'aloneness', 'merciless solitude', the 'secrecy' of characters who are all essentially 'secret agents': 'He was alone, I was alone, every man was alone where he stood'.[19] George Eliot was the author Lawrence acknowledged as providing the model for his first novel *The White Peacock*, an influence perhaps there exhausted and not subsequently reworked, and Conrad was the author he said he could not forgive 'for being so sad and for giving in' (*SLC*, p. 132). It is understandable that Lawrence cannot feel fundamentally in sympathy with authors anxious to register the alienating consequences of the very ideology of individualism a chorus of Lawrentian voices promote.

III

The argument so far has indicated that we can perhaps read Lawrence as Fredric Jameson reads Henry James, as fixed within a paradox peculiar to capitalism whereby the form in which personal alienation is criticised itself serves further to reproduce that alienation:

The fiction of the individual subject – so-called bourgeois individualism – had of course, always been a key functional element
in the bourgeois cultural revolution, the re-programming of individuals to the 'freedom' and equality of sheer market equivalence. As this fiction becomes ever more difficult to sustain (or, to
use the somewhat mythic terminology of the Frankfurt School, as
the old 'autonomy' of the bourgeois subject is increasingly lost
under the effects of disintegration and fetishisation), more des-
perate myths of the self are generated, many of which are still
with us today. The Jamesian point of view, which comes into
being as a protest and a defense against reification, ends up fur-
nishing a powerful ideological instrument in the perpetuation of
an increasingly subjectivized and psychologized world, a world
whose social vision is one of a thoroughgoing relativity of
monads in coexistence and whose *ethos* is irony and neo-Freudian
projection theory and adaption-to-reality therapy.[20]

The argument is here parallel to that of Deleuze and Guattari who in
Anti-Oedipus: Capitalism and Schizophrenia protest at what they see as
the pernicious individualising of experience unleashed by the nineteenth century that leads Freud to shrivel the socially and politically
generated neuroses of his patients to individual traumas securely
located within the primal triangle of 'Mummy, Daddy and me'. This
neurotic psychology predicated upon absence, castration and envy
is in fact the internalisation of the basic problematic of a capitalism
itself predicated upon a collective fear of loss. All individuals under
capitalism, which works by the strategic engineering of scarcity –
slumps, bankruptcies and poverty are as essential to it as personal
wealth – are driven by the neurotic desire to possess capital/the
phallus and avoid loss/castration. In fact Lawrence's quarrel with
Freudianism runs along similar lines. *Fantasia of the Unconscious* is
his own *Anti-Oedipus* suggesting, if obliquely and diffusively, that
'Oedipus' is not something inherent to the child, but the foisting
upon the child of the guilt of a social formation. But, this being
Lawrence, the argument is muddied by a recalcitrant individualism
whose absoluteness effectively negates neighbouring insights: 'There
is only one clue to the universe. And that is the individual soul
within the individual being' (*FU*, p. 150).

In his reading of Delueze and Guattari David Musselwhite has
given Lawrence fulsome praise for his 'brilliant' critique of Freud as
'possibly the best introduction to the kind of account of libidinal

energy that Deleuze and Guattari are elaborating in their work'.[21] But frankly it is very difficult to find even oblique continuity between the familiar Lawrentian individualism of the *Fantasia* and Musslewhite's impeccably post-modern account of identity, 'The self is not an original identity, but the produced effect, mobile rather than static, nomadic rather than fixed, of fabulous plays of differences'.[22] Lawrence positively fetishises those *bêtes noires* of postmodernity which Musselwhite refutes – origin, originality, fixity, locatedness, self-identity, 'The intrinsic truth of every individual is the new unit of unique individuality which emanates from the fusion of the parent nuclei', 'the new individual, in his singleness of self, is a perfectly new whole . . . he is something underived and utterly unprecedented, unique, a new soul', 'the original nucleus . . . remains always primal and central, and is always the original fount and home of the first and supreme knowledge that *I am I*. This original nucleus is embodied in the solar plexus' (*FU*, pp. 30, 30–1, 35).

It is fair to add that elsewhere Lawrence does make himself available to a reading such as Musselwhite's of the *Fantasia*. In his enthusiastic review of Trigant Burrow's *The Social Basis of Consciousness* Lawrence agrees with the whole tenor of the work as evidenced in its title and particularly Burrow's rejection of Freudian 'sex-repression' as the root of 'the neurosis of modern life' and concurs that 'The real trouble lies in the inward sense of "separateness" which dominates every man.'[23] He finds in Burrow's characterisation of contemporary consciousness the presentiment of his own thought, and even perhaps of his own biography,

> Suddenly aware of himself, and of other selves over and against him, man is a prey to the division inside himself. Helplessly he must strive for more consciousness, which means, also, a more intensified aloneness, or individuality; and at the same time he has a horror of his own aloneness, and a blind, dim yearning for the old togetherness of the past. (*SP*, pp. 468–9)

I am prompted to say biography here by Alasdair Gray's comments on Lawrence's life which, with its famous pilgrimages, or 'Flitting' as a chapter title of *Women in Love* puts it, Gray reads as fuelled by the need to replace the lost community, 'the old togetherness of the past', Lawrence only experienced in youth. Socially, his shift from

Midlands miner's son to fêted author meant degeneration from 'community' to 'clique'.

> In the mining town where he grew up he had known a community: people who accepted each other for what they had in common as workmates, neighbours, chapel-goers. His mother wanted her children *not* to be common, but professional and moneyed. By his talents he had become these things, and found that the professional, talented, wealthy folk he now mixed with, though good friends who recognised his uniqueness, had no community beyond cliques based on love-affairs and conversations about art and ideas. So he went searching through Australia, New Mexico and Italy for a working community like the Eastwood of his childhood, but not based on wage slavery, and with room for a free spirit like his own.[24]

'Cliques based on love-affairs and conversations about art and ideas' exactly characterises the milieu of the rootless intelligentsia of *Women in Love*. Perhaps Ursula is more deeply autobiographical a figure for Lawrence than Birkin. Like him she moves, in the shift from *The Rainbow* to *Women in Love*, from rural, working 'community' to cosmopolitan, bohemian 'cliques', forging in the process a resolute creed of self-protective individualism, 'striving for more consciousness', which proves both blessing and curse. 'The Bitterness of Ecstasy' is the title of the chapter in which, contemplating a cell through a microscope, she has her epiphanic intuition of the splendour of her own isolation. Lawrence's poignant 'Autobiographical Sketch' testifies to the emotional deracination which has exchanged a deeply social 'blood-affinity' for cliques and 'consciousness'. 'I cannot make the transfer from my own class into the middle class. I cannot, not for anything in the world, forfeit . . . my old blood-affinity with my fellow-men and the animals and the land, for that other thin, spurious mental conceit which is all that is left of the mental consciousness once it has made itself exclusive' (*SLC*, p. 5).

The obverse of Lawrentian individualism is loneliness, illusion, failure expressed through a self-cancelling futility which condemns its own condemnation of 'conceit' as itself 'conceit'.

> 'This achieved self, which we are, is absolute and universal. There is nothing beyond. . . . At this crisis there is a great cry of loneli-

ness. Every man conceives himself as a complete unit surrounded by nullity. And he cannot bear it. Yet his pride is in this also. The greatest conceit of all is this cry of loneliness.   ('The Crown', *SLC*, p. 435)

So that my individualism is really an illusion. I am a part of the great whole, and I can never escape. But I *can* deny my connections, break them and become a fragment. Then I am wretched.   (*A*, p. 126)

But I feel, somehow, not much of a human success. By which I mean that I don't feel there is any very cordial or fundamental contact between me and society, or me and other people. There is a breach.   ('Autobiographical Sketch', *SLC*, p. 4)

Self-obsessed and self-tormented, Lawrence can be seen as simultaneously the critic, the promoter and the victim of that most essentially bourgeois of conceptions described by Adorno as 'the bottomless fraud of mere inwardness'. His life and work dramatise the crisis identified by Adorno when he says that an art,

wholly at the service of individual claims and dedicated to the glorification of the self-sufficient individual, thereby reduces the latter to a mere receptive organ of the market, an imitation of arbitrarily chosen ideas and styles. Within repressive society the individual's emancipation not only benefits but damages him. . . . If today the trace of humanity seems to persist only in the individual in his decline, it admonishes us to make an end of the futility which individualises men, only to break them completely in their isolation.[25]

NOTES

1. F. R. Leavis, *D. H. Lawrence: Novelist* (Harmondsworth: Penguin, 1973).
2. D. H. Lawrence, *Studies in Classic American Literature* (Harmondsworth: Penguin, 1986) p. 8; hereafter referred to as *SCAL*, with page references given in the text.
3. D. H. Lawrence, *Kangaroo* (Harmondsworth: Penguin, 1988), p. 312; hereafter referred to as *K*, with page references given in the text.
4. D. H. Lawrence, *Apocalypse* (Harmondsworth: Penguin, 1976) p. 124; hereafter referred to as *A*, with page references given in the text.

5. G. J. Zykaruk and J. T. Bolton (eds.), *The Letters of D. H. Lawrence* (Cambridge: Cambridge University Press, 1981) vol. 2, p. 182.

6. D. H. Lawrence, *Fantasia of the Unconscious and Psychoanalysis and the Unconscious* (Harmondsworth: Penguin, 1986) p. 35; hereafter referred to as *FU*, with page references given in the text.

7. D. H. Lawrence, *The Rainbow* (Harmondsworth: Penguin, 1981) p. 441; hereafter referred to as *R*, with page references given in the text.

8. D. H. Lawrence, 'John Galsworthy', in A. Beal (ed.), *Selected Literary Criticism of D. H. Lawrence* (London: Heinemann, 1969) pp. 120–1; hereafter referred to as *SLC*, with page references and essay-titles given in the text.

9. D. H. Lawrence, *Lady Chatterly's Lover* (Harmondsworth: Penguin, 1988) pp. 65–6 and p. 109; hereafter referred to as *LCL*, with page references given in the text.

10. D. McLellan (ed.), *Karl Marx: Selected Writings* (Oxford: Oxford University Press, 1977) p. 233.

11. F. Engels, *The Condition of the Working Class in England* (Harmondsworth: Penguin, 1987) p. 69.

12. J. S. Mill, *On Liberty* (Harmondsworth: Penguin, 1982) p. 127.

13. C. Dickens, *Great Expectations* (Harmondsworth: Penguin, 1986) p 471.

14. E. Brontë, *Wuthering Heights* (New York: Norton Critical Edition, 1972) pp. 33–4 and p. 81.

15. W. Benjamin, *Charles Baudelaire: A Lyric Poet in the Era of High Capitalism* (London: New Left Books, 1973) p. 50.

16. D. Musselwhite, *Partings Welded Together: Politics and Desire in the Nineteenth Century Novel* (London: Methuen, 1987) p. 146.

17. C. Dickens, *A Tale of Two Cities* (Harmondsworth: Penguin, 1988) p. 44.

18. G. Eliot, *Middlemarch* (Harmondsworth: Penguin, 1981) pp. 289, 668, 698, 759, 564, 253 and 698.

19. J. Conrad, *The Shadow-Line* (Harmondsworth: Penguin, 1986) p. 130.

20. F. Jameson, *The Political Unconscious: Narrative as a Socially Symbolic Act* (London: Methuen, 1986) pp. 221–2.

21. Musselwhite, *Partings Welded Together*, p. 230.

22. Ibid., pp. 49–50.

23. D. H. Lawrence, *A Selection from Phoenix*, ed. A. A. Inglis (Harmondsworth: Penguin, 1979) p. 471; hereafter referred to as *SP*, with page references given in the text.

24. A. Gray, *Gentleman of the West* (Harmondsworth: Penguin, 1986) pp. 132–3.

25. T. Adorno, *Minima Moralis* (London: Verso, 1974) pp. 149–50.

10

I. A. Richards and the Problem of Method

BARRY CULLEN

Nobody will dispute that the degree of theoretical sophistication required of a critic today is likely to be far in excess of that expected in critics of the past. Even opponents or detractors of theory as a relevant or necessary condition of critical argument are likely to display a command of theoretical weaponary superior to that of even major critics of the recent past.[1] Current deprecations of traditional Shakespeare criticism, say by Hawkes or Drakakis, the Belsey–Eagleton attack on Leavis, or, in more general (and less provocative) terms, Williams' critique of the Coleridgean–Arnoldian tradition, all emphasise the ideological inadequacy of the critical performance under review. To be a critic now is to be an ideologue not, as then, an ideal reader, who vanished in the mid 1960s, the time of the Johns Hopkins structuralist symposium. Before then twentieth-century, Anglo-American criticism was 'innocent' (meaning guilty of course) of its ideological determinants and co-ordinates. Since then, criticism has come of age and all haste is being made to repair the negligence of earlier decades in respect of ideological awareness and hermeneutical expertise. Little interest is shown in the history of theory in this country before the 1960s for it is assumed that there was none.

To challenge this assumption it is only necessary to consider the work of I. A. Richards. Unlike Leavis, or the sundry hapless 'orthodox' critics who now fall regularly under the Eagletonian axe, Richards is a figure who has largely escaped hostile attention, probably because few people know much about his work. Yet he is perhaps more central to the current criticism versus theory argument than virtually any of his Cambridge contemporaries, if only because he was at the centre of a similar debate in the 1920s and 1930s, which pivoted around the question of whether to look at

literature as an autonomous form of knowledge or as a social practice, identified by theory as a cultural determinant for ordering and
stabilising rapid social change. Richards (who favoured the latter)
didn't stay to finish the argument and retired to leave Leavis and
Empson to fashion their own kind of responses to the problems that
emerged. But Richards was the first to raise the issue in these terms
and the question of why he failed to establish his argument more
effectively or successfully remains, and is – or should be – part of the
current debate.

I want to argue that a study of Richards' early theoretical work
serves as something of a cautionary tale as to how far criticism can
usefully look to philosophy for its methods, and that without some
very clear idea of how these will serve the literary objectives of the
critic the result can be disappointing and largely unsatisfactory. In
Richards' case there were two influential factors at work in his
turning to philosophy as a source of inspiration and guidance: the
recent revolution in British philosophy initiated by Russell and Moore
(and consolidated by Wittgenstein); and the recent birth of the
English school at Cambridge from the parent body of the Modern
Language tripos.

Well before Richards came up to Cambridge in 1911, a major
change had overtaken British philosophy which was to have far-
reaching implications for British culture. Until the end of the nineteenth-century idealism has been the dominant mode of academic
philosophy, a metaphysical system of ideas that stressed the relativity of all knowledge, including that of physical reality. The effect of
this was to deny science a sound epistemological basis for its operations. However vigorously objectivity was pursued in practice there
was no satisfactory account of it as long as idealism was logically
invulnerable. In consequence, science held firm to only one of a
number of possible realities, the phenomenal world of objects as
opposed to the metaphysical reality of the Absolute and its manifestations. Effectively the concept of 'objectivity' had no secure intellectual basis; it represented only a possible perspective out of many.
This provided an intellectual climate in which a number of meta-
physically-based outlooks could flourish, including the aesthetic,
although, as Arnold noted, the encroachments of science into traditional provinces of the arts in Victorian times posed potential threats
to the existential security of these activities. However, by the turn of
the century, Russell had fatally weakened the logical basis of British
idealism (which relied heavily on classical predication models for its

epistemological underpinning) to the extent that the primacy or objectivity of physical reality could be ensured, with a concomitant enhancement of the prestige of the native empirical tradition in philosophy generally and the especial endorsement of positivism as the exclusive proprietor of the 'objective'. It is difficult now to realise what a prize such an achievement must have seemed at the time, but it is apparent from the writings of early twentieth-century humanists (such as Russell himself) that the securing of a clear and demonstrable division between the world of the objective and the world of the subjective was tantamount to getting within sight of the promised land of a reconstructed social world free from religion and other superstitious errors.[2]

In other words there was an ideological, as well as intellectual dimension to this revolution. What had begun as an exercise in technical logic, the solving of a particular problem, became in a short time a swelling tide of confidence that a major change in the nature of knowledge had taken place. Truth was no longer the exasperatingly part-sense, part-idea unattainable of metaphysics but was readily available in the only form which mattered: factual, measurable, verifiable. A clear line had been drawn between the subjective, the personal, the emotional on the one hand, and the objective, the impersonal, the rational on the other. Art – in so far as it relied on idealism for its justification – was weakened; science, both natural and social, strengthened.

This is the context in which Richards came to switch from history to philosophy in his first term at Magdalene and which, eight years later, was to lead him to accept Mansfield Forbes's invitation to lecture in the English School. His main interests were in the sciences: biology, chemistry, neurophysiology, and psychology, and those fields that the new learning was opening up: psychoanalysis, gestalt theory, semantics, semiotics, communication theory and psycholinguistics. Judging from the correspondence to Forbes in 1919, when he was preparing his lectures, Richards had read relatively little literature (he found the preparation of a novel course 'a bother') but he was enthusiastic at the prospect of the other course he'd been asked to prepare: lectures on the principles of criticism.[3] It was presumably this interest that Forbes detected when at a chance encounter they fell into the conversation that resulted in Richards being recruited to the English school. From their conversation emerged Richards' conviction that literature had an academic future only if the traditional aestheticism associated with *belles lettres* was abandoned and a new aesthetic, one aware of and in contact with the anti-metaphysical spirit of the day, took its place.

The construction of such an aesthetic was challenging and few even at Cambridge were qualified to undertake it. Certainly not Forbes himself, an engaging but eccentric critic, whose main interests were in architecture and mountain walking, nor any other recent recruits to the English school, most of whom were ex-classicists looking for not a very demanding route to a fellowship.[4] Yet there was an outstanding figure in the university at the time who could represent a precedent for what Richards was being asked to do. As an undergraduate, Richards had been most impressed with G. E. Moore. He was another Cambridge man at the centre of the revolution in British philosophy; he had quite independently and uniquely challenged idealism with his imperturbable but pertinacious common-sense scepticism, inspiring Russell, in turn, to challenge idealism at its logical roots. Moore's philosophy was an unusual, almost idiosyncratic, form of realism which employed rigorous analysis of language to reveal the bedrock elements of reality. But Moore was not a materialist of any kind; his 'reality' was a reality of the 'propositions' revealed through an analysis of the way language is used, propositions themselves being the closest we can get to ultimate reality. Thus, Moore's reality is a propositional reality but one which is wholly objective; he rejected the traditional view of British empiricism where propositions are subjective mental states. This position enabled Moore to argue for the quite independent existence of entities such as beauty or goodness, and to argue that, once located, these entities were known, like the meaning of propositions, directly by intuition. Although it was his emphasis on analysis of language as a philosophical technique that impressed Moore's professional colleagues, it was very largely his justification of and appeal to intuitionism that made Moore the doyen of Bloomsbury criticism, and which appealed to all those seeking to save aesthetic appearances in the face of positivistic scepticism at the turn of the century. Moore, in fact, appealed to both sides of the art/science divide (although for quite different reasons), and it may have been this, as much as his pedagogic and forensic skills, which tempted Richards to emulate his Cambridge colleague.[5]

In fact, in his first published work, Richards argued for a position close to that of Moore. He saw art as based, like science, on truth, but whereas science is verified 'empirically', art is based on intuition and individual experience. Following Moore, by employing the notion of an ultimate reality supporting the propositional character of language, he argues that science is based on a nominalist system of signs that relate directly to a verifiable physical reality whereas art has a more oblique relationship to truth: art is autotelic and is 'tested against the whole dynamic of mind and feeling, a single individual's interiority'.[6] This was not to remain Richards' position for very long and was soon to be replaced by a more extreme physicalist philosophy of both mind and language. It is important, however, to register Richards' initial position, because it stays in his thought throughout, as a way in which art and science can both be said to occupy an 'objective' relationship to reality, and, although his notion of art changes over the years, there is a sense in which it could be said to be a series of variations on this basic position.

If Moore provided the model for Richards' aim of reconciling poetry and science, another Cambridge figure was instrumental in finding the means by which this was to be done. Unlike Moore, C. K. Ogden seems to have been both a shadowy and a notorious figure in Richards' Cambridge. He was known as a pacifist who throughout the 1914 War ran a radical periodical, the *Cambridge Magazine*. Richards had been friendly with Ogden since his undergraduate days and they had worked together in a minor way in the 'Heretics', a club Ogden had founded before the war at which various papers were read expounding the case for civil liberties, internationalism, co-education, birth control, etc. Ogden owned a Cambridge bookshop which provided an outlet for progressive publications and various projects associated with the establishment of Basic English. An incorrigible eccentric, he had several addresses where he seldom lived, used a number of pseudonyms, was excessively secretive, and had a disconcerting habit of meeting people wearing a mask which he might change several times in the course of an interview. Richards thought highly of Ogden's abilities: 'Ogden was a very good scholar, good enough for a chair in classics and destined for one – but he was interested in too many other things.'[7] More work needs to be done on the influence that Ogden had on Richards' thinking at this formative period. What can safely be said is that Ogden struck a chord with Richards at their first meeting as undergraduates,[8] and that Richards was much taken with the free-thinking, uninhibited progressivism of his senior. Richards himself had adopted similar views at school, but meeting Ogden at Cambridge helped to give him the intellectual confidence he needed to foster the radicalism already searching for an outlet.

When Richards took on the task of becoming literary philosopher to the infant English school he had in practice very little idea of where he was going. Forbes appointed him in the spring of 1919 to the post of lecturer, asking him to teach a course of lectures on the novel and the 'principles of criticism'. The outline sketch of the criticism course shows the *Principles of Literary Criticism* text at an early stage of development (i.e. no cultural diagnosis or value theory) but already possessing a characteristic psychological orientation.[9] Equally suggestive is an undated letter to Forbes probably belonging to the next academic year (1920) which indicates the kind of influence that Ogden was beginning to exert:

I'm making a dead set at fundamental grammar. If it can be properly approached I am clear that it would provide the best intellectual training-field possible. Further it is with poetry and Art the only *universal* form of education; but I haven't quite got hold of the main thread yet, and so many people have missed it, I hope you will hit off Symbolism. The guts are there in spite of the fleshy epidermis. Do not bother about 'What is a Fact?' That is not an application though it looks as though it were. We did it first and the logical part is really the best thing we have done, from it all the Canons etc. sprang.[10]

This attempts to explain parts of what was later to become *The Meaning of Meaning* (1923)[11] to Forbes who presumably had been sent a draft of early forms of chapters IV and V. 'Fundamental grammar' would translate in today's terms into 'linguistics' and acts as an acknowledgment of an important shift in Richards' perception that poetry – once properly explained and supported by theory – could play a central educational or ideological role. Ogden's inspiration was to form the basis for Richards' interest in the more specialised field of 'symbolism' (semiotics and semantics), which in turn was to lead to the psycho-linguistic poetics of *Principles of Literary Criticism*, the cultural theory and apologetics of *Science and Poetry*,[12] and the celebrated reader-response protocols of *Practical Criticism*.[13] Ogden was convinced that most of the world's ills (including war) could be traced to a failure of communication, the inability of human beings to convey accurately to each other what they actually felt and thought. The chief villain in this scenario was language, or rather people's propensity to hypostatise language, to objectify it, in a way that cut them off from control of their own meanings and delivered them over to the power of the unscrupulous: metaphysicians, priests, politicians *et al.* The antidote to this was a science of language which would enable people through an understanding of how language works to move to a higher plane of social relationship and harmonious being.

The core of the theory outlined in *The Meaning of Meaning* was its then radical claim that language is a social institution based upon a conventional use of signs, and not an immutable reflector of reality. Failure to conceive of it as such leads to various 'thought-diseases' such as 'word-magic' (hypostatisation of meaning which conceals from us the instrumentality of language), proper-name superstitions (words as things or controlling things), and various forms of idealism associated with the western philosophical tradition from Plato onwards. Even the formalism of Russell and Wittgenstein is not immune from the Ogden-Richards razor because by locating breakdown of communication in the imperfect nature of language rather than in the conditions of its use – the used not the user – they perpetuate misunderstandings which only contribute to further obscurity. The solution is to look at language as a system for generating meanings and then to understand how meanings are generated principally through use in psychological contexts. Contexts give words meanings like bells provide stimuli for Pavlov's dogs so 'the meaning' of a word will always be haunted by its previous contexts. Meaning is a mental not a phenomenal event and has to be understood primarily and finally in psychological terms: the situation of use (the physical and psychological contexts in which words are uttered) determine meanings, not principles of logic. Logic is a science of systematic symbolisation but language is not systematic: symbols (i.e. linguistic 'signs') are used in a wide variety of situations, many of which are partially or entirely emotive. Thus the appropriate study of language is through psychology not logic.

Psychology's ability to explain and describe meaning in mental terms is what brings language for Ogden and Richards into the field of social science and makes possible a new understanding of both communication (the field of general usage and thus the province of Basic English) and literature (the field of emotive meanings used in a purposive and highly effective way). Literature, specifically poetry, has no referential value (which is not to say it has no cognitive content) because it is language used at the opposite pole to that of scientific statement, that is in a purely emotive way. What 'emotive' means in relation to poetry is the subject of *Principles of Literary*

Criticism. Building on the premises established or outlined in the earlier work Richards emphasises the affective nature of human experience and the central role that language has to play, or fails to play, in regulating and ordering this. Words are used to construct an internal emotional equipoise, but command of language is usually so imperfect that much of the inherent complexity of experience is too psychologically overwhelming. The result is waste, frustration, unhappiness, and a general low-key functioning of our emotional lives.

Richards' solution is to ask where language is used most effectively: the answer, poetry. For Richards the poet, any artist in words, writes poetry not out of a need to 'communicate' something (there is nothing to communicate if 'truth' is a wholly scientific concept) but out of a need to order his or her emotional life, to find the appropriate expressive strategy for whatever experience poses as a challenge to successful inner integration:

> It is never what a poem *says* which matters, but what it *is*. The poet is not writing as a scientist. He uses these words because the interests whose movement is the growth of the poem combine to bring them, just in this form, into his consciousness as a *means of ordering, controlling and consolidating* the uttered experience of which they are themselves a main part. The experience itself, the tide of impulses sweeping through the mind, is the source and the sanction of the words. They represent this experience itself, not any set of perceptions or reflections, though often to a reader who approaches the poem wrongly they will seem to be only a series of remarks about other things. But to a suitable reader the words – if they actually spring from experience and are not due to verbal habits, to the desire to be effective, to factitious excogitation, to imitation, to irrelevant contrivances, or to any other of the failings which prevent most people from writing poetry – the words will reproduce in his mind a similar play of interests putting him for the while into a similar situation and leading to the same response.   (*SP*, p. 33; italics as in original)

This passage epitomises a poetics aimed at bridging the arts/science gap. Poetry is like science a form of communication but unlike science it has no truth to convey in the usual sense of the term: it communicates an 'experience', a psychic totality whose import is in its psychological structure, a structure of linguistically ordered 'interests'. Exactly why the poet needs to *communicate* his or her inner adjustments is not addressed here but the need to make explicit is central to the theory and is the obverse of the reader's role as an internaliser of experience which is so pronounced in this passage. The poet like the reader has an inner need to find a satisfactory state of adjustment for a psyche built out of competing and conflicting impulses but, unlike the reader, has a need to do this through expressive means, means which take the form of poems. Conversely non-poets (the rest of us) have equally strong adjustment needs but, lacking the expressive drive of the poet, depend entirely on the limited resources of our language competence to find relief. Fortunately for the rest of us the poet's experiences of inner conflicts of impulses which are resolved in the writing of poetry can be found to match the character of the inner conflicts which we all experience as part of our normal social lives, and which therefore can be assimilated by us through reading.

Put like this it is easy to see the socio-cultural bearing of Richards poetics. The source of value in this account is not the poem, the poet or the reader, it is the language that everybody uses to respond to the flux which is the social and physical world of everyday life. Yet Richards shows relatively little interest in pursuing the social dimension of language. He is primarily interested in 'experience', which is the basic unit of value in this theory. The quasi-ethical character of language matters most to him because it is language which converts sensation into experience. Richards sees experience as the order and shape given to the multiplicity of psychic events flowing incessantly in upon us. Our lives are valuable to the extent that they are 'experienced'; otherwise we cease to live, to be consciously alive. Poems are only valuable to the extent that they facilitate this experiential awareness which is a condition of living a larger, fuller life.

At this point Richards' links with the larger tradition of Victorian and Edwardian secularism become clear, and the problem of 'belief' moves to the forefront of his concerns. Confident that he has brought mind, language and art within a framework of materialistic explanation, he proposes, in *Science and Poetry*, that the affective comforts previously supplied by metaphysical systems such as religion can be dispensed with and replaced by the more explicitly emotional securities of poetry. Because, from his position, religion had no positive content anyway, and was little more than a species of bad poetry, Richards regards it as a straightforward matter to replace it with good poetry, poetry which is recognised as justified by its affective character. Richards accepts that much poetry in the past has been explicitly religious in both content and outlook and he deals with this in one of two ways: either by suggesting that the beliefs on which it appeared to depend are not in fact essential to it, not intrinsic to its nature as poetry; or by admitting frankly that it never was poetry, that it was some form of utterance which was rooted in a belief subsequently discredited, and that its capacity to organise or adjust attitudes or impulses was never sufficiently great.[14]

It is for this reason that the poetry of the modern period holds such a central place in Richards' aesthetic. Poetry is to be judged on its success in dealing with the emotional verities of human existence, the enduring realities: birth, life, death. 'Modern' poetry is poetry which confronts these truths head on, which, in facing these verities, has not only severed its reliance upon belief but which makes such severance the subject of the verse. On Hardy:

> he is the poet who has most steadily refused to be comforted in an age in which the temptation to seek comfort has been greatest. The comfort of forgetfulness, the comfort of beliefs, he has put both these away. Hence his singular preoccupation with death; because it is in the contemplation of death that the necessity for human attitudes to become self-supporting, in the face of an indifferent universe, is felt most poignantly. Only the greatest tragic poets have achieved an equally self-reliant and immitigable acceptance. (*SP*, p. 69)

and on T. S. Eliot's *The Waste Land*:

> Both bitterness and desolation are superficial aspects of his poetry. There are those who think that he merely takes his readers into the Waste Land and leaves them there, that in his last poem he confesses his impotence to release the healing waters. The reply is that some readers find in his poetry not only a clearer, fuller realisation of their plight, the plight of a whole generation, than they find elsewhere, but also through the very energies set free in that realisation a return of the saving passion. (*PLC*, p. 295)

In an original footnote to *Science and Poetry*, Richards complimented Eliot even further to the effect that in writing 'The Waste Land' he had 'effected a complete severance between his poetry and all be-

liefs', but this was removed in later editions when Eliot protested
that he could not understand what Richards meant (*SP*, p. 64).

Clearly the generic paradigm that underlies this poetic is tragedy,
which, in fact, occupies a prominent place in Richards' literary
thinking:

> The essence of tragedy is that it forces us to live for a moment
> without [the suppression of impulses]. When we succeed we find,
> as usual, that there is no difficulty; the difficulty came from the
> suppression and the sublimations. The joy which is so strangely
> the heart of the experience is not an indication that 'all is right
> with the world' or that 'somehow, somewhere, there is Justice'; it
> is an indication that all is right here and now in the nervous
> system.   (*PLC*, p. 246)

Tragedy is paradigmatic because it is *essential* poetry, which in
Richards' view forces us to confront life. For Richards, this is what
most people fail to do by evading situations which, if confronted
successfully, would enhance their lives. Tragedy does not permit
such evasion. It is poetry which cannot be written or read without
psychological conflict, and without recognising the conflict as the
heart of both the psychological experience and the literary expression which gives it being. (Hence the emphasis on ambiguity, irony
and complexity of utterance as distinctive poetic features in Richards'
thinking.) In this way it is felt that tragedy bridges the gap between
the aesthetic and the psychological; it is at once a form of literature
and an outlook or attitude to life. But all depends upon it being read
as such. Good reading depends, Richards claimed, on the right theory
of art – knowing what not to expect in poetry (like objective truth) –
and on a proper practice which in turn depends upon the right kind
of information about reading being available.

So Richards' other formative work of criticism, *Practical Criticism*,
aims to remove the obstacles to 'right' reading by demonstrating the
inadequacies of even quite sophisticated and well-educated readers.
The plan of the book is well known: unseen, unsigned poems were
distributed to a university audience for comment, which was then
collected and analysed by Richards for discussion in subsequent
lectures. The results were then codified so as to provide analytical
tools to improve reading techniques, such as the four types of meaning: sense, tone, feeling, and intention. The object of the book was to
be a demonstration of how cultural transmission is cut off at source

by imperfect reading habits. But in fact beneath a not very heavy veneer of analytical exposition the overall feeling is one of exasperation and complaint: a sense of frustration at the general obtuseness of these educated readers to see the seriousness of the issues at stake:

> The verbal expression of this life, at its finest, is forced to use the technique of poetry; that is the only essential difference. We cannot avoid the material of poetry. If we do not live in consonance with good poetry, we must live in consonance with bad poetry. And, in fact, the idle hours of most lives are filled with reveries that are simply bad private poetry. On the whole evidence I do not see how we can avoid the conclusion that a general insensitivity to poetry does witness a low level of general imaginative life. There are other reasons for thinking that this century is in a cultural trough rather than upon a crest.   (*PC*, pp. 319–20)

This impression seems to be enforced by the loss of rhetorical control that Richards shows in later chapters where the critic's mediation of literature and the role of the critic as judge is dismissed as so much irrelevance before the need for exposure to the soul-healing therapies of great art. Ten years before Richards had seen himself as seizing the new instruments of psychological science to establish principles of criticism on a sound theoretical basis, but the impression given by *Practical Criticism* is that any theory is relatively impotent in the face of entrenched misconceptions about the nature of art. Only by use of much more drastic methods, such as the imposition of Basic English in the classroom, could these be defeated. Receiving no encouragement or sympathy for such a draconian solution in England, in 1930 Richards went off to China to pursue his experiments.

Richards' construction of a new aesthetic was wholly in the spirit of his day, a time when scientism was the answer to age-old problems and there appeared to be nothing that science could not solve. From today's perspectives this might look naive but in fact there is no reason to think that it is essentially different to the confidence that many critics have today in the superiority of understanding conferred upon them by a grasp of literary theory. Both positions look outside art to find a body of ideas which 'explain' art either as psychological phenomena or ideological product; both share a conviction of having reached some position of knowledge which, if not complete, is securely irreversible from which, in a sense, they can look down on art and place it as a known product. And it is this *hauteur* which suggests some vulnerability in Richards' position: it was too inflexible from the start, too fixed a stance to respond sensitively to the mutations that modern art was to undergo as it reacted creatively to the disorientating changes initiated at the turn of the century (Richards' view of 'The Waste Land' now looks both simplistic and anachronistic). Scientism was a bolt-hole, not the empire of certainty that Richards took it to be, and a basic criticism that has to be made of his theoretical drive is that he tried to lock up the idea of art in a nineteenth-century castle of positivism instead of looking to bring it into the wider world of modern understanding.

Richards' confidence in the persuasive effect of argument rooted in physicalism and supported by positivistic method seems to have waned at the end of the 1920s (which saw the rise of *Scrutiny* as well as Logical Positivism) but there is no reason to think that his conviction of the essential validity of the method itself came into question. British philosophical thinking at the time was still being swept along by a surge of enthusiasm for scientific method as a key to truth. Cambridge was at the centre of this impetus and Richards was only one of a number of distinguished figures there to associate themselves with belief in science as the key to progress in all areas of human thought. Russell is such a figure and Wittgenstein, although he had no declared affiliations, lent the weight of his growing reputation in Cambridge to scientism through the publication of *Tractatus Logico-Philosophicus*.[15] The difference between such work as theirs and that of Richards is, however, considerable. They were doing seminal work to establish the primacy of scientific method in epistemology; Richards was utilising the success or prestige of such work to justify the application of positivistic techniques in an unrelated field, that of art and literature. There is no question that he displayed considerable ingenuity and imagination to do so; and there can be little doubt that without unusual intellectual ability and a wide ranging knowledge of current developments in a variety of fields his whole project would have collapsed into ignominious failure. It took some courage as well as remarkable competence for Richards to mount the campaign he did.

Yet scientific progress is not only a matter of campaigns or courage; it depends upon patient and meticulous assembling of relevant facts to support either a hypothesis which may or may not be verified by such data or from which valid inferences or hypotheses may be made. This applies just as much to the social sciences as to the natural ones. The problem in social science, however, is to determine the status of a 'fact', to be clear about what is validly factual and what is not. Much of the philosophical work done by Russell, Moore and Wittgenstein had a direct bearing on this and led to Logical Positivism's claim that statements were factual only if they could be objectively verified by physical observation. Richards anticipated and adopted this position both in *The Meaning of Meaning* and *Principles of Literary Criticism*. He related the function and acquisition of language, and its application in aesthetic contexts, to processes which were in principle observable and measurable. 'In principle' is the operative phrase because much of the essential evidence needed to support such a position has never been produced and probably never will. The 'mind-language' complex which Richards took in the 1920s to be the subject of psychology and subsequently made the focus of his theory has been largely ignored by that science, which is interested chiefly in human behaviour.

This is not only a matter of Richards' imperfect prediction of the future course of psychology. His readiness to anticipate developments (which subsequently did not happen) and then project far-reaching conclusions upon them is endemic throughout his first books and is symptomatic of what can only be called an essential indifference to the spirit as well as the letter of scientific method. The unsatisfactory nature of this approach is well brought out by one of Richards' ablest commentators, W. H. N. Hotopf.[16] Hotopf, who writes as a psychologist sympathetic to Richards' achievements, points out that Richards is one of the worst offenders against his own theory that confusions of thought are the result of confusions of language because much of his argument is obscured or negated by his inability or unwillingness to distinguish clearly what he is talking about. An instance of this is the five 'canons of symbolism' which are used in *The Meaning of Meaning* to justify the scientific approach to language, but which are used in two disparate and conflicting ways: as a system of prescriptive norms and as descriptive categories, neither usage being noted or distinguished from the other. Hotopf notes a general tendency throughout this book for the argument to oscillate between relativist and absolutist position. Just as questionable in a 'scientific' argument is the cavalier attitude that Richards shows for distinctions of logical category. The key term 'reference' for instance is at various points in *The Meaning of Meaning* treated (i) as an object of the referring process; (ii) as the referring process itself; (iii) as a synonym for beliefs, ideas, concepts, thoughts and thinking; (iv) as propositions. The verb 'to refer' can also mean 'to be adapted to, to be directed to' or 'to be similar to what has been caused by'.[17] The different senses required of these terms is sometimes evident from the context but the point is not that Richards uses the same term with different senses but that he shows no awareness that for the purposes of demonstrative argument such senses have to be carefully and explicitly distinguished if they are to perform effectively the clarifying function he requires of them.

A more serious example of the same kind of indifference is to be found in Richards' use of the term 'impulse' in *Principles of Literary Criticism*. The idea of the 'impulse' is the cornerstone of Richards' psychological model and central to his theory of value as psychic equipoise. The impulse is the basic unit that constitutes 'appetencies' or 'interests', which in turn form the building blocks of 'experiences', those maximal positions of psychological efficiency which all psyches seek to attain. An impulse is defined as 'The process in the course of which a mental event may occur, a process apparently beginning in a stimulus and ending in an act, is what we have called an impulse' (*PLC*, p. 86). The context in which this appears makes clear that this is a description of a physical process: by a 'stimulus' is meant a sensory impingement upon the central nervous system which then reacts accordingly. But Richards also uses 'impulse' in a context such as the following:

> With the exception of some parents and nursemaids we have lately all be aghast at revelations of the value judgements of infants. Their impulses, their desires, their preferences, the things which they esteem, as displayed by the psycho-analysts, strike even those whose attitude towards humanity is not idealistic with some dismay.   (*PLC*, p. 45)

Here it is apparent that an impulse is something very much less precise, a type of preference or desire that is not descriptive of a physical event but of some psychological-cum-ethical process of choice. Normally there would be little danger of confusing these quite different senses. But it is clearly part of Richards' rhetorical strategy to conflate them, to claim that the psycho-ethical motivations and drives that are characteristic of the human psyche are identifiable with neurophysical activity of impulses upon which the integration of the central nervous system depends. J. P. Russo, in his recent biography of Richards, points out that here Richards is adapting C. P. Sherrington's work on the nervous system, where impulses (units of electro-chemical activity) are described in terms of subordinate or priority groups which are regulated into an integrated system by means of common paths of expression. Richards adopted the Sherrington model virtually unchanged so that he could construct a mechanistic psychological model of 'impulses', all striving for harmony in the discharge of their psychic energy. He generalises nerve-integration at a particular point ('the final common path' of Sherrington) to explain all mental activity in terms of an ordering and subordinating movement. In other words, he converts an explanation of *involuntary* impulse activity into a description of psychological process so as to suggest that the one is objectively indistinguishable from the other.[18]

The unacceptable practice of identifying mental with neural events is evident enough here. Richards appears not to have been concerned about this, finding no apparent difficulty in making an identification of the psychological with the physiological nor regarding this distinction as a serious obstacle to resolution of the problem of mind/brain dualism in materialist terms. Many people no doubt will share his belief that eventually some suitably convincing materialistic explanation of mind and consciousness will be found. But, as an argument purporting to demonstrate that mind is fully comprehensible as an integrative psychological process, functioning according to known and (potentially) predictable norms, his reliance on 'impulse'-psychology was little more than a superior form of wish-fulfilment. It showed neither a sound logical nor empirical basis upon which to develop a philosophy of mind or to erect a theory of art as a form of psychological enhancement and superior communication. As an example of scientific method applied to solve problems of art and its value it appears to be woefully ill-equipped and inadequate

The point at issue is not whether Richards was a good social scientist. The central question is whether he justified his claim that social-scientific method was the sole route to truth in the field of art.[19] The evidence of his own performance must be that he failed to establish the case to any convincing extent. Indeed by adopting such an uncompromisingly positivistic position, but without the appropriate investigative rigour to support it, all he succeeded in doing was to expose the shortcomings of a quasi-scientific poetics in a comprehensive way. This leads to a larger question: whether this failure was due to the nature of the method itself, or to the adoption of an inadequate or inappropriate version of it. It is clear that Richards' notion of scientific method is too crudely positivistic and that a more refined or sophisticated notion of how to proceed may well have led to a more sophisticated argument. What is not clear is whether this would have led to any substantially different conclusion; the problem of trying to redefine art in terms that do not largely empty 'literature' of meaning would remain essentially what it has always been. By trying to materialise the basis of art into psycho-physiological processes, potentially capable of quantification and measurement and thus to remove it from the field of interpretation and judgement, Richards did not bridge the gap between art and science as he intended. He merely shifted the ground of discussion to be a different framework of ideas, one which underlined the ideological and therefore controversial nature of art.

NOTES

1. A number of recent works have drawn attention to the intrusive claims of theory to be the prior conditions of general critical discussion ranging from comic or semi-comic treatments, such as M. Bradbury, *Mensonge* (London: André Deutsch, 1987) and P. Washington, *Fraud: Literary Theory and the End of English*, to more serious discussions as found in, say, A. D. Nuttall, *A New Mimesis* (London: Methuen, 1983) or S. Olsen, *The End of Literary Theory* (Cambridge: Cambridge University Press, 1984).

2. For a comprehensive account of this change see D. Bell, 'Philosophy', in C. B. Cox and A. E. Dyson (eds.), *The Twentieth-Century Mind* (London and New York: Oxford University Press, 1972) vol. 1.

3. Undated letters from Richards to Forbes are included as an Appendix in H. Carey, *Mansfield Forbes and his Cambridge* (Cambridge: Cambridge University Press, 1984).

4. Ibid., pp. 67–8, for further details about some early recruits to the English School.

5. G. J. Warnock gives a concise summary of Moore's thought in *English Philosophy Since 1900* (Oxford: Oxford University Press, 1958). For Moore's influence on Bloomsbury see J. M. Keynes, 'My Early Beliefs' and L. Woolf, 'Cambridge Friends and Influences', both in S. P. Rosenbaum (ed.), *The Bloomsbury Group* (Toronto: University of Toronto Press, 1975) pp. 48–65 and pp. 92–109.

6. J. P. Russo (ed.) *I. A. Richards Complementarities* (Manchester: Carcanet Press, 1977) p. xii.

7. Ibid., pp. 260–1.

8. Richards' account of his first meeting with Ogden is described in interview in R. Brower *et al.*, *I. A. Richards: Essays in His Honour* (New York: Open University Press, 1973) pp. 19–20.

9. I. A. Richards, *Principles of Literary Criticism* (London: Routledge, 1960); hereafter referred to as *PLC*, with page references given in the text.
10. Carey, *Mansfield Forbes*, p. 151.
11. C. K. Ogden and I. A. Richards, *The Meaning of Meaning* (London: Routledge, 1949).
12. I. A. Richards, *Poetries and Sciences* (London: Routledge, 1970) p. 33. This is a revised and retitled version of the text first published as *Science and Poetry* (London: Kegan and Paul, 1926)' hereafter this will be referred to as *SP*, with page references given in the text.
13. I. A. Richards, *Practical Criticism* (London: Routledge, 1929); hereafter referred to as *PC*, with page references given in the text.
14. For further illustration of Richards' views on 'belief' in poetry see chapter VII of *Poetries and Sciences*.
15. Russo suggests that Richards had ambitions to rival Wittgenstein as a philosopher of language and mind in the early stages of his career. Hence the dispatch of a copy of *The Meaning of Meaning* to Wittgenstein in 1923 together with an Appendix critical of the picture theory of meaning. It was received with a polite but crushing response to the effect that Richards and Ogden had missed the point of what he was trying to do. See J. P. Russo, *I. A. Richards: His Life and Work* (London: Routledge, 1989) pp. 140–3.
16. W. H. N. Hotopf, *Language, Thought and Comprehension* (London: Routledge, 1965).
17. Ibid., pp. 306–7.
18. See Russo, *Complementarities* , pp. 179–88.
19. The claim is implicit in most of Richards' early work and is close to being made explicit in the early chapters of *Principles of Literary Criticism* and *Science and Poetry*.

11

George Orwell: The Practical Critic

ANTHONY CRABBE

George Orwell's view of knowledge was avowedley practical. If you want to know what it is like to be a tramp, live as one – to be working class, then labour with them – to fight in a civil war, then enlist in an army.

Many have noted that Orwell was unusually hostile towards anyone who thought they could grasp his kind of issue through abstract theorising, rather than practical experience.[1] At worst such people were 'pansy left', 'nancy poets', 'fascists', or 'snobs', at best they had failed in what Orwell took to be their responsibilities; they were corruptible hypocrites, concerned more with their own self-preservation and sheltering within 'smelly little orthodoxies'.

John Wain has claimed 'every orthodoxy smelt bad to Orwell'.[2] Others have remarked that this is very much the posture of the tradition (or orthodoxy?) to which Orwell himself seemed to belong.[3] But it is also an approach that befits a man whose first literary métier was journalism. And it was through this métier that Orwell first came to build up a substantial body of literary criticism.

So in examining this body, we are confronted from the outset with four significant issues. First, given Orwell's own literary career, what he saw the nature of literature to be; second, how far Orwell explicitly took note of established critical theory and tradition; third, how far we might detect implicit systems or orthodoxies in his own critical approach; and fourth, at the end of the day, what insights Orwell affords into both his chosen subjects and the practice of criticism in general.

In consideration of the first issue, it is notable that Orwell never gave a sustained argument for his own definition of literature – it has to be gleaned from many diverse writings on subjects ranging from British food to W. B. Yeats. Judging from this range of topics, Orwell had a broader view than most of his contemporaries about the kinds of writing that counted as 'literature'. Accordingly, his critical attention was focused in equal measure on popular culture subjects like Boys' Weeklies and Thrillers, as well as high culture ones like Shakespeare and Dickens. This seems to foreshadow recent developments in criticism, but as we shall see, it disconcerted many of his contemporaries.

Moreover, Orwell, approached all his writing 'with a regard for (literary) form', which in his own view often competed with his journalistic instinct to 'tell the whole truth'.[4] Orwell was particularly interested in the question of form and content. He regarded Kipling as a great stylist whose work was flawed by an unattractive ideology; Carlyle as a clever man 'without the wit to write in plain straightforward English' ('Good Bad Books', *PE*, p. 325); Dali as a brilliant draftsman of abhorrent subject matter ('Benefit of Clergy: Some notes on Salvador Dali', *PE*), and so forth. However, in 'Good Bad Books', Orwell argues that works like *Raffles* and *King Solomon's Mines* 'escape literature' to survive only as 'light literature' because their intellectual value is inferior – regardless of their blend of stylistic skill and creative fertility. Hence intellectual worth is the one prerequisite for prose to attain the status of 'literature', whilst style is essential to its literary survival.

This brings us to Orwell's notions of that which made literature worthwhile. He saw prose writing in particular as a polemical activity: 'Above a quite low level, (prose) literature is an attempt to influence the viewpoint of one's contemporaries by recording experience' ('The Prevention of Literature', *PE*, p. 340). For the journalist, 'experience' amounts to an honest record of both how things happened and how the journalist reacted to them at the time. For the imaginative writer of prose, the invention of a story must be directed by an honest representation of the writer's 'subjective feelings'.

Poetry he saw rather differently: 'A poem is an arrangement of sounds and associations, as a painting is an arrangement of brush marks. For short snatches, indeed as in the refrain of a song, poetry can dispense with meaning altogether' ('Prevention of Literature', *PE* p. 340). Correspondingly, Orwell's criteria for assessing poems turn out to be rather different to those he used for prose.

It is not surprising to discover that this general view of prose accords with Orwell's analysis of his own work, discussed in one of his last essays, *Why I Write*. There Orwell identifies four motives found in varying degrees in all writers:

> Sheer egoism. Desire to seem clever, to be talked about, to be
> remembered after death. . . . Aesthetic enthusiasm. Perception of
> beauty, pleasure in good literary style. . . . Historical impulse.
> Desire to see things as they are, to find out true facts. . . . Political
> purpose. Desire to push the world in a certain direction, to alter
> other peoples' idea of the kind of society they should strive
> after.   ('Why I Write', *PE*, pp. 9–10)

He believes the measure in which each will be found in a given
writer's work is determined both by their personal nature and by the
nature of times in which they live. Orwell claims that, naturally, he
was more inclined to the first three motives, but the nature of his
epoch had 'forced' political purpose to dominate his work.

In his essay 'The Prevention of Literature' Orwell had actually
generalised this idea somewhat further: 'There is no such thing as a
genuinely non-political literature, and least of all in an age like our
own, when fears, hatreds and loyalties of a directly political kind are
near to the surface of everyone's consciousness' ('The Prevention of
Literature', *PE*, p. 346). Orwell also demanded a sense of honesty
and realism about political purpose:

> It seems to me nonsense in a period like our own, to think one can
> avoid writing of such [political] subjects. Everyone writes of them
> in one guise or another. It is simply a question of which side one
> takes and what approach one follows. And the more one is con-
> scious of one's political bias, the more chance one has of acting
> politically without sacrificing one's aesthetic and intellectual
> integrity.   ('Why I Write', *PE*, p. 11)

Oddly, he did not extend this call for self-awareness of personal
inclination to the practice of criticism. Criticism seems to have been
just another thing that Orwell 'did' in order to earn a crust. As we
shall see, this lack of self-consciousness presents some difficulties in
following Orwell's critical thrust.

Putting all these ideas together, then, we may see Orwell as making the following case about the nature of literature: literature 'proper'
should engage us aesthetically through its form; it *must* also engage
us intellectually. To achieve the latter it must be honest (true to
personal experience) and realistic (historically and politically aware).
Such qualities cannot be developed by detached imagining or theor-

ising, they are best nurtured through personal involvement and experience (practical knowledge), as well as sense of open commitment.

So Orwell's view of literature is inherently prescriptive rather than descriptive. And the prescription is highly personal, nakedly related to Orwell's view of his own literary motives.

Given such premises, it becomes easier to understand the kind of critical criteria Orwell seems to have deduced from them. We see these criteria hard at work in perhaps his best known critical essay 'Inside the Whale'. A notable feature of the essay is its historical grouping together of authors. This appears to be an essential preliminary to passing any critical judgement. For what Orwell then proceeds to do is judge the appropriateness of each author's work to the period in which he or she was writing. Through this means, Joyce, for instance, emerges with certain reservations as a worthwhile author, since his experience was essentially Edwardian and a novel like *Ulysses* owes its distinct aesthetic form to a particular 'vision of life' pertinent to that age. Orwell's reservations about Joyce really seem more directed to the nature of the age itself: 'When one looks back at the twenties, nothing is queerer than the way in which every important event in Europe escaped the notice of the English intelligentsia' ('Inside the Whale', *PE*, p. 121).

Hence, Joyce, Eliot, Lawrence *et al.* are castigated for their 'defeatism' – an inward-lookingness and longing to escape their own society by directing our eyes 'to Rome, to Byzantium, to Montparnasse, to Mexico, to the Etruscans, to the subconscious, to the solar plexus – to everything except the places where things are really happening' ('Inside the Whale'. *PE*, p. 120). Lawrence comes off worse than Joyce because Orwell finds his life vision 'a lost cause . . . a wish that things would happen in a way they are manifestly not going to happen' (Inside the Whale', *PE*, p. 123). Orwell makes no apologies for judging these authors by their subject matter.

> In cultured circles art-for-art's saking [was] extended practically to a worship of the meaningless. Literature was supposed to consist solely in the manipulation of words. To judge a book by its subject matter was the unforgiveable sin, and even to be aware of its subject matter was a lapse of taste . . . [commending a Punch cartoon] an intolerable youth is pictured informing his aunt that he intends to 'write'. 'And what are you going to write about,

dear?' asks the aunt. 'My dear aunt', says the youth crushingly, 'one doesn't write about anything, one just writes'. ('Inside the Whale', *PE*, p. 121)

So Orwell ignores Lawrence's stylistic skills because Lawrence's subject matter is seen to be meaningless, in the sense that it has no contemporary relevance. Orwell seems unprepared to consider that Lawrence's 'escapism' was itself a meaningful political gesture – to him it was 'defeatism'.

Here we see a major limitation of Orwell's prescriptive notion of literature. Perhaps because of his journalistic background, he tended to see history and society as comprised of sets of 'facts', which the writer had a responsibility to confront. This can only be true in the limited sense, say, that history concerns a record of events. But beyond that, history is concerned with the *significance* of these events, and is thus an intellectual construct as much as a 'true' record. Orwell's condemnation of Lawrence amounts to saying that Lawrence's work failed to address the significant facts of the day – as construed by George Orwell.

Yet, evidently, Lawrence characters like the Brangwen sisters did confront significant issues. For instance, they sought to break with the social mould that had been cast for them as wives and lovers by moving from home, taking employment, exploring unconventional sexual relationships and so forth. In this respect their predicament reflected the wider plight of women at that time. Lawrence didn't have to cast them as suffragettes in order to develop this theme of individuals in opposition to social and political expectations. Had he done so, he would have made the Brangwens typical of women of the period, and so lessened the general truth of their plight. More typically, Lawrence's novels show the Brangwens seeking emancipation through very personal routes, *irrespective* of orthodox social dictates.

Thus, there is political significance to their apolitical conduct, and there seems no good reason to chide Lawrence because he didn't hammer that point home in polemical style. Indeed, there is the indication here, as elsewhere in Orwell, that an author is condemned for his or her *intention*. Unfortunately, Orwell's prescriptions for moral and political purpose impose those same 'crippling' restrictions on 'honest records' which Orwell advised against in 'The Prevention of Literature'.

Whilst Lawrence is condemned for his irrelevant vision, Pound and Wyndham Lewis are hammered as 'fascists', Lewis in particular, as a witch-hunter of Bolsheviks. At the other end of the spectrum, Auden, Spender, Day-Lewis, MacNiece *et al.* are seen to be 'orthodoxy sniffers' of a different kind – 'Sniff, Sniff. Are you a good anti-Fascist?' ('Inside the Whale', *PE*, p. 132). Moreover, they are viewed as armchair communists, who (here Orwell plays his trump card) unlike him, only knew their subject-matter from a distance, having failed to gain first hand experience. They came to embrace their orthodoxy (communism) purely for the sake of something to believe in. Accordingly, they tend to compromise their 'aesthetic and intellectual integrity'. As an instance, Orwell cites Auden's poem 'Spain' where he talks about accepting guilt if murder is necessary and Orwell morally rebuts this on account of his own experience of killings in the Spanish War.

Initially, Henry Miller seems to come out well by comparison to the aforementioned. Orwell applauds his frankness and also praises Miller's innovation of a prose form appropriate to the 'third class carriage' subject matter of *Tropic of Cancer*. He repeatedly recommends the acquisition of the novel to his readers, and he also reiterates the claim that Miller 'is the only imaginative prose writer of the slightest value who has appeared among the English-speaking races for some years past' ('Inside the Whale', *PE*, p. 139).

Then, in the last sentences of the essay, Orwell reveals that this praise has been the build-up to an ironical dénouement which he then unleashes with sadistic fervour:

> Even if that is objected to as an overstatement, it will probably be admitted that Miller is a writer out of the ordinary, worth more than a single glance; and after all, he is a completely negative, unconstructive, amoral writer, a mere Jonah, a passive accepter of evil, a sort of Whitman among the corpses. . . . It is a demonstration of the impossibility of any major literature until the world has shaken itself into its new shape.   ('Inside the Whale', *PE*, p. 139)

Here we see the measure of just how prescriptive Orwell's view of literature was. Intellectual worth required more than just Miller's kind of honesty. Intellectual activity had to be directed by a sense of moral purpose. On the whole, this was not a novel perspective – it belongs to the ancient tradition that art must be morally edifying.

Orwell seems to have updated this approach only insofar as he saw political awareness as a moral imperative for his own age.

Orwell's view of authorial 'experience' also seems embedded in an established intellectual tradition. His notion that the writer would best discover 'the true facts' of history and society through direct observation and participation firmly belongs to British empiricism. Not only is this view open to familiar objections – that the 'truth' obtained by such means cannot be free from preconceptions – but it is also inconsistent with Orwell's own view that a writer should recognise from the first his or her own political instincts.

As for Orwell's awareness of critical traditions, it is notable that two of his longer essays on Dickens and King Lear developed out of his readings of criticism of their work. In its general structure, 'Charles Dickens' is one of Orwell's more orthodox pieces of criticism, with his discussion developing out of quite a wide ranging survey of Dickens criticism. 'Lear, Tolstoy and the Fool' is a very different proposition. As a prelude to his rebuttal of Tolstoy's assessment of Lear, Orwell writes:

> In reality there is no kind of evidence or argument by which one can show that Shakespeare, or any other writer is 'good' . . . Ultimately, there is no test of literary merit, except survival, which is itself merely an index to majority opinion. Artistic theories such as Tolstoy's are quite worthless because they not only start out with arbitrary assumptions, but depend on vague terms ('sincere', 'important' and so forth) which can be interpreted in any way that one choses. Properly speaking one cannot answer Tolstoy's attack.   ('Lear, Tolstoy and the Fool', *PE*, p. 410)

Here we catch a glimpse of a different Orwell to the one discussed so far. His own criticism in essays like 'Inside the Whale' clearly suggests a consistent set of critical criteria. Yet as soon as Orwell consciously reflects upon the nature of critical activity, he seems instinctively to rubbish any idea that there could be rules governing such a thing. A year after this, he wrote:

> I often have the feeling that even at the best of times literary criticism is fraudulent, since in the absence of any accepted standards whatever – any external reference which can give meaning to the statement that such and such a book is 'good' or 'bad' – every literary judgement consists in trumping up a set of rules to justify

an instinctive preference. One's real reaction to a book, when one has a reaction at all, is usually, 'I like this book' or 'I don't like it' and what follows is a rationalisation. ('Writers and Leviathan', *PE*, p. 459)

Presumably Orwell isn't here objecting to the idea that criticism involves justifying and rationalising one's own preferences and instincts. He merely refutes the notion that the critic can justify any judgement without 'trumping up' sets of rules by way of argument.

This claim presents considerable difficulties for Orwell and his readers alike, as may be seen when he uses it to rebut Tolstoy's criticism of Lear. He makes the case that Tolstoy's arguments can be invalidated by showing them to born of malice as well as Tolstoy's unwitting recognition of Lear's follies in his own behaviour.

Now here it is hard to decide whether Orwell thinks his invalidation of Tolstoy's arguments demonstrates (i) that all critical arguments are trumped up, or (ii) that only bad arguments are. If (i) were the case then at worst we would have to see Orwell's own critical endeavours as a demonstration of the essential insincerity of critical argument, or at best, as an intentionally ironic demonstration of that fact. Alternatively, if (ii) were the case, then Orwell would have to concede that there could be critical arguments which provided worthwhile insights into the critic's preferences.

Naturally, it would be in everyone's best interests if (ii) were the case. Yet we have already seen the ferocious irony underlying 'Inside the Whale', the conclusion of which questions the very possibility of anyone writing what Orwell sees to be literature. It is hard then, to ignore the corresponding implication that in 'this age' the critic cannot practise genuine literary criticism. Perhaps the proper reading of 'Inside the Whale' is that the critic has to step outside the confines of conventional critical approaches and appeal to our moral and political consciousness in order to reveal both literature and criticism for what they really are.

Indeed, this was what many contemporary critics sensed Orwell to be doing. Q. D. Leavis argued that Orwell was a critic of literature as opposed to a literary critic.[5] Edmund Wilson thought Orwell's criticism of 'serious writers' was 'semi-political, semi-sociological' (although he thought his work on popular culture first rate). Both these critics thought Orwell's work generally failed to examine its texts in sufficient depth; and certainly it's true that Orwell provides very little in the way of textual evidence for his judgements. Yet both critics enjoyed the 'refreshing' directness of his approach, with Leavis in particular sharing many of his partialities, not to say prejudices.

Wilson sees Orwell's limitations as a critic arising from his stance as a moralist, for instance, his tendency to generalise *ad hominem* about authors' careers, without following their 'artistic development'. It is interesting that Wilson – whose critical concerns were seen to be close to Orwell's is thrown by Orwell's appeals to the historicity of the text, and that his own objection implies a belief in the transcendence of artistic merit. This also seems to apply to another of Wilson's objections, that Orwell tended to apply the same approach to serious literature as to the popular kind.

Some years later, John Wain took this last point further in complaining that 'if we had nothing but Orwell's criticism to go on, we should never be able to tell, from reading it, that Shakespeare was as far superior to the amiable author of the Magnet as, in fact, he is. So it isn't "literary criticism", in the real sense, that one reads Orwell's essays on books.'[6]

Here, Wain correctly senses that Orwell's view of literature is far broader than his own – just as we may see that Orwell's broader scope makes him much closer to the contemporary critic than Wain. If Wain's remarks had been addressed to contemporary criticism, it would indeed invoke the current debate about the usefulness of criticism which, in substituting 'analysis' for 'judgement' and 'cultural norms' for 'artistic merit', permitted as much critical attention to be focused on comics as Shakespeare. However, Wain fails to recognise that Orwell openly shared his own hierarchical view of literature, manifested in Orwell's prescriptive definitions. Very likely, Wain *chooses* to ignore this aspect of Orwell's work in order to disqualify undesirable subjects from creeping into the critical canon.

So we see a consensus among the critics above that Orwell couldn't be regarded as a 'proper' literary critic, because of his leanings towards 'beside the point', 'semi-political-sociological' observation made at the expense of textual 'discrimination' and 'sensitivity'. Judgements of this kind show they chose not to pick up the gauntlet thrown down with such a crash by Orwell, as when he rubbishes 'art for art's sake'. Orwell's strident demands for renewed concentration on subject matter could not be construed as incidental. In both their tone and content they have to be seen as an attempt to compensate for a purported imbalance of interest in conventional criticism. Far from defending their approaches against this shift of emphasis, critics like Leavis, Wain and Wilson simply ruled it out of court as not being a literary critical argument in their sense.

In fact, as Q. D. Leavis noted, Orwell could 'close read' a text when so inclined. But given Orwell's desire to refocus attention on subject matter, this must have seemed something of a distraction from his own critical thrust. Instead, Orwell showed greater inclination to close read political, rather than literary texts, as in 'Politics and the English Language' and his appendix on 'Newspeak' in *Nineteen Eighty-Four* reveals an understanding of how language can predetermine thought and action, which seems far in advance of most of his British contemporaries.

Moreover, Orwell would probably be the first to anticipate such a response from the literary establishment, which makes his claims about the fradulence of literary criticism less perplexing. Given the expectations of mainstream critics, Orwell could hardly identify his critical method with theirs. Thus he distances his own approach and highlights it by resort to a favourite polemical device – impassioned overstatement (even at the expense of subordinating his subject to consideration of style, a failing he freely acknowledged). The rough and tough style, the demands for practical experience and so forth, were not just necessary instruments for cracking open the contemporary predicament. Egotism played its part in this as he frankly admitted. But more than this, it was a virile posture that fits well with the swingeing tradition of British commonsense criticism of John Dennis, Dr Johnson, Macaulay *et al.*

This is a tradition where an individual can make a name for himself by standing up against prevailing highbrow opinion, fearless of its ridicule. Hence a philosophical theory can be refuted by repeatedly kicking a rock. Such individual actions can be sanctioned by reference to common sense – the thoughts and values of ordinary people – and thereby serve to liberate the public from the tyrannies of highbrow fads.

In his discussion of Orwell's common sense standards, Edmund Wilson is far more effective than when he challenges Orwell's position as a literary critic. He recognises that Orwell's criticism is at its most vulnerable on those occasions when he appeals to common standards. An outstanding example is Orwell's essay on Salvador Dali – 'a dirty little scoundrel' – whose antics succeeded in getting an often hilarious rise out of Orwell. Orwell claims that 'any investigation' of Dali's work should start out from the 'fact' that 'they are diseased and disgusting' – an assertion that hardly promises a convincing critical argument. However, that is often the price the common sense critic has to pay for his public-spirited act of appealing to the orthodoxies of the masses.

Orwell, however, is not abashed about his own readiness to shoulder public responsibilities. He talks of 'a writer' (not unlike himself) having to be 'prepared to deliver lectures in draughty halls, to chalk pavements, to canvass voters, to distribute leaflets, even fight in civil wars if it seems necessary ('Writers and Leviathan', *PE*, p. 463). But beyond that such a writer never writes for anyone but himself, otherwise, the individual becomes compromised by the group and there will be the danger that 'any thought which is freely followed up may lead to the forbidden thought. ('The Prevention of Literature', *PE*, p. 340) So a writer must operate as an individual, an outsider, at the most an unwelcome guerilla on the flank of a regular army. Orwell is prepared to conceded that facing up to public responsibilities may force the writer into collaborative actions incompatible with his or her personal beliefs. But this only makes it important that writing should be the product of the saner self that stands aside.

In the same vein, Orwell's jibe that literary merit (ability to survive) was 'merely an index of majority opinion' could be seen as a rejection of the Eliot/Leavis view of critical activity. This proposes criticism as 'a co-operative labour', where the critic 'should endeavour to discipline his personal prejudices and cranks – tares to which we are all subject – and compose his differences with as many of his fellows as possible in the common pursuit of true judgement'.[7]

Clearly, for Orwell, the truth of any judgement could not be decided by consensus. You could appeal to consensus views, as with Dali's work, but you had to do so out of your own choosing, not because you felt your collaborators expected it of your. Your choice would be determined by an honest recognition, and then exposition of your personal reaction to literature and events. Only on these terms could Orwell's individual contribute to a common pursuit.

Of course, the Dali case is but one demonstration that a critic's reactions are hardly a matter of 'free' discovery, but rather, heavily determined by one's cultural background. As Edmund Wilson saw, the Blimpish part of Orwell's background couldn't resist rising to the bait offered by that 'diseased', 'disgusting', 'antisocial' little 'cad'. And so Dali gets off lightly by provoking critical reactivity in place of critical activity.

So, when viewed as a theory, Orwell's critical approach suffers from its emphasis on the primacy of individual experience, despite foreshadowing later criticism in other respects. Where it does offer a strong challenge to the Eliot/Leavis view of consensus is in its insistence upon the importance of subject matter.

Compare for instance, Orwell's and F. R. Leavis' discussions of the Houyhnhnms in Gulliver's Travels.[8] Both cite pretty much the same material and agree that the Houyhnhnms (representatives of the Augustan virtues) are unattractive creatures. Leavis attributes this to Swift's sharing of 'the shallowest complacencies of Augustan common sense: his irony might destroy this, but there is no conscious criticism'. Leavis closely examines the language of Swift to reveal its ironic method. He thinks that it is only the 'force' of Swift's genius for the ironic method that makes the Houyhnhnms credible. The 'power' of Swift's satire then, is explained by appeal to the transcendental 'quality' of its literary form.

Orwell, however, recognises that satire operates in an historical and political context. The Houyhnhnms are unattractive because Swift is seen to be a political reactionary. His political stance is so negative and misanthropic that he is incapable of inventing an attractive utopia, represented by Houyhnhnm society. Swift can offer 'no conscious criticism' of their virtues, because he has no genuine concept of social virtue. And here Orwell is able to open up his assessment of Swift to contemporary parallels. Houyhnhnm society resembles a totalitarian regime, where nobody is free because all agree. Swift can make his creatures credible because, like a Catholic or Communist, he can pick out 'a single hidden truth' and then 'magnify and distort it' with a 'barely sane' conviction and 'intensity of vision'. Thus Orwell does not seek to explain the enduring attraction of Swift by reference to some transcendental quality, but rather by relating the quality to political themes relevant as much to contemporary society as to Swift's. Regardless of whether we agree with Orwell's analysis, he does seem to offer us a reason why we should read *Gulliver's Travels* today that looks more pertinent and tangible than F. R. Leavis'.

Orwell's own highly individual sense of conviction precluded pursuit of consensus views. The conformity we seem to find in his critical approach is the search for conformity between personal experience and action. In this respect, 'experience' denotes the individual's raw reaction to texts and events, and 'action' his effort to explore honestly and confront the reasons for the given reaction. In

the case of a writer, 'action' carries the added sense of purposefully
striving to convince others of the reasons. In the case of Orwell, this
was something that could be pursued through all avenues of his life:
journalism, essay and novel writing, and even soldiering if the need
arose.

NOTES

1.   See, for example, Edmund Wilson, in *New Yorker*, 25 May 1946, re-
     printed in J. Meyers (ed.), *George Orwell: The Critical Heritage* (London:
     Routledge & Kegan Paul, 1975) pp. 224–7.
2.   J. Wain, 'George Orwell as a Writer of Polemic', in R. Williams (ed.),
     George Orwell: A Collection of Critical Essays (Englewood Cliffs, N.J.:
     Prentice-Hall, 1974) p. 100.
3.   See, for example, N. Arvin, *Partisan Review*, September 1946, in J. Meyers,
     George Orwell, pp. 232–5.
4.   G. Orwell, 'Why I Write', in *The Penguin Essays of George Orwell* (Lon-
     don: Penguin, 1984) p. 12. All the Orwell essays referred to appear in
     this volume; hereafter referred to *PE*, with titles of essays and page
     references given in the text.
5.   Q. D. Leavis, in *Scrutiny*, September 1940, in J. Meyers, *George Orwell*,
     pp. 187–90.
6.   J. Wain in R. Williams, *George Orwell*, p. 100.
7.   T. S. Eliot quoted in F. R. Leavis, *The Common Pursuit* (London: Chatto
     & Windus, 1952) p. v.
8.   F. R. Leavis, 'The Irony of Swift', in *The Common Pursuit*, pp. 73–8; and
     G. Orwell, 'Politics vs Literature', in *PE*, pp. 376–93.

12

Reason, Rhetoric, Theory: Empson and de Man

CHRISTOPHER NORRIS

On the face of it William Empson and Paul de Man have little in common beyond their obvious concern with the complexities of literary language and the close-reading of texts. One's sense of the contrast might be summarised in terms of R. P. Blackmur's mythical opposites, the Prolific and the Devourer.[1] Empson is the 'creative' critic, one who opens up new and exciting possibilities of sense in texts worn smooth by habitual reading. This quality is seized upon by admirers and detractors alike. To the latter it is a species of misapplied imaginative licence, a habit of response which substitutes mere ingenuity for the discipline of trained judgment. To the former it is a liberating gesture which throws off the protocols of scholarly method and it puts criticism back in touch with the energizing sources of poetic creativity. Aside from such differences of viewpoint there is widespread agreement among the commentators that Empson is a critic of extraordinary zest, inventiveness and brilliance. In de Man's case the usual impression is of a powerful but rigorously negative intelligence applied to the business of undoing, rather than creating, fresh possibilities of sense. The vulgarised image of deconstruction as a free-for-all interpretative romp is patently wide of the mark when set against de Man's scrupulous practice.

Empson's method is to multiply meanings to the point where methodical distinctions collapse in a seemingly endless proliferation of sense. His vaunted seven types of ambiguity are really little more than a series of pegs on which to hang a mass of examples whose meaning constantly outruns and upsets any tidy logical sequence.[2] What holds his book together is the sheer imaginative energy and drive by which language is made to yield up ever more diverse subtleties of meaning. In de Man the anomalies of logic and sense are the upshot of a *theory* which persistently seeks them out and refuses

153

to settle for any assurance of achieved method or meaning. Deconstruction in this rigorous form would seem to be the active antithesis of everything that Empson most strikingly represents. Its effect is to problematise the act of reading to a point where language can only reveal its incapacity to say what it means or mean what it says.

Where Empson finds language exceeding the powers of plain prose statement, his response is to try out a whole variety of paraphrastic hints and roundabout suggestions which may at least help to focus the reader's mind. The most rewarding ambiguities are those that create the maximum challenge to a critic's desire for orderly, cut-and-dried patterns of sense. Yet Empson hangs on to the basic rationalist conviction that poetry is, after all, a species of communicative language and ought to make sense enough not to be treated as some kind of holy mystery. Hence – among other things – his dogged attempt in *Seven Types of Ambiguity* to extract some kind of rational prose sense from Wordsworth's 'shuffling and evasive' grammar in the lines from 'Tintern Abbey' (*STA*, pp. 151–4). What Empson won't allow is the idea that language may create problems of logical accountability beyond all reach of intelligible prose statement. And this is precisely what de Man sets out to demonstrate over and again in his deconstructive essays. As he puts it in a much-quoted sentence from *Allegories Of Reading:* 'rhetoric radically suspends logic and opens up vertiginous possibilities of referential aberration'.[3] And again: in so far as there exists such a thing as 'literary language', it can only be equated with those aberrant effects of rhetorical figuration which put such obstacles in the way of logic and reference. De Man's is, in short, a singular technique for creating disturbances wherever thought tries to get on equable terms with its own linguistic character.

But then, turning back to *Seven Types*, one finds that Empson often comes up against disturbances of a similar kind. He sets out explicitly to provide a machinery of rational explanation, the 'general assurance' (as Empson describes it) 'which comes of a belief that all sorts of poetry may be conceived as explicable' (*STA*, p. 256). Such an attitude strikes him as preferable to the kind of 'esthetic' squeamishness which refuses to analyse poetry for fear of destroying the reader's delicate responses. Besides, Empson argues, 'normal sensibility is a tissue of what has been conscious theory made habitual and returned to the pre-conscious, and, therefore, conscious theory may make an addition to sensibility' (*STA*, p. 254). *Seven Types* is there-

fore addressed to those who have the courage of their rational convictions, who want to understand their responses to poetry and not
give way to mystified 'intuitive' creeds. It is in this spirit that Empson
holds out against the more extreme kinds of poetic unreason. Unlike
the American New Critics, he refuses to accept that paradox is the
chief merit and defining characteristic of poetry, so that any attempt
to spell out its meaning in more or less rational terms is bound to do
violence to the poem.

Thus Empson chides Wordsworth for his fuzzy logic and 'shuffling' argumentation, even while protesting that he enjoys the poetry
and that 'probably it was necessary for Wordsworth to shuffle, if he
was to maintain his peculiar poetical attitude (*STA*, p. 154). It is here
– and in similar passages throughout *Seven Types* – that Empson
notes a disturbing tendency for rhetoric to upset the normative
patterns of grammar (or logic) and insinuate a deviant pattern of its
own. Of course he never goes so far as de Man, for whom the object
of reading is precisely to tease out such ultimate collisions of sense
between the 'grammatical' and 'rhetorical' dimensions of a text.
Nothing could be further from Empson's attitude of sturdy rationalist conviction. But the fact that he returns so often to poems which
problematise most of his own working assumptions is a sign that
close-reading in Empson's manner cannot be immune to such textual complications.

It is in the last chapter of *Seven Types* that Empson raises these
problems most explicitly in reflecting on the larger implications of
his method. The chapter is designed as a defence of 'analytic' criticism against those who would reject the whole approach as nothing
more than a species of reductive rationalist machinery. Empson, as
we have seen, comes down firmly on the side of analysis, theory, and
conscious understanding. To this extent he identifies with the prevailing scientific culture of his day, rather than the ill-defined 'literary' outlook which pins its hopes to the truth-claims of unaided
intuition. Even so, as he admits, there is a sense in which understanding poetry is *not* like understanding events in the physical
world, since 'the act of knowing is itself an act of sympathising;
unless you are enjoying the poetry you cannot create it, as poetry, in
your mind' (*STA*, p. 248). And this leads on to the further reflection
that modern science, after all, has produced a more complicated
picture of what goes on in any 'normal' transaction between knower
and known. Empson's early poems are evidence enough that he had
absorbed the new scientific ideas and set himself to work out their

moral and imaginative bearings.[4] Among them was the notion that 'truth' might always be a matter of probabilistic inference from the partial and strictly undecidable evidence provided by observation. In subatomic physics, for instance, any event that might be claimed as evidence for this or that theory could also be seen as a product of the experimental conditions set up to determine its nature. The speculative range of the new physics, together with its problems of verification, were such that often no clear line could be drawn between fact and theory, experimental truth and hypothetical construct.

A part of Empson's case is therefore to argue that science itself is undergoing a change in what counts as 'scientific' method. Those who so zealously resist its encroachment into other domains (for instance, that of literary criticism) are perhaps ignoring this decisive shift of viewpoint. On the old, positivistic model: 'the scientific idea of truth is that the mind, otherwise passive, collects propositions about the outside world; the application of scientific ideas to poetry is interesting because it reduces that idea of truth (much more intimately than elsewhere) to a self-contradiction' (*STA*, pp. 248–9). That is to say: the activity of reading a poem (of 'creating it, as poetry, in your mind') is a process so complex as to deconstruct all naive antinomies of subject and object, acts of understanding and literary texts. It becomes a strictly undecidable issue as to how far meaning is in and of the text, and how far a product of reader involvement. And this suggests in turn that the critic is ambiguously placed when it comes to deciding what 'rational' standards to apply in the explication of poetic language. Empson tends to assume on principle that any good poem will make at least some kind of logical sense without forcing the interpreter back into regions of paradox or abnormal psychology. Thus 'any contradiction', according to Empson, 'is likely to have some sensible interpretation; and if you think of interpretations which are not sensible, it puts the blame on you' (*STA*, p. 197). But this attitude of flat good sense is always coming up against its limits with the kind of poetry which responds best to Empson's techniques of close-reading. The most memorable pages of *Seven Types* are devoted to poets (George Herbert, Wordsworth, Hopkins, and others) whose language presses ambiguity to the point of downright logical contradiction. And it is here that Empson's commentary registers that sense of a certain tension at work between rhetoric and grammar, the figural power and the rational constraints of language.

This tension results from Empson's deep-grained resistance to the powers of unreason which he finds often lurking in the more extreme forms of paradoxical expression. In *The Structure of Complex Words* he set out to provide nothing less than a full-scale logical semantics of language based on a theory of multiple meaning.[5] Empson had clearly come to feel that his own earlier methods were inadequate or positively dangerous, in so far as they encouraged an irrationalist drive to ignore the virtues of plain prose sense and embrace all manner of mind-bending paradox. *Complex Words* has a number of specific targets in view. It is intended partly as a rationalist rejoinder to Orwell's grim prognosis, in *Nineteen Eighty-Four*, of the ways in which language can be kidnapped and perverted by the powers of totalitarian thought-control.[6] Empson admits that such perversions exist, and that language has the rhetorical means of encoding many varieties of irrational paradox. Moreover, these devices have something in common with certain forms of 'literary' language which collapse the normal logic of semantic entailment and simply conflate the different senses of a word. But to find such deviant rhetorics at work is also to see that they only *make sense* against a background of normative rational assumptions. Hence, the main thrust of Empson's argument (in *The Structure of Complex Words*), contrary to Orwell's: 'the human mind, as expressed in language, is not irredeemably lunatic, and cannot be made so' (*SCW*, p. 83n.). Hence also his insistence that 'complex words' are not simply cases – like those of 'ambiguity' – where the meanings pile up in a vaguely associative manner. Empson's point is that words can carry a kind of 'compacted doctrine', a structure of equations or logical entailments, such that their meaning can be analysed in truth-functional terms. Thus he rejects the notion of I. A. Richards, that the language of poetry is strictly 'emotive', having nothing to do with veridical truth-claims or logical forms of thought.[7] For Empson, there is a 'grammar' of complex words which may run into problems in coping with some kinds of poetry – Wordsworth's for instance – but which nonetheless provides the essential basis for a rationalist theory of language and interpretation.

Perhaps the best examples of this theory in action are the chapters in *Complex Words* devoted to the key-word *sense* and its various structures of semantic implication. The point about 'sense', as Empson argues, is that its meanings span the whole range of human cognitive claims, from 'sense = sensory experience' (or sense-data) to 'sense = ultimate knowledge through imaginative insight'. The word can thus be used to imply a variety of different ideas about the powers and limits of human understanding. There is a typical eighteenth-century rationalist usage which suggests that one should 'concentrate on the middle of the range, the man-sized parts where we feel most at home' (*SCW*, p. 262). This amounts to a common sense belief that reason gets along well enough on the evidence of the senses without going in for any kind of transcendental truth-claims. The word can suggest all this, Empson writes, because 'the simple use of the trope (which is now taken as a pattern) is an appeal to you to sow a normal amount of good judgement, "like everyone else," ' (*SCW*, p. 262). How the emphasis falls from one context to another will depend on the particular equations imposed by the period (or individual) style. But in so far as the word has a common sense or normative structure, it will tend to focus on the middle-range meanings which support the idea of plain 'good judgement'.

As a rationalist himself, with no great liking for religious or other kinds of paradox, Empson is clearly well disposed toward 'sense' in this particular semantic guise. His whole approach in *Complex Words* rests on the assumption that we *do* interpret language – at least as far as possible – in a rational or common sense way. Empson's equations (the 'bits of machinery' as he calls them) tend to work best where the words make sense according to rational norms, and not where they rest on purely intuitive or transcendental claims. On the other hand he does devote several chapters to exploring some deviant cases of just that kind. In *Measure for Measure*, as Empson reads it, there is a running debate on the senses of 'sense' which pushes the word into some very dark corners of irrational paradox. From its three chief meanings ('sensuality', 'sensibility', 'sensibleness') the play generates a series of questions which resist any straightforward rational solution. Thus: 'Are Puritans hard? (Is not-one not-two?) Are they liable to have crazy outbreaks? (Is not-one not-three?) Is mere justice enough? (Is three two?)' (*SCW*, p. 270). According to Empson, it is the extreme and contradictory nature of the equations thus produced that makes *Measure for Measure*, by common assent, something of a problem play. The semantics of sense come down in the end to 'an examination of sanity itself, which is seen crumbling and dissolving in the soliloquies of Angelo' (*SCW*, p. 270).

Thus it seems that language can take on irrational or pathological powers of suggestion even in the case of words like 'sense' which apparently resist such uses. Empson characteristically stresses the resistance and still finds a kind of rock-bottom sanity in the way these paradoxes work themselves out. *'Measure for Measure,'* he writes, 'is one of the most striking cases where the feelings in the words jib at a wholehearted acceptance of the story' (*SCW*, p. 271). Or again: the dominant equations move over from 'sensuality' to 'sanity', by which crucial shift 'the action is forced round to a happy ending' (*SCW*, p. 287). What Empson wants to do is provide an argued alternative to the kind of 'neo-Christian' reading which fastens on the themes of perverted 'sense' to extract a message of contempt for all merely human values. This is why he insists that the middle-ground meanings – the common sense equations that stress 'good judgement' – are still actively at work even where the word is being forced to paradoxical extremes. There is a rational grammar of complex words that the reader has to grasp, at least subliminally, if the deviant uses are to make any sense.

Empson sees this as a definite advance over his earlier notion of poetic ambiguity. That term had tended to imply that 'the reader is left in doubt between two readings' with no need to work out the logical relations between them. Ambiguity, he writes, 'is more or less superseded by the idea of a double meaning which is intended to be fitted into a definite structure' (*SCW*, p. 103n.). This shift seems motivated chiefly by Empson's resistance to interpretative methods like those of the American New Critics which make a virtue of paradox and other forms of poetic unreason. His objection to Orwell – that 'language is not irredeemably lunatic and cannot be made so' – is therefore very much in line with his reading of *Measure for Measure*. In both cases it is a question of restoring confidence in the common sense grammar of semantic implication, such that instances of deviant usage can be seen as departures from the rational norm.

The problematical relationship between *grammar* and *rhetoric* is likewise a major theme in de Man's *Allegories of Reading*. Critics who evade this problem assume that rhetorical figures like metaphor and metonymy can be simply absorbed into a generalised typology of tropes creating no problems of structural classification. They have ignored the possibility that these two dimensions of language may not lend themselves to the same kind of analysis, or, more pointedly, may produce conflicts of logic and sense which cannot be resolved by any clear-cut system of description. The rhetorical question (as in Yeats' line: 'how can we know the dancer from the dance?') is de

Man's chief example of the way in which rhetoric works to suspend the normal relation between grammar, logic, and sense. Does the question honestly seek an answer, thus implying that common sense distinctions hold and that language cannot be entirely given over to the Symbolist fusion of figure and context? Or does the question rhetorically deny that any such knowledge is possible, since all distinctions appear to drop away in the moment of imaginative truth? It cannot be a case of simply deciding between these rival interpretations. 'The one reading,' as de Man puts it in *Allegories*, 'is precisely the error denounced by the other and has to be undone by it' (*AR*, p. 12). Neither is it a case of ambiguity in the sense that one might hold both readings comfortably in mind without any conflict developing between them. The example from Yeats is enough to suggest that 'two entirely coherent but entirely incompatible readings can be made to hinge on one line, whose grammatical structure is devoid of ambiguity, but whose rhetorical mode turns the mood as well as the mode of the entire poem upside down' (*AR*, p. 12). Such is the divergence between 'grammar' and 'rhetoric' which theorists are prone to ignore when they attempt – in the classic structuralist fashion – to work out a unified typology of figural devices.

There would seem to be two main sources of confusion, according to de Man. On the one hand critics assimilate rhetoric to grammar, assuming too readily that figural language obeys the same logic as commonly applies to the analysis of well-ordered prose statement. This fails to account not only for rhetorical questions but for all those cases where meaning exceeds or complicates a straightforward structural account. De Man follows Peirce in arguing that rhetoric points toward a process of displacement (or 'unlimited semiosis') which cannot be reduced to the clear-cut concepts and categories required by a putative 'grammar' of tropes. On the other hand there is an equal and opposite temptation to privilege certain rhetorical figures (especially metaphor and symbol), and ignore the quasi-grammatical structures which call their claims into question.[8] Such readings typically work to promote a mystified esthetic ideology, the notion that language can achieve a state of pure, unmediated vision transcending the antinomies of subject and object, mind and nature. De Man sets about deconstructing this mystique in a number of passages from *Allegories of Reading*. In particular he shows how the high claims of metaphor and symbol are effectively undone by a reading that reveals their covert dependence on chains of metonymic detail. Metonymy is the master-trope of deconstruction in so far as it lays bare the signifying mechanisms of a language endlessly condemned to rehearse the noncoincidence of sense and logic, rhetoric and grammar. To accept the claims of metaphor on their own self-mystifying terms is to cultivate a blindness to the workings of language that amounts to a form of ontological bad faith. Deconstruction has the power to resist such readings by a patient attention to the ways in which language works to cover its own rhetorical tracks. More specifically, it shows how the privileged status of metaphor and symbol rests on a blindness to those other, more mechanical figures like metonymy whose workings are not thus valorised. Hence de Man's argument – based on the analysis of a passage from Proust – that 'precisely when the highest claims are being made for the unifying power of metaphor, these very images rely in fact on the deceptive use of semiautomatic grammatical patterns' (*AR*, p. 16).

Empson is at one with de Man in putting up a certain principled resistance to the suasive powers of metaphor and symbol. This comes out most clearly in Empson's dealing with the pantheist doctrine confusedly asserted (as he reads it) in Wordsworth's nature poetry. The semantics of 'sense' are here pressed to the point of a hypostatic union which collapses all merely logical distinctions and insists on 'the one life, within us and abroad'. The word moves across as its various contexts demand, from 'sense = sensory experience' to 'sense = the divine imagination given by love'. In so doing it cuts out the middle range of meanings where the process of rational understanding can best get a hold. In *Seven Types* Empson had puzzled at length over Wordsworth's elusive grammar and semantics, while compelled to admit that he enjoyed the poetry despite its rhetorical designs on the reader. By the time of *Complex Words* this resistance is more sharply focused in terms of the semantic grammar which Wordsworth both exploits and subtly undermines. His most striking uses of 'sense' belong to the class of what Empson calls 'Type IV' equations. That is to say, they function by a species of active false logic which brings together two different senses of a word without any hint of the rational grammar by which those senses might be related. Wordsworth, in short, creates an impression of philosophic depth 'through the firmness and assurance with which he used equations of Type IV; equations whose claim was false, because they did not really erect a third concept as they pretended to' (*SCW*, p. 305).

De Man brings a similar pressure to bear upon the privileged tropes of metaphor and symbol. A deconstructive reading gives

grounds to question the assurance of pure, self-authenticating sense
which sustains such figures. It sets out to demonstrate the sheer
impossibility of language attaining to its wished-for condition of
unmediated commerce between mind and nature, 'sense' in its inward and outward aspects. Interpreters in the Romantic tradition
who ignore this nonidentity of meaning and intent are effectively
colluding in the same process of rhetorical mystification. Far from
achieving its visionary aims, such language involuntarily betrays the
discrete or necessarily disjunctive character of thought, meaning,
and perception. De Man's favored tropes are those which hold out
against the Symbolist drive to aesthetic transcendence, as in this
passage from *Blindness and Insight*: 'Whereas the symbol postulates
the possibility of an identity or identification, allegory designates
primarily a distance in relation to its own origin, and, renouncing
the nostalgia and the desire to coincide, it establishes its language in
the void of this temporal difference'. ('Rhetoric of Temporality', *BI*,
p. 207). Metonymy likewise resists the undifferentiating drift toward
metaphor by remaining stubbornly attached to the mere contiguities
of outward, sensory experience. It shows up the strains and
antinomies that persist in any attempt (like Wordsworth's) to project
a unified self through metaphors drawn from the natural world.
These conflicts result from 'the illusory priority of a subject that had,
in fact, to borrow from the outside world a temporal stability which
it lacked within itself' ('Rhetoric of Temporality', *BI*, p. 200). Metonymy, allegory, and irony are the tropes which de Man most often
singles out as reflecting this hard-won knowledge. They each bear
witness to the *differential* structure of meaning, in the twofold
Derridean sense of that word: the fact that language is always caught
up in a play of 'difference' and 'deferral' beyond the grasp of any
pure, self-present identity.[9] Interpretation is faced with the choice
between 'a conception of the self seen in its authentically temporal
predicament' and 'a defensive strategy that tries to hide from this
negative self-knowledge' ('Rhetoric of Temporality', *BI*, p. 208).

Empson, like de Man, finds cause to mistrust the prematurely
totalising claims of metaphor and symbol. One could press the comparison further by remarking that both critics make a cardinal point
of the distinction between 'rhetoric' and 'grammar', the latter conceived as exerting a restraint upon the powers of irrational suggestion vested in figural language. Empson has a chapter on Pope's
Essay on Criticism which nicely demonstrates this process at work in
the operative key-words *wit* and *sense* (*SCW*, pp. 84–100). The poem

rings changes on the various meanings of 'wit', from 'mere ingenuity' to 'force of intellect' or 'imaginative power'. At the same time it
shows a constant deference to the superior claims of 'sense', a word
whose semantic range encompasses the great Augustan virtues of
sobriety, commonsense, and rational judgement. The importance of
'sense', Empson writes, is 'to provide a steady bass note in contrast
to the high gyrations of wit' (*SCW*, p. 99). The poem therefore serves
as an object-lesson in the reading of its own exemplary strategies of
argument. The semantic grammar of complex words is sufficient to
imply the whole structure of judgement required to make sense of its
witty language. Pope's tricks of style are always in touch with this
larger, implicitly normative dimension. They make great demands,
as Empson says, on 'the "common-sense" which is to become adequate to the task of criticism' (*SCW*, p. 100).

It is on the basis of this generalised common sense assurance that
Empson can show how Wordsworth effectively short-circuits the
grammar of semantic implication. For de Man there is no such assurance to be had, since the 'grammar' in question is not so much a
structure of logical assumptions as a system of repetitive or 'quasi-
automatic' rhetorical functions which deconstruct the drive toward
consistent sense. Thus the 'grammatisation of rhetoric' is a process
which admits of no confident appeal to the laws of rational thought.
It is always liable to go into reverse, so to speak, and erase the very
distinction between grammar and rhetoric which theorists from Aristotle to Genette have constantly sought to impose. 'We are back at
our unanswered question' de Man writes: 'does the grammatisation
of rhetoric end up in negative certainty or does it, like the rhetorisation
of grammar, remain suspended in the ignorance of its own truth or
falsehood?' (*AR*, p. 17). Any answer to this question – such as Empson
most certainly sets out to provide – could only figure to de Man's
way of thinking as a premature attempt to foreclose on the problems
engendered by literary texts.

In the end there is this deep divergence of methodical intent
between Empson and de Man. It can best be described in terms of
those categories (logic, rhetoric, and grammar) which de Man takes
over from the classical trivium. Logic and grammar have always
been seen as largely coextensive, since grammatical patterns appear
to map directly onto the forms of logical thought. This correspondence has then been taken as a formal guarantee that ideas (or the
logic of representation) match up with the structure of perceived
reality. In his essay 'The Resistance to Theory', de Man remarks that

'grammar stands in the service of logic which, in turn, allows for the passage to a knowledge of the world'.[10] Rhetoric, on the other hand, works to upset this self-assured structure of representation. The study of tropes cannot be contained within tight disciplinary bounds, but tends to complicate other dimensions, especially that of grammar. Difficulties arise according to de Man, when 'it is no longer possible to keep it [rhetoric] in its place as a mere adjunct, a mere ornament within the semantic function' ('The Resistance to Theory', *RT*, p. 14). And this disturbance extends from the interface of rhetoric and grammar to the region of cognitive truth-claims where logic supposedly articulates the deep 'grammar' of thought.

Deconstruction thus becomes the undoing of theory, a 'project of rhetorical analysis that will reveal the inadequacy of grammatical models of nonreading' ('The Resistance to Theory', *RT*, p. 15). Theories which assimilate rhetoric to a structural typology or 'grammar' of tropes are precisely ignoring the difficulties placed in their way by the problematic status of figural language. 'Rhetoric, by its actively negative relationship to grammar and to logic, certainly undoes the claims of the trivium (and by extension, of language) to be an epistemologically stable system' ('The Resistance to Theory', *RT*, p. 15). Hence (de Man argues) the resistance to deconstruction among philosophers and critics who stake their enterprise on a firm categorical distinction between grammar and rhetoric. This includes those structuralist thinkers – like Genette – whose elaborate taxonomies of figural language fail to account for the tensions that develop in the close-reading of their own (otherwise exemplary) texts. Theory is undone by such a reading precisely in so far as it needs to repress these signs of rhetorical disruption.

That Empson takes a very different line is obvious enough from his working faith in the rational grammar of complex words. His argument has three main premises, each of them challenged directly by de Man's attitude of extreme epistemological scepticism. He assumes that grammar is indeed very largely coextensive with logic; that rhetoric is subject to logical restraints upon its powers of implication; and that the semantics of complex words can therefore be described in terms of a logical grammar of sense. Such is the epistemological basis for Empson's strongly rationalist theory of language. It is a theory designed, as he says, to answer a seemingly straightforward question: 'how in the world we come to do such a thing, what intellectual machinery we have . . . to approach the actual words on the page . . . without merely feeling that they don't fit'

(*SCW*, p. 57n.). In this respect it bears some resemblance to the kind of 'ordinary language' philosophy practised by J. L. Austin and his followers. Indeed, there is a striking similarity of views between Empson's chapters on 'sense' an the line of argument adopted by Austin in the lectures published as *Sense and Sensibilia*.[11] What Empson and Austin have in common is a will to coax language down from the heights of irrational paradox and lead it back to a healthy sense of commonplace meanings and distinctions. For Austin, the paradoxes mostly take hold through the bad philosophical habit of forcing language into specialised jargons completely out of touch with ordinary usage. For Empson, the case is more complicated in so far as he needs to admit that poets like Wordsworth can create all manner of sense-bending paradox and yet strike the reader as somehow conveying important truths. There is a footnote to *Complex Words* which addresses this problem in summary fashion. One must, Empson says, 'distinguish a "fallacy", which depends on your not noticing the logical contradiction, from a "paradox", in which it is recognised and viewed as "profound"' (*SCW*, p. 53n.). But this allowance goes distinctly against the grain of Empson's rationalist semantics. More typical is Empson's comment on Wordsworth: that 'what is jumped over is "good sense"; when Wordsworth has got his singing robes on he will not allow any mediating process to have occurred' (*SCW*, p. 304).

Given the book's extraordinary range of argument, it is a singular fact that *Complex Words* has received so little attention from critical theorists over the past three decades. The likeliest explanation is that Empson's rationalist premises run counter to the modes of rhetorical criticism which have flourished during that period. To 'old' New Critics it was a high point of principle that poetry possessed an imaginative logic of its own, a source of intensified meaning and perception irreducible to plain prose statement. Ambiguity, irony, and paradox were the favored rhetorical devices upon which to base these programmatic claims for the uniqueness of poetic language. For Cleanth Brooks in *The Well-Wrought Urn* it is an item of critical faith that 'what Wordsworth wanted to say demanded his use of paradox . . . [and] could only be said powerfully through paradox'.[12] Empson concurs up to a point. He allows that the false logic of Wordsworth's Type IV equations may have been the only available means of expressing his rich but confused ideas about God, mind, and nature. All the same he insists that those ideas *were* confused, and should not be accepted on their own peculiar terms by critics over-willing to embrace all manner of irrational paradox. It is hardly surprising that *Complex Words* was greeted with scant sympathy by those among the New Critics who had responded so keenly to *Seven Types of Ambiguity*. The earlier book had opened up whole new dimensions of rhetorical close-reading. In the sequel Empson seemed to turn his back on this liberating prospect and leave small room for the high claims now advanced on behalf of ambiguity, paradox, etc.

The comparison with de Man also brings out his continuing distance from the newer deconstructionist modes of rhetorical analysis. Empson shares the will to demystify figural language in so far as it denies, represses, or distorts the grammar of semantic implication. To this extent his enterprise has something in common with de Man's. What sets them at odds is the assumption crucial to Empson's argument, that grammar (the structure of semantic implication within complex words) is closely related to logic and not, as de Man would have it, everywhere subject to rhetorical subversion. As an example of the 'persistent symbiosis between grammar and logic' de Man in 'The Resistance to Theory' cites a passage from A. J. Greimas[13] which rejects the idea of 'constructing a grammar for each particular text', and identifies the 'science' of semiotic method with its claim to universal validity. For Greimas, quite simply, 'grammar is an isotope of logic' ('The Resistance to Theory', *RT*, p. 13). De Man, on the contrary, regards such claims as yet another species of nonreading, of that deluded mastery over texts that avoids engaging their full rhetorical complexity. No doubt Empson's rationalist semantics would earn a similar rebuke. His approach could only strike de Man as a technique for sinking the difference between grammar and logic, and thus for keeping rhetoric safely within bounds. Indeed there are passages in *Complex Words* where this motive becomes quite explicit. Thus Empson remarks that 'there is plenty of backing for the idea that we use false identity; the difficulty is in applying it to verbal analysis in a definite enough way to be useful' (*SCW*, p. 43). This 'usefulness' can only be a matter of discovering some logical structure of sense at work within the more resistant forms of rhetorical language.

It so happens that Empson makes this point while discussing a text from Proust. The passage has to do with Françoise and her attitude to the Guermantes family, whose 'greatness' she deduces at once from the 'number of its branches' and the 'brilliance of its connections'. Proust goes on to analyse the source of her confusion in terms which lend themselves to Empson's purpose: 'For since there was but the single word "great" to express both meanings, it seemed to her that they formed a single idea, her vocabulary, like cut stones sometimes, showing thus on certain of its facets a flaw which projected a ray of darkness into the recess of her mind' (*SCW*, p. 43). Empson calls this ' a very beautiful image' but treats it as an instance of clearly-marked logical bewilderment. 'A word has two uses normally separate; there is a case where they can be used together; an assertion is added that they normally come together or even are the same' (*SCW*, p. 43). There is no question here of treating the confusion as pointing to some deep insight or transcendental truth.

De Man's chapter on Proust in *Allegories of Reading*, which requires no detailed summary here, turns on the failure of Proustian metaphor to sustain its own imaginative truth-claims, a failure not merely local or contingent but, as de Man would argue, characteristic of all such language. Proust sets up a range of thematic oppositions whose structural contrast devolves upon the two main figures of metaphor and metonymy. On the side of metaphor are the associated properties of inwardness, presence, imagination, and *reading* as the act of absorbed self-communion wherein these conditions are most perfectly attained. Metonymy, on the other hand, looks to a world of external relationships and chance contiguities upon which to build up a sense of lived experience. It therefore stands at the opposite pole from metaphor, denying access to the realm of authentic self-presence or inwardness which Proust equates with the superior activity of pure imagination.

In de Man's reading these structured oppositions break down and momentarily erase the distinction between metaphor and metonymy. The idealised figures of imaginary self-presence inevitably depend on random, contiguous details from the outside world. The effect is to complicate those metaphors and resist their prematurely totalising drift toward an ethos of Romantic transcendence. 'A rhetorical reading of the passage reveals that the figural praxis and the metafigural theory do not converge and that the assertion of the mastery of metaphor over metonymy owes its persuasive power to the use of metonymic structures' (*AR*, p. 15). Such is the 'grammatisation of rhetoric' that de Man finds at work wherever the truth-claims of metaphor or symbol are pushed to the limit. But the upshot of his reading is not to insist, like Empson, that such cases of 'false identity' can only be interpreted in light of a logical grammar against which to measure their deviant sense. For de Man, there is always the further possibility that metaphor may prove the constitutive figure of narrative involvement as such. The best efforts of rhetorical close-reading would then be unable to undo the illusion, though they might indeed reveal its constitutive blind spots. It is here that deconstruction has to acknowledge the seductiveness and force of an opposed (and by no means simply a naive) reading. 'By an act of memory or of anticipation, the narrative can retrieve the full experience of the moment. We are back in the totalizing world of the metaphor. Narrative is the metaphor of the moment, as reading is the metaphor of writing' (*AR*, p. 68). De Man is committed to resist such readings by his attitude of rigorous epistemological scepticism. But he is equally suspicious of the rationalising drive which would seize upon their moments of cognitive blindness to assert the superior truth-claims of grammar or logic. For de Man, it is the chief and characterising feature of literary language to press beyond the point at which distinctions between 'logic' and 'rhetoric' possess any kind of clear-cut explanatory force.

Clearly there is no question of finally adjudicating the issue between Empson and de Man. They stand as two of the most resourceful modern spokesmen for antagonistic ways of thinking about language, truth, and logic. Empson sets out the rationalist case against those forms of active false logic which interpreters are apt to raise into wholesale rhetorical creeds. De Man pursues such arguments up to a point, but finally doubts whether logic itself can be exempted from the omnipresent figural drive within language. Both critics are deeply engaged in what de Man describes as the principal task now facing literary theorists: that of distinguishing the 'epistemology of tropes' from the 'epistemology of grammar'. That they arrive at such sharply divergent conclusions is all the more reason for reading them together.

NOTES

1. R. P. Blackmur, *A Primer of Ignorance* (New York: Harcourt Brace, 1967).
2. W. Empson, *Seven Types of Ambiguity*, 2nd edn (Harmondsworth: Penguin, 1961); hereafter referred to as *STA*, with page references given in the text.
3. P. de Man, *Allegories of Reading: Figural Language in Rousseau, Nietzsche, Rilke and Proust* (New Haven, Conn.: Yale University Press, 1979) p. 9; hereafter referred to as *AR*, with page references given in the text.
4. See W. Empson, *Collected Poems* (London: Chatto & Windus, 1955).

5. W. Empson, *The Structure of Complex Words* (London: Chatto & Windus, 1951); hereafter referred to as *SCW*, with page references given in the text.

6. See also W. Empson, 'Christianity and *1984*', in J. Haffenden (ed.), *Argufying* (London: Chatto & Windus, 1987) pp. 601–4.

7. See especially I. A. Richards, *Principles of Literary Criticism* (London: Kegan Paul, Trench, Trubner, 1926).

8. See also P. de Man, 'The Rhetoric of Temporality', in *Blindness and Insight: Essays in the Rhetoric of Contemporary Criticism* (London: Methuen, 1983) pp. 187–228; hereafter referred to as *BI*, with essay-titles and page references given in the text.

9. See J. Derrida, 'Difference', in D. B. Allison (tr.), *'Speech and Phenomena' and Other Essays on Husserl's Theory of Signs* (Evanston III.: Northwestern University Press, 1973) pp. 129–60.

10. P. de Man, 'The Resistance to Theory', in P. de Man, *The Resistance to Theory* (Minneapolis: University of Minnesota Press, 1986) p. 14; hereafter referred to as *RT*, with essay-titles and page references given in the text.

11. J. L. Austin, *Sense & Sensibilia* (Oxford: Clarendon Press, 1961).

12. C. Brooks, *The Well-Wrought Urn* (New York: Harcourt Brace, 1947) p. 198.

13. For the passage in question, see A. J. Greimas, *Du Sens* (Paris: Seuil, 1970) p. 13.

13

About Being and Necessity: The Work of Christopher Caudwell

MICHAEL HAYES

Writing about any critic can be disparaged as writing about writing; the parasitic act of someone unable to create. Furthermore, writing about a Marxist critic like Christopher Caudwell in the wake of the dramatic collapse of communism in Eastern Europe might be seen as ghoulishly disturbing the bones in a pauper's grave. But what the disapproval misses is both the indeterminate and mysterious relation between each of these writings, and the provoking ambiguity that exists between 'writing' as an act and 'writing' as a page of text – the doing and the being.

Similarly, between Marxist theory and the communist state there is an intriguing space between the thinking and the actual implementation, the doing. The question is, are we imposing our structure of ideas on the actuality we are theorising about, or does the theory genuinely arise from the actuality – does it represent the real processes? Society is in a constant state of change, it is a seamless continuum, any theory about it carries with it the danger of being an imposition; a focus that enables observation and understanding but one which obscures more than it reveals. Alternatively, society is so complex in itself that we can hardly know anything about it, except inconsequential details unless we have recourse to the deeper perspective that theory can give us.

Broadly speaking, there are two views of Claudwell's applications of Marxist theory: (a) they are inept; (b) they are impressively powerful and wide ranging.

The former view states that Caudwell did not, for perfectly good historical reasons, have at his command a sufficiently developed theory. He was working, so the argument goes, in isolation, separated from continental developments and the version of Marxism that he explicates is deficient in its understanding of superstructures.

170

This meant that he was unable to locate literature adequately within the social framework, he merely saw a crude relationship between fundamental social processes and the practice of literature. The latter view, valuing Caudwell's contribution and supported, for example by E. P. Thompson, points to the tremendous energy and scope of Caudwell's research and thinking: the bibliography for *Illusion and Reality*[1] alone cites over four hundred items covering a wide range of academic interests. My own view is that Caudwell was certainly man of his time with all the insights and limitations that that entails. But he was also, by sensibility, a poet and it has always been the task of the poet to explore language as the territory where the word becomes act and the act is the word: 'writing' in all its ambiguity. Given this perspective, Marxism, for Caudwell, is simply the best means available for writing about the nature of poetry and the contents of what we might generally call consciousness. The very first sentence of the introduction to *Illusion and Reality* reads 'This is a book not only about poetry but also about the sources of poetry' (*IR*, p. 13). Marxism presented Caudwell with the means to explore literature in new, and what were for him, more dynamic ways. It granted a whole new vision and rigour to writing about writing.

We are so familiar now with works of literature trailing clouds of criticism that we often fail to recognise the nature of the possible relationship between literature and criticism. But in a piece such as this the nature of the writing about writing takes pride of place. Two questions result. First, does Caudwell give us readings of literature which enhance our understanding? Second, does he put at our disposal lines of enquiry which allow us to read with more understanding and sensitivity for ourselves?

The first question is the more familiar one. The 'expert' reads for us. S/he guides us through the literature exploring its patterns and felicities to make us better readers. (Some critics also presume better people!) Historically, the role of the critic was that of the priest, guiding the neophyte through the rarified rituals of true art, for the critic naturally doubled as teacher when the most important examples of literature were in Latin and Greek. Critical commentary was necessarily bound up with textual exegesis at a sophisticated level. When 'reading literature' changed its meaning, as it did during the course of the nineteenth century, from reading the classics to reading English literature, the critics did not give up their magisterial function. Instead of arguing for the existence or otherwise of the digamma in ancient Greek they started handing down their interpretations of Milton's 'blind mouths' and Tennyson's 'liquid l's'. Unfortunately, their authority for such pronouncements was far less tangible than that of their classical predecessors, who were at least expert in another language. Their authority was based on the acceptance of their authority, their comments valid because it was *they* who made them.

After the Great War the need for authority in English Studies, which had started at the end of the nineteenth century with the appointment of the first professor of English Literature, quickly gathered momentum. It became obvious that criticism had to stand in a principled and rational relationship to literature. The premises under which it operated had to rest on something more substantial than the mere word of an individual critic.

The big three, as usually viewed, are Richards, Eliot and Leavis. Richards' approach was in many ways the most scientifically modelled. He decontextualises the literary work, like a frog pinned to a board on the laboratory table, the site for a critical dismemberment; a process carried even further by the American New Critics. The aim was to demonstrate the inter-relationship of the parts and their contribution to the whole; Coleridge's organic metaphor realised through a critical approach based on a rather basic and partial biological methodology. Eliot is possibly the most interesting of the three even though he excludes himself by claiming that his criticism is simply a by-product of his poetry and is really meant for his fellow practitioners. Like Richards, his work is 'scientific' – the measure of the work lying in what he calls the 'objective correlative'. The parallel drawn is from the physical sciences where the objective correlative is mathematics. If for example we measure a field and three sides are of equal length but the fourth is not we know we have a problem – either we have measured the field wrongly or Euclidean Geometry needs further development. So, for Eliot, the measure of literature was what the literature grasped from the world outside itself. For Leavis criticism was the process of disputation about literature. Engaging in controversy about literature was for him not only revealing of the work but was also a way of refining the mind and preparing for life, hence the frequently acrimonious and ill-natured accounts of the works of others that commence his essays.

Each of the three provide lively and often provocative accounts in answer to our first question 'does the criticism enhance our readings of literature?' Does Caudwell equally offer such enlightenment? The answer to this must be a rather hesitant 'yes'. That admitted, it would be very rash not to see real interest in some of his more detailed commentary; his strength lies in exactly the area where the others are weakest. In answer to the second question 'does he make available the means by which we can read with more understanding for ourselves?', the answer is a resounding 'yes'. The richness of this thought, the depth and scope of his contextualisation of literature, gives us a framework within which we can grasp the real implications of literature. He has articulated a theory which allows us to make sense of literature within the complex continuum we call society. Furthermore, it gives us insights not only as regards literature but also other social manifestations as various as physics and psychoanalysis, in other words the contents of consciousness.

In his account of the development of the natural sciences Max Muller, the nineteenth-century philosopher, sees three stages: the empirical, which is the documentation of instances; the classificatory, which is the orderly cataloguing of instances; and finally the explanatory, which is the construction of theories. There is a particular tension between stages two and three, if the classifications are not also soundly theoretical they obscure more than they reveal. But the theoretical has to be based on the solid results of the earlier stages or it is merely a polite fiction. For Muller the process is orderly, but this does not mean that each preceding stage has to be completed (as if it ever could be) before the next is embarked on. For him it is 'the quick eye of genius' that elaborates the empirical and classificatory stages into a theory. Where the big three, Richards, Eliot and Leavis, provide us with criticism located in the first two stages, it is Caudwell who possesses 'the quick eye of genius'. Richards certainly went much further into theory than the other two, but his psychological account requires far more experimentation and knowledge than is current even today.

So the claim I am making for Caudwell is that he is an important theoretician about literature. This importance does not lie simply in his espousal of Marxism but in his grasp of the possibilities that Marxism affords. If we are looking for a doctrinaire Marxist we will be disappointed because Caudwell is first a poet and the drive and subtlety he brings to his work is the need to wrest a unified vision from the chaos of human development. Marxism has pride of place in that struggle because it was the most articulate statement concerning the nature of being and necessity that was open to him. But the real key to his position is the understanding of mind and imagination as the presiding arbitrators between being and necessity.

Viewed in this way the reservations that many Marxists have about his work and the difficulties that others find become obvious. He leaps from one insight to another at times leaving the relationships implicit, at other times distracting us from one thought by the vitality of another so that we, not he, lose sight of the overall thesis. Language is for use and the customary restrictions we place on it in intellectual discourse are continually broken by his lively awareness of its protean possibilities. His central concern is the interplay of being and necessity, but some detailed textual examination is necessary to underline problems that arise from his style of writing. Before doing that I need to clarify my view of his Marxism and why writers as diverse as Forster in the 1930s and Eagleton in the 1980s have had serious, though different, reservations about it.

For many writers working within a theory the theory becomes the determinant of their writing. The result is an analysis which is virtually a dialogue with the theory; where the theory is inadequate the writing is an attempt to elaborate and extend the theory. For Caudwell, Marxism is not the determinant of his writing – that is provided by the problem of human existence. Rather Marxism is the condition of his writing – he sees Marxist theory as self-evidently the broadest statement of the human context, the expression of a core truth. At the same time he is aware that other discussions, such as anthropology and psychoanalysis, are also important discussions and formulations of the same problem. It is undeniable, for example, that the Christian religion was the dominant paradigm for discussions of the human condition for well over a thousand years, but ultimately he sees it as a failure. It has failed not simply because it is the 'opium of the people' but rather because, unlike the mythology from which it grew, it has become static. Religion, unlike mythology, demands assent and in doing so loses the flexibility and openness to change which characterise myth. In religion, 'mythology ceases to grown and change and contradict itself, and is set up as something rigid and absolutely true' (*IR*, p. 45). Once the world of collective emotion, which mythology expresses, has to demand assent by faith it has lost touch with the reality of people's lives.

Marxism has for Caudwell the great advantage that it presupposes constant change and tries to give an account of that change which remains in touch with reality. Earlier I discussed the paradox of theory – that it is both necessary and dangerous. Caudwell is vitally alive to this danger, in his essay on D. H. Lawrence he sees it as inherent in the very nature of language itself.

But in language reality is symbolised in unchanging words which give a false stability and permanence to the object they represent. . . . This frigid character of language is regrettable but it has its utilitarian purposes. It is probably the only way in which man, with his linear consciousness, can get a grip on fluid reality.[2]

While the relationship between reality and language implicit in this account is no longer tenable, the net result that in spite of its 'frigid character . . . it has its utilitarian purposes' remains true. Those purposes are fulfilled because in spite of its seeming 'frigidity' the word can be seen as 'a dynamic social act' (*IR*, p. 159). Its nature may appear fixed but in contexts of use between people it constitutes social behaviour and therefore has a communicative potential.

Too often theories are viewed as master plans demanding that their insights be enacted. Marxist societies from the Baltic to the South China Seas have regrettably, on occasion, operated on such a principle. But theories can also be seen as the conditions of thinking within which greater understanding and clarity can be achieved. This is how Caudwell employs Marxist theory to tackle his main concern which is not only about consciousness and its capacity to confront the necessities of existence but also the manifestation that most particularly interests him, namely poetry and the sources of poetry. As he says in the introduction to *Illusion and Reality*, 'There is only one sound sociology which lays bare the general active relation of the ideological products of society with each other and with concrete living – historical materialism' (*IR*, p. 18). Marxism provides the ground rules or the conditions within which his various discussions take place. Within that framework a whole variety of psychoanalytical, logical, anthropological and literary theories can be harnessed to provide explanations.

'Poetry is clotted social history, the emotional sweat of man's struggle with Nature' (*IR*, p. 147). The need for subsistence demands that men act in unison, that is the collective that takes responsibility for deriving a living from the earth. Poetry is the heightened language that men in unison use to express their collective emotion. It is most simply and clearly exemplified by the tribal songs celebrated at the festivals where the group's inter-dependence is extolled and confirmed. Of course, as division of labour enters into the conduct of society so the nature of the collective spirit alters and poetry alters – but its fundamental purpose remains, the articulation of collective emotion.

This need for collective emotion is not self-evident; it demands explanation. Where there is real danger naturally the tribe responds to the immediate situation but where the threat remains potential the group has to prepare itself in readiness. Caudwell believed that men could change each other and the world through poetry, for it makes the potential world more real and so spurs on men to make the efforts necessary to realise the possible world.

With division of labour different classes emerge so different groups in society are placed in a different relation to the basic task of survival as well as to each other. We see the poets of the 1930s, Day-Lewis, Auden and Spender, as bourgeois artists. They can then relate to the proletariat in one of three possible ways: opposition, alliance or assimilation. In spite of being bourgeois they chose the road of alliance; any discussion of their work would, for Caudwell need to be articulated within this framework. The basic role of poetry as the enunciation of collective emotion remains, but its expression is complicated by the divisions and illusions that a complex society creates. Historical materialism allows us to trace the realities through the confusions.

One of the problems of *Illusion and Reality* is the three chapters – IV, V and VI – on the English poets. Basically Caudwell is writing, not so much about the English poets, but about the canon: those names elevated for special study by tacit academic agreement. Furthermore the rather general commentary which sees them as bourgeois artists responding to the overall economic developments of the time fails to explicate their expression of the collective emotion that he sees as the true meaning of poetry. What I am suggesting is that Caudwell's discussion of the sources of poetry and its need to express itself in different ways at different times is full of critical possibility. However, his actual treatment of particular works and poets does not realise this possibility: though this does not mean that his commentary is without interest. For example, when discussing Keats, he writes: 'The Keatsian vocabulary is full of words with a hard material texture – all crimson, scented, archaic, still, jewelled and anti-contemporary. It is as vivid as missal painting. Increasingly this world is set in the world of feudalism, but is not a feudal world. It is a bourgeois world' (*IR*, p. 109). The discussion of the vocabulary and its implications opens up interesting possibilities as to the nature of the dream world Keats wants to make real. To state merely that it is 'regressive' in character is to fail to do justice to the original insight.

A few of the questions that the theory seems to pose are: what role does the narrator see himself having in relation to productive society; what view is taken in the work of medieval division of labour; and how does the vocabulary relate to the ideology of the poetry? Naturally a number of the questions arising are clearly posed by modern developments in Marxist theory, but it seems naive to suggest that they are not implicit in Caudwell's basic formulation. And this throws us back to the fundamental problem in relation to Caudwell's thinking, that the reader has to do a great deal of the work. It is not that the ideas are undeveloped so much as their expression is channelled through a variety of different discourses. As I said earlier, the explanatory stances Caudwell adopts within this basic Marxist framework read like metaphors in a poem.

To demonstrate some of the demands Caudwell makes on his readers I will look at the final paragraph of *Illusion and Reality*. It may seem an unfair choice since implicit in the paragraph are the understandings arrived at throughout the book, but it is also a fair choice in that its analysis should help explicate the gap between Caudwell and his readers: the third writing interposes between the first two 'writings about writing'.

a. Therefore the still of art endures as
b. long as man. The fountain dwindles
c. away only when men are rent
d. and wasted by a sterile conflict,
e. and the pulsing movement of
f. society is halted. All this movement
g. is creative because it is not a
h. simple oscillation but a development
i. unfolded by its very restlessness.
j. The eternal simplicities generate
k. the enrichment of art from their
l. own bosoms not only
m. because they are eternal but
n. also because change is the
o. condition of their existence.
p. Thus art is one of the conditions
q. of man's realisation of himself,
r. and in its turn is one of the
s. realities of man.   (*IR*, p. 329; my layout)

The first sentence (a and b) draws on the convention of self-conscious poetic language, it is stilted and archaic. The poetic tone is maintained by the opening of the next sentence, (b) 'The fountain dwindles', but the meaning is the complete opposite, dwindles versus endures. Before we have time to absorb the relation between the two, 'only' appears not just to condition the opposition but also to expand on 'dwindles' with 'rent' 'wasted' and 'sterile'. The words are forceful, as they are intended to be, but they introduce three dissimilar perspectives; men as a group are divided from each other, mankind's economic efforts are wasted and the resulting conflict is unproductive. The final movement of the sentence (e to f) introduces yet another image, the idea of society as living, 'pulsing' being. In our commitment to the theory about society and conflict the initial image of art as a fountain is lost – poetic image is submerged under Marxist theory. This, of course, is an enactment of the process, but the demands on the reader are extraordinarily complex. The third sentence (f to i) ignores the conflict situation that introduced the second sentence to amplify the rationale and commitment enshrined in the author's use of the word 'pulsing'. The fourth sentence (k) re-introduces conventional poetic language, 'The eternal simplicities', to restore the discussion of art that started the paragraph. Again there is an unexpected paradox 'eternal', which we take as persisting in time, is said to include 'change' as part of its condition of existence. This re-conditioning of our ideas which the book undertakes is possibly not best served by using a language redolent of the most fixed attitudes it seeks to radicalise. The final sentence affirms in clear and concise terms the thesis of the book.

The rapid changes in focus, the movement between the different clauses make much of Caudwell's writing difficult to read. The easy judgement would be to suggest that written at speed, as it was, the writing is not very good. This, as I have suggested earlier seems to miss the point of Caudwell's style. Although he is engaged in presenting an argument, the wealth of detail from various points of view likens the finished work to an impressionist painting. Viewed at a distance or subjected to a first reading, the painting looks pleasing enough, the words come sonorously off the page. Scrutinised close-up, however, the painting disintegrates into a hectic welter of diverse splashes of varied colour, the writing fragments into discordant perspectives and rapid changes of direction. But if we persevere we come to appreciate the vibrant life of the picture, if we commit ourselves to a careful reading the subtlety and complexity of the thought becomes apparent.

Up to this point I have tried, by focussing on his theory, to place Caudwell among the group of post First World War critics for whom the study of literature could no longer be taken for granted. Furthermore, he alone of the group (with the possible exception of I. A. Richards) struggled to locate literature in a comprehensive and systematic theory of human behaviour. His chosen ground for such a theory was man as a part of the group whose fundamental aim was the struggle for subsistence. This struggle either with nature or, unhappily, with other men, he considered to be the well-spring of all our acts of consciousness, whether scientific or artistic. At the scientific end of the spectrum our sense of the world is subject to rigorous checks by the real world, at the artistic end of the spectrum the check is the capacity of the art to express the social or collective determination of the group.

One of the problems with Caudwell is the dizzying breadth of his argument. He sees both physics and literature as part of the whole of man's conscious encounter with the world, he argues for what he calls 'phantasy' or, in more conventional terms, ideology as the core which, under different conditions, becomes different understandings. It is within this vast panorama that the poet, writer of detective novels, commentator on physics and expert on aviation as well as political activist places literature.

Having set literature, however, within a new agenda which offers exciting though extremely difficult and demanding prospects for our scrutiny of it, what does he himself offer by way of readings of particular texts? As suggested earlier, in this more customary role of the critic his remarks, certainly in *Illusion and Reality*, are highly provocative but incomplete. The commentaries on the English poets are more like slogans used to defend his thesis on historical materialism than a new reading in the light of his version of historical materialism. Having proposed a theory of art in which literature and poetry are the prime examples, his actual discussions of the work of individual authors is limited by the immediate needs of his polemic.

This rather sketchy treatment of individual authors is not merely haste or carelessness, it stems from the nature of his theory itself, as we can see from his essay on Lawrence. The sub-title, 'A Study of the Bourgeois Artist', presents Lawrence as already framed by the class circumstances of the period. Being in such a position Lawrence is isolated within notions of individual freedom. His response is quite right from Caudwell's point of view – to be 'a man hating cash – relationships and the market, and profoundly interested in the relations between persons' (*CF*, p. 19). Where he goes wrong is in believing in the attainment of individual freedom through a Fascist rather than a Communist solution. This drives him into a regressive retreat into more primitive communities in Mexico, Sicily and Etruria. What he fails to realise is that the individual artist is a part of the whole 'in fact that artist does not express himself in art forms, he finds himself therein' (*CF*, p. 17).

In turning against intellect and consciousness Lawrence retreats from his potential for contributing fully to the expansion and development of consciousness, which is the only hope for adapting to the changing environment. His potential is not as an individual artist at all but as part of a collective consciousness. It is not individual relations that must be changed but 'social relations must be changed so that love returns to the earth and man is not only wiser but more full of emotion' (*CF*, p. 27).

At the core of Caudwell's work the individual artist is of little interest except as a species of case study. The real interest lies in artists' confrontation with their time to re-define the collective emotion necessary to power adaptive change to meet new circumstances. His theory not only relocates literature within the widest frame of human reference but suggests that a radical review of critical practice is necessary. The critic is no longer the judge or guardian of the memory of the individual artist, rather the sounding post of the new emergent consciousness – the task is a new one and we are all yet children. 'The child would love to return to the womb, but it must become adult and face the strenuous and bracing tasks of life' (*CE*, p. 27).

NOTES

1. C. Caudwell, *Illusion and Reality* (London: Lawrence & Wishart, 1977); hereafter referred to as *IR*, with page references given in the text.
2. C. Caudwell, 'D. H. Lawrence', in *The Concept of Freedom* (London: Lawrence & Wishart, 1977) p. 15; hereafter referred to as *CF*, with page references given in the text.

14

W. H. Auden as Critic

HELENA BLAKEMORE

In setting up my brass-plate as a critic,
    I make no claim to certain diagnosis,
I'm more intuitive than analytic,
    I offer thought in homeopathic doses
    (But someone may get better in the process)
I don't pretend to reasoning like Pritchard's
Or the logomachy of I. A. Richards.[1]

A good deal of what is written about literary critics centres on their
'approach' – the framework or ideology upon which their work is
based, be it Marxist, feminist, structuralist or whatever. An attempt
to do this with Auden's criticism is doomed to failure. On the face of
it, this comes as a great surprise: surely, like the rest, he is a scholar
who applies his knowledge and his intellectual ability to a wide
variety of literary texts in order that others may benefit from his
greater understanding of them? Is this not what the likes of F. R.
Leavis and Raymond Williams are also concerned with? Well, yes it
is, but I believe there is a substantial difference between Auden's
approach and that of the other members of the 'critical canon'. Reading through *The Dyer's Hand and Other Essays*[2], one is constantly
struck by the difficulty of categorising his approach, the breadth of
his knowledge and the variety of styles he uses, which range from
a series of aphorisms ('Reading') to a broad discussion of contextual
issues ('Brothers & Others') and to a detailed textual analysis or
'close reading' ('Don Juan').

His essays continually raise questions about the function of the
critic and what literary criticism is 'for', an issue he himself discusses
in, for example, 'Reading': 'So long as a man writes poetry or fiction,
his dream of Eden is his own business, but the moment he starts

writing literary criticism, honesty demands that he describe it to his readers, so that they may be in the position to judge his judgements' ('Reading', *DH*, p. 6). He then relates his vision of Eden by means of a breakdown of geographical, social, cultural and economic ideals: climate, religion, domestic furniture and so on. This may seem merely light-hearted, but it does not sit uncomfortably in the context of a body of work within which no perspective or source of information is to be deemed irrelevant or extraneous. And anyway, who is to say that a little light-heartedness is out of place? Auden's opening remarks in his essay 'Don Juan' on the distinction between art which is boring and art which is a bore makes very amusing reading as well as being food for thought: one immediately has the urge to add a personal selection to his classifications.

The key, I feel, to gaining an understanding of Auden's concerns lies with the fact that he was primarily a practising artist. This implies that as an artist he thereby had a greater understanding of 'art' and how it is produced – that his own work would give him a special insight into the work of others which is unavailable to the 'common critic'.

There is, however, one difference between 'the artist' and the traditional literary critic which is quite simply the way in which they work. The academic critic is most frequently to be found in a university – before 1950, most likely Oxford or Cambridge – ensconced in comfortable academia, gathering the 'tools of the trade' around him/her, with a long-term career in writing and teaching both behind and ahead of him/her. Auden's life has been well documented, notably in Humphrey Carpenter's *W. H. Auden: A Biography*.[3] It does not take the reader very long to realise that very little of his time was spent in comfortable academia; when he returned to Oxford in 1972, it was because he was 'getting rather old to live alone in the winter and I would rather live in a community. . . . I am going back to England solely because of my age.'[4] He spent a great deal of his life moving around, living variously in Berlin, New York, Italy, Austria and Oxford as well as at a number of American colleges and he also spent lengthy periods in Iceland and China. Equally, his essays were only a small part of his output: acknowledged as a poet, he also wrote libretti and operettas, plays (with Christopher Isherwood) and pamphlets.

Geographically and intellectually speaking, therefore, the areas in which he worked varied enormously, and so it is hardly surprising that his writing encompassed this range of interests and influences.

He may not be quite what we have come to expect from a critic, but his eclecticism leads to a broadening out from the text as opposed to the more usual funnelling into it; as a 'learning experience', to quote a now hackneyed phrase, it can only be enlightening.

A closer look at some of his essays may help to explain this process. In 'Reading', the first essay in *The Dyer's Hand and Other Essays*, Auden outlines what, in his opinion, are the prime functions of a critic:

1. Introduce me to authors or works of which I was hitherto unaware.
2. Convince me that I have undervalued an author or a work because I had not read them carefully enough.
3. Show me relations between works of different ages and cultures which I could never have seen for myself because I do not know enough and never shall.
4. Give a 'reading' of a work which increases my understanding of it.
5. Throw light upon the process of artistic 'Making'.
6. Throw light upon the relation of art to life, to science, economics, ethics, religion, etc.   ('Reading', *DH*, pp. 8–9)

He goes on to explain how the first three of these demand scholarship, and the second three a superior insight. The reader may disagree with the conclusions reached by a critic, but would find it hard to ignore the questions. The question is, does Auden fulfil his own criteria?

In the foreword to *The Dyer's Hand and Other Essays* Auden states that 'there is something, in my opinion, lifeless, even false, about systematic criticism' (*DH*, p. xii). His own approach may be singular and unsystematic, but I believe that it is no less illuminating for that. As a commentary it is certainly entertaining and, as criticism, it is both instructive and contentious: it can provoke a lively response (surely one of the most fruitful elements of the best literary criticism) whilst at the same time offering insights – 'throwing light' – onto a particular work or genre in order to increase understanding.

It is not unreasonable to describe Auden's critical essays as a collection of unsupported statements, generalisations and opinionated remarks, shot through with ragged categorisations – and indeed his critical work has frequently been referred to in these terms. Equally, however, it is not completely accurate nor, by extension, completely fair. The inference is that criticism should *not* be opinionated or personal, but rather that it should be wholly balanced, impersonal, objective and 'correct': definitive assertions of the 'truth' of a work – the critic, under these restrictions, being merely a medium through which the 'truth' of a text is revealed. Of course, this can never be the case. Critics bring to their work as much baggage as any artist; much of this can be identified and discarded along the way, but it is inevitable that some will be retained. And the critic also has an additional restriction, as Auden also noted in the aforementioned Foreword: 'I have never written a line of criticism except in response to a demand by others. . . . The trouble with writing commissioned criticism is that the relation between form and content is arbitrary' (*DH*, p. xi). The critical piece, in other words, does not arise spontaneously, and the subject matter and length of the piece are not in the hands of its creator. Unlike other critics in this volume, Auden was not an academic. He wrote critical essays because he was asked to by people who believed that what he had to say would be interesting, or, perhaps more accurately, because he needed the money.

Auden's claim, in the excerpt from 'Letter to Lord Byron', that his critical writing is 'more intuitive than analytic' suggests that his responses were purely subjective and does not acknowledge that he was extremely well read and a considerable classical scholar. It does, however, serve to illustrate his approach both to writing and to the written word: bold brush strokes on a huge canvas.

Monroe K. Spears has suggested that the critical consensus of opinion was that Auden, through his poetry, was shown to be 'guilty' of 'immaturity, frivolity, irresponsibility, and other vices, and is therefore not to be taken seriously'. He then continues: 'There is a certain irony in the fact that [*The Dyer's Hand*], with its massive demonstration of Auden's maturity, seriousness and moral responsibility, has already done a good deal to dispel the myth that these qualities are lacking in the poetry.'[5] He believes that there was a misunderstanding as regards his approach – his generalisation and panoramic views are just a different way of looking. This phrase would seem to tie in closely with my earlier reference to the difference between Auden and more traditional critics: Auden's way is just a different way of looking.

Rather than close textual analysis, the essays tend to be more concerned with general considerations: using literary texts to examine larger questions of a more philosophical or broadly historical nature. He does concern himself with straightforward analysis of literary forms and styles, as in 'Don Juan' or 'The Guilty Vicarage', in which he examines the internal workings of detective stories by identifying their five elements: the milieu, the victim, the murderer, the suspects and the detective. (As a matter of interest, he considers there to have been only three successful fictional detectives: Sherlock Holmes, Inspector French and Father Brown.) More frequently, however, Auden considers literary texts in terms of their relationship to larger issues, as in 'Brothers & Others', in which *The Merchant of Venice* is used as the framework for comparing socio-economic conditions in England and in Shakespeare's plays (feudal, mercantile, etc); examining the contradictory nature of the two settings in the play – Venice (commercial reality) and Belmont (fairy story) – and the traditional symbolism they imply; the history of Jews in literature; and an analysis of usury, especially in terms of the various historical and theological attitudes towards it.

The reason for outlining all this is that 'Brothers & Others' demonstrates admirably the way Auden, in the course of one essay examining the work of one dramatist (Shakespeare), and predominantly one text, combines literary appreciation with scholarly and intelligent comments from the fields of history (economic and sociological, ancient, medieval and modern) and theology (Christian and Jewish).

While it is impossible for literary criticism ever to be an exact science, it can be structured and methodical – but is this really enough? Auden's criticism, on the other hand, is an intensely personal, selective and subjective commentary, but this belies the fact that the essays are frequently problematic for student and academic alike. Much of his writing appears on first reading to be very straightforward (a good example is 'The Virgin and The Dynamo'), and indeed his writing style does 'read' very easily and is not, superficially at least, difficult to comprehend. Beneath the surface, however, one finds the essay to be a series of ideological complexities, written more or less in note form, the sequence of which is hard to follow for all but the most determined and knowledgeable reader. This is because Auden has a tendency to use terms without defining them. In 'The Virgin and the Dynamo' he refers to man 'as soul and body' being an individual, and 'as mind and spirit' being a member of society, without going much further to enlighten us as to what exactly he means by these concepts either philosophically or in reality ('The Virgin and the Dynamo', *DH*, p. 65). Furthermore, he has an annoying habit of not concluding his essays. They begin, roam widely and wildly around their subject(s) – and any others which come to

mind – and end. They are not exercises in formulaic literary precision but statements of personal ideology; not systematic analyses
but opinionated and scholarly discourse.

The Poetic Art of W. H. Auden[6] includes a chapter by John Blair
entitled 'Poet and Parable' in which he discusses the way in which
Auden sees himself as a teacher – and his work (centrally his poetry,
but including his essays) as the medium through which he communicates. Auden's own list of 'critical criteria' ('throw light', 'show',
'introduce', as opposed to the more commonly used literary critical
terms such as analyse, examine or demonstrate) make it evident that
he is not interested in making pedantic or dogmatic statements in
order to 'solve' a text but to chuck ideas about, make suggestions
and possible connections, encourage debate. It is perhaps ironic that
his way of making bald statements which almost beg to be contra-
dicted – perhaps this is what one should expect from a truly didactic
writer – frequently read like a series of undergraduate essay-titles
(they might well be followed by 'Discuss'):

> The artistic failure of 'Childe Harold' is due in large measure to
> Byron's disastrous choice of the Spenserian stanza.   ('Don Juan',
> *DH*, p. 395)

> Given a few more years of Othello and of Emilia's influence and
> [Desdemona] might well, one feels, have taken a lover.   ('The
> Joker in the Pack', *DH*, p. 269)

> One often hears it said that only in this century have the writers of
> the United States learned to stand on their own feet and be truly
> American, that, previously, they were slavish imitators of British
> literature.   ('American Poetry', *DH*, p. 355)

In the foreword to *Twentieth-Century Literary Criticism*, editor David
Lodge states that 'Works of literature have their meaning, and their
very existence, in a continual stream of human conversation about
them, which at its most formalized and articulate we call literary
criticism.'[7] With this criterion it is perhaps not surprising that Auden's
name is unlikely to be one of the first to come to mind when consid-
ering the tradition of British literary criticism; he was, of course,
primarily a poet, and as a critic his writing was rarely formalised and
often inconsistent; he was also preoccupied with categorisation (Ariel
types and Prospero types, Alice types and Maud types), strong on

aphorisms and generalisations and weak on supporting evidence. That being said, however, his critical output was considerable, and despite the fact that he saw his critical writing as a means of paying bills – writing on demand – his individual approach to literature is frequently more accessible, and certainly more refreshing, than much of the weighty outpourings of the more systematic professional critics.

The most profitable way of reading Auden's work is to view him as a teacher. His concerns are with encouraging his readers to think, not telling them what to think, hence John Blair's interpretation of his work as parables. As a poet, he used a very broad range of poetic styles, reinforcing his sense of the importance of history not in terms of a linear series of events but as a well of knowledge into which we can dip at random for reinforcement and illumination of ideas. As a critic, he made use of the same techniques in order to reveal what he saw as the richness of our intellectual heritage. It might be somewhat rash to recommend Auden's essays as the sole source of criticism on a text, but perhaps seen in conjunction with other work his refreshing eclecticism would encourage wider perspectives and less restricted approaches:

> Blessed be all metrical rules that forbid automatic responses, force us to have second thoughts, free from the fetters of Self.[8]

NOTES

1. W. H. Auden, 'Letter to Lord Byron' (Part III, ll. 15–21), in *Collected Poems* (London: Faber & Faber, 1976) p. 88.
2. W. H. Auden, *The Dyer's Hand and Other Essays* (London: Faber & Faber, 1963); hereafter referred to as *DH*, with essay-titles and page references given in the text.
3. H. Carpenter, *W. H. Auden: A Biography* (London: Allen and Unwin, 1981).
4. Ibid., p. 439.
5. M. K. Spears, *Auden: A Collection of Critical Essays* (New Jersey: Prentice-Hall, 1964) p. 4.
6. J. Blair, *The Poetic Art of W. H. Auden* (Princeton: Princeton University Press, 1965).
7. D. Lodge (ed.), *Twentieth-Century Literary Criticism: A Reader* (London: Longman, 1972) p. xvii.
8. From 'Shorts II', in *Collected Poems*, p. 642.

15

'I thought I had provided something better'[1] – F. R. Leavis, Literary Criticism and Anti-Philosophy

BARRY CULLEN

Leavis once said that he wished he knew enough about philosophy to keep it out of literary criticism, a sentiment that perhaps a significant number of contemporary critics would say amen to, if it weren't for the peril of appearing out of touch with things, especially the post-1960s shifts in criticism which have converted many English university departments into progressive philosophy rings. The new critical orthodoxy demands a high degree of theoretical-cum-philosophical awareness about the nature of language, the status of knowledge, the metaphysics of subjectivity and other such arcana – unfortunate the teacher who cannot tell his/her *aporia* from an *a priori*. In this climate Leavis' comment will appear to some only to confirm his irrelevance to discussion about recent critical practice, and to indicate the extent of the breach that now exists between contemporary criticism and that of the 'modern' Cambridge critics of the early years of this century. It was these critics, I. A. Richards, F. R. Leavis and William Empson, together with T. S. Eliot, who established the intellectual basis of English teaching over half a century, and amongst whom Leavis was generally recognised as the formative figure as far as university teaching of English was concerned. In the current debate about the future direction of English studies his hostility to, or indifference toward theory will appear to emphasise the methodological inadequacy that English literary criticism has hitherto displayed, particularly in respect of its ideological orientation. For many, Leavis and theoretical philistinism will be synonymous, underlining the need for urgent and drastic reform of a teaching system still too heavily indebted to a postulated Leavisite tradition of 'practical criticism' and moral earnestness.

A typical example of this approach is to be found in Belsey's *Critical Practice*,[2] a first critical resort for many unsuspecting students. For Belsey, Leavis is naive expressive-realist whose criticism manifests itself as 'a recurring slide from text to author'[3] and who is so ideologically innocent as to lose sight of the objectivity of the text entirely in his pursuit of the writer's qualities of mind: 'literary inadequacies are seen as a direct expression of [the author's] personal inadequacies'.[4] A postulated critical naivety is presented here as an index of theoretical naivety, by which is meant an unawareness of the critical relevance of questions such as 'do ideas exist outside discourse?' or 'in what sense is fiction "true"?'[5] questions which – it is implied – Leavis would have much benefited from being aware of if he had had the advantages of a philosophical training. Even a nodding acquaintance with the notion that criticism is an ideological activity, and therefore inscribed within the realm of philosophical discourse, would have rescued Leavis from the simplistic, so the argument runs. To anyone who knows Leavis' work as it developed over nearly fifty years, with its constant preoccupation with the status of critical judgment, or with the essential difficulty of enforcing critical valuations, or, towards the end of his life, with the explicit task of justifying a mode of subjectivity that could challenge the pervasive positivism of the British philosophical tradition, such a claim appears woefully ill-informed. Only someone who confuses theoretical flag-waving with critical intelligence, or who has taken no steps at all to discern the intellectual basis upon which Leavis' classical status as a critic depends, could advance intellectual naivety as his salient weakness.

Belsey's position should not be taken seriously (although, as Leavis might have said, it is significant). But other critics from the left represent an altogether different level of intellectual challenge to those who believe that Leavis' seminal influence as a critic rests on more than a muddled mission to preserve middle-class morality. Francis Mulhern, for instance, in an influential account of the origins and growth of the *Scrutiny* movement,[6] argues that Leavis developed the humanist inheritance of the Cambridge positivists in an effective but ultimately contradictory way. By harnessing Eliot's concepts of tradition and impersonality to a socio-cultural politics of conservatism Leavis aligned literary and cultural debate along an axis of anti-political thought and criticism. The contradictory nature of this is epitomised for Mulhern by 'the logical paradox of an

insistent metaphysical vocabulary combined with a positivist methodology'[7] lying at the heart of Leavis' criticism. This paradox is in his
view largely verbal but is symptomatic of a general epistemological
confusion between subjectivism and empirical realism that is held to
be central to Leavis' thinking.

The contours of this argument are visible in an earlier and consid-
erably more doctrinaire form in Eagleton's *Criticism and Ideology*[8].
Eagleton presents *Scrutiny* as both a radical and reactionary movement in that it was a 'progressive vanguard' and an 'elite', at once
responsible for disturbing established valuations and simultaneously
consolidating a position of intellectual privilege for its members.
This contradiction straddles a philosophical divide characterised as:

> the 'philosophy' of *Scrutiny* went beyond sensuous empiricism,
> and necessarily so. Just as, for Eliot, such empiricism proved
> ideologically insufficient, demanding its sublation into doctrinal
> Christianity, so *Scrutiny* stood in objective need of a metaphysic
> whose intuitive force was in inverse proportion to its theoretical
> articulateness. Such a metaphysic was provided by the work of
> D. H. Lawrence. Lawrence's idealism did not undercut sensuous
> empiricism: on the contrary it lent it nothing less than ontological
> status. Furnished with this metaphysic, then, *Scrutiny* was able to
> lambast the varieties of utilitarian empiricism from the standpoint
> of an absolute idealism, while at the same time assaulting 'abso-
> lutist' systems (including, naturally, Marxism) from the view-
> point of a thoroughly 'English' liberal empiricism. The position
> was invulnerable in direct proportion to its irrationality. Since the
> metaphysical underpinning slipped by definition through the net
> of language (so that to demand its demonstration was to reveal
> oneself in that very act as unregenerate) it was shielded from
> scrutiny [*sic*], but it was by the same token, theoretically sterile.[9]

In other words the *Scrutiny* 'philosophy' is a thoroughly bogus one,
a facade concealing mutually conflicting philosophical positions cob-
bled together to suggest the presence of a coherent system of ideas
but whose primary purpose is to act as an enabling device for various kinds of partisan attacks and evasions. Yet – so the claim runs –
this metaphysic is simultaneously sufficiently persuasive and intellectually satisfying for *Scrutiny* contributors (around a hundred and
fifty of them over twenty years) to remain unconcerned by its polit-

ical duplicities and inherent irrationality; to be sufficient explanation for those who wrote regularly to overlook the methodological contortions of switching from 'absolute idealisism' to 'liberal empiricism' and back again over a period of many years. All this was carried out as part of a misguided mission to protect an obsolescent elitism. Leavis, never of course named in this account, is nevertheless assumed to be the ringleader of this particular cabal, and as such is credited with powers of persuasion and influence akin to the miraculous when it comes to concocting such a philosophical *pis aller*.

The overall implausibility of this is evident enough, yet Eagleton's readiness to see Leavis as an intellectual illusionist, although misconceived, is looking along a perspective others less politically dogmatic have adopted over the years. It focuses upon the problem of characterising the nature of the 'metaphysic' that is inherent in the expression and formulation of Leavis' critical judgements. And it suggests that this is not likely to be straightforward because of the difficulty of identifying the philosophical coordinates in Leavis' thinking. Idealism, empiricism, utilitarianism, and positivism are all drawn into Eagleton's picture as he attempts to identify the determining characteristics of the thought. As a Marxist he needs to characterise Leavis' criticism in doctrinaire terms and his conventionalised simulcra of dialectical oppositions is his way of getting the conundrum to make sense. But others less disposed to accept the dictates of the dialectic have also been prompted to enquire along related philosophical lines, if only because the thinking that is so very obviously active in Leavis' work is that of a major intelligence and should, one assumes, be translatable into discursive terms. Leavis himself appeared at times to give encouragement for such a view, especially in the writings leading up to and succeeding *The Living Principle*.[10] It would seem all the harder to understand, then, why no one has successfully achieved a satisfactory adumbration of his critical position in theoretical terms, also why attempts to do so have been resisted and in most respects denigrated by Leavis over the years. As long ago as 1937 Leavis was correcting efforts to identify his 'philosophy' of criticism, while some of the last writing he ever did forty years later was devoted to the same purpose. If it was a familiar problem to him, that seems to have been because it was also an important problem for him, one with a bearing on the value and standing of his life's work as a critic. If it was one which he could never satisfactorily resolve it was also one which, characteristically, he refused to abandon and to the end of his life he was wrestling with ways in which to represent the relationship between his critical vision and a theoretical version of it that would securely establish the integrity of the former in the face of a demand for the latter that might misrepresent or overwhelm it. The character of his difficulties and the nature of the problem need to be better known.

A well-trodden but still convenient avenue into discussion of this question is provided by the exchange with René Wellek which took place in the pages of *Scrutiny* in the Spring of 1937.[11] This has become widely known as the locus for a discussion of views about how far Leavis had provided a 'philosophical' account of his critical practice by providing a discursive exposition at first hand of what he understood literary criticism to be. Critics have been divided over it because the tone and attitude of his contribution, as much as its explicit content, made clear that Leavis was mounting some kind of principled critique of methodological enquiry as such, without making wholly clear what those principles were, or what criteria he was appealing to in making such a critique. It was not until many years later that he chose to make these more explicit. As it was, he addressed himself, on this occasion, to the question which Wellek put to him, namely what was the yardstick by which he had arrived at his critical judgements as laid out in the recently published book, *Revaluation*.

Wellek's position was that Leavis, in developing the critical thesis enunciated in *Revaluation*, had not provided any account of the theoretical framework within which his critical judgement was operating and that if he had done so his critical argument (which Wellek claimed to be in agreement with) would have been strengthened. He also thought that because he (Leavis) had a 'norm' by which all his judgements were validated, it was incumbent on Leavis 'to defend this position more abstractly, and to become conscious that large ethical, philosophical and, of course, ultimately, aesthetic *choices* are involved'.[12] Wellek then went on to claim that because Leavis was some kind of realist in philosophical terms this made him unsympathetic to, and largely ignorant of, the idealism that underpinned romanticism in general and the English romantic poets in particular, and that, for instance, 'the chapter on Wordsworth, excellent as it is in fine critical discrimination, shows the same lack of interest in romantic philosophy [as in the case of Blake, Shelley *et al.*].[13]

To the latter point Leavis' reply was to the effect that romantic philosophy was one thing, but romantic poetry quite another; that any attempt to read poetry in terms of its philosophical constituents was likely to fail to read it for what it was doing as poetry: giving complex emotional and intellectual experiences a defining precision and reality which they would not otherwise have. This discussion correlated with the earlier part of the essay which took the form of a description by Leavis of how the critical reading of literature was quite unlike that postulated in the theoretically-governed model that Wellek had proposed. Leavis claimed that Wellek did not understand what literary criticism was if he thought of it in terms of abstractly statable norms that could be applied to texts as testing criteria:

> The critic – the reader of poetry – is indeed concerned with evaluation, but to figure him as measuring with a norm which he brings up to the object and applies from the outside is to misrepresent the process. The critic's aim is, first, to realize as sensitively and completely as possible this or that which claims his attention; and a certain valuing is implicit in the realizing. As he matures in experience of the new thing he asks, explicitly and implicitly: 'Where does this come? How does it stand in relation to. . .? How relatively important does it seem?' And the organization into which it settles as a constituent in becoming 'placed' is an organization of similarly 'placed' things, things that have found their bearings with regard to one another, and not a theoretical system or a system determined by abstract considerations.   (*LCP*, p. 61)

A striking feature of this description of critical reading is the emphasis placed on 'realization', the 'making real' of the objects of attention. Another striking feature is the philosophical complexity of this: just what exactly is the status of the object 'realized'? Does this 'realizing' process imply some 'unreality' in the object so identified? Is it an object that exists only in potential? Does it require the intervention of the mind to bring it to realisation, as in some forms of idealism? If so, what does 'mind' mean here: reason? judgement? imagination? And does it then seem reasonable for Wellek to think of Leavis as some kind of realist? Is such a position consistent with Leavis' declared belief in a 'human world', a world independent of the individual? Yet the role of the subject, the reader, also looms large in this account. 'A certain valuing is implicit in the realizing.' How? If the process is akin to grasping a perception – which it seems to be – then in what sense is this a valuing process? Does it matter that the perceptions in question are *linguistically-conditioned*, or is language assumed to be transparent in this account? Is the critic wrestling with the capacity of language to deliver alternative realities or is it the character of reality itself which imposes such 'realizing' requirements upon the reader? Such questions confirm, if confirmation were needed, that Leavis' critical postulates are far from unsophisticated ones. And yet, such is the force and precision of the argument, the deployment of these ideas, that no sense of confusion or insecurity of grasp on the one hand or a contrasting sense of display of virtuosity on the other is allowed to prevail. These ideas receive measured but not undue acknowledgment as working premises that could receive extensive treatment if such were needed in another context. But here, in the immediate context of exposition and debate, they are not pressing issues; the thrust is to emphasise for explicit recognition that 'literary criticism and philosophy [are] quite different disciplines' and that 'the business of the literary critic is to attain a peculiar completeness of response and to observe a peculiarly strict relevance in developing his response into commentary' (*LCP*, p. 61). In other words whatever theoretical sophistication is manifested in the essay it is not there to justify some philosophical pretension; it exists to reinforce the claim that to practice as a literary critic requires intellectual skills at least equal to those required for the practice of philosophy and that whatever analytical skills may be required in formulating the abstractable norms that Wellek looked for, they are not superior to and may be – Leavis is discreet here – inferior to those required every day by the literary critic.

Wellek was not the man to press Leavis profitably on these issues and such reply as he did make largely confirms Leavis' much later comment that he did not seem to be particularly intelligent about literature. But Wellek's challenge was not entirely nugatory. Although Leavis made short work of the claims that were made about his ignorance of romantic philosophy, he does not dismiss or in any way impugn the seriousness of the issue that Wellek raises in respect of the 'norms' that are operating in literary criticism. On the contrary he opens by thanking him 'for bringing fundamental criticism to my work' (*LCP*, p. 59), and goes on to suggest that in fact he (Leavis) had hoped for such a challenge so that he could bring out the fact that his book's avoidance of abstract argument was not due to ignorance or lack of theoretical expertise but was an essential part of the book's thesis:

> If, as I did, I avoided such generalities, it was not out of timidity; it was because they seemed too clumsy to be of any use. I thought I had provided something better. My whole effort was to work in terms of concrete judgments and particular analyses: 'This – doesn't it? – bears such a relation to that; this kind of thing – don't you find it so? – wears better than that', etc.   (*LCP*, p. 63)

'I thought I had provided something better.' The challenge to theory – the theory of Wellek and Warren and the *Theory of Literature* (which appeared in 1949 – is made explicit here. As early as the 1930s Leavis could see that the 'theory industry' was well under way in America, and with characteristic resolution he was determined to oppose its establishment in England. But not, as 'Literary Criticism and Philosophy' makes plain, in any defensive, negative or apprehensive spirit. The tone of this essay, unlike some others, one has to say, is not combative, polemical or strident; it is one of assurance, of knowing that the case for criticism is a good one and that an understanding of literature which is quite so firmly rooted in the actualities and realities of literary experience is not going to be discomfited or embarrassed by the superior understanding of the philosopher.

No doubt this way of putting it confers a status upon Wellek that is, philosophically speaking, inappropriate, and modern theoreticians would have questioned Leavis more searchingly than Wellek could do. But the importance of this exchange was not a matter of the degree of philosophical sophistication displayed on either side but of the opportunity it provided for Leavis to register his awareness that at some crucial points literary criticism and philosophy come into contact and that the ideological consequences of this register themselves in terms of priorities: either criticism is dependent – in some sense – upon philosophy for its methods, its tools of analysis, its conceptual apparatus, or it is not. If it is, then literary criticism could not in any serious sense be regarded as a separate discipline; it would have no *sui generis* mode of enquiry and procedure, no methodology which was recognisably a *literary* method and not a philosophical one. This was not Leavis' position, which is why he welcomed Wellek's intervention as he did: it provided an occasion for the elucidation of some essential principles which, where the institutionalised study of literature is concerned, are always in danger of slipping from sight.

At this point two related questions press for consideration because they arise, explicitly or implicitly, from Leavis' account. First, in what sense does criticism as Leavis described it in his essay fall outside the province of philosophy? Is there anything in his account that would distinguish *critical* activity applied to the reading of literary texts from a *philosophical* activity applied in the same direction? And second, should it matter whether literary criticism is regarded as a separate discipline or not? Is literary criticism capable of becoming a *discipline*, a distinct mode of enquiry and understanding, if it eschews dependence upon philosophy or history or some other methodology and relies only upon its contact with literature? The answers to both questions are implicit in the 1937 essay but it is not easy to elucidate them as it stands. The essay – like nearly all Leavis' criticism – is essentially *d'occasion*, an exercise in relevant exposition which in this case required close concentration upon the critical act of reading; relatively little, except for what is implied in the larger discussion, is said on the nature of literature itself, and the stress on language which was to become such a central part of Leavis' later apologetic is wholly missing. In this sense the essay is incomplete and needs to be supplemented with explanation from the later work, especially that contained in, and arising from, *The Living Principle*.

Before turning to this, one point does need to be made about Leavis' application of the term 'philosophy' in general. Leavis was brought up, intellectually speaking, in the Cambridge of Moore, Russell and Wittgenstein. Their philosophy was in the central tradition of the British enlightenment, which, originating with Locke and Hume and consolidated by Bentham and Mill, manifests itself as a rationalistic form of empiricism, an empiricism which by Leavis' time had become predominantly analytical and scientific in its preoccupations. Although Leavis had not read philosophy at Cambridge he was very familiar with the work of I. A. Richards who had, and Richards was a self-confessed positivist who looked to the prevailing tradition of Cambridge realism to supply him with the methodological justification for a 'psychologistic' method of literary enquiry. Richards' example, though not widely followed as a method, was influential in the encouragement it gave to the establishment of a social science ethos in literary studies, one which Leavis had initially absorbed and supported. It is not surprising, therefore, if in this climate Leavis' notion of philosophy was heavily influenced by its links with positivism. For him, philosophy, in the sense of the academic discipline practised in British (and American) universities through most of his lifetime, was a form of enquiry dominated by preoccupations with analytical method, by questions about the relationship between investigation procedure and objects of attention, by considerations of what could be identified as real in language, and what was the result of subjective misconception and what was not.[14] Continental developments in phenomenology or existentialism, which provide quite a different view of what can or might be investigated, and therefore of what language is, were largely ignored by British and American philosophers in the interwar years, and Wittgenstein's later work, although germane here, was still very little known, even in Cambridge, until after the Second World War.

However, the relevant consideration is not that Leavis formed his sense of the nature of philosophy as an educational discipline from the Cambridge academic milieu in which he lived. That is only to be expected. More pertinent is that throughout his lifetime he saw no reason to change it. It is on this latter point that he is likely to appear most vulnerable, for few today could be unaware that over the past twenty years or so major changes in attitude towards that tradition have taken place in philosophy. Any suggestion that philosophical interests today are dominated by the kind of respect paid to the Logical Positivists in the 1930s can be discounted; the impact of structuralism, post-structuralism, phenomenology and hermeneutics, as well as a refurbished Marxism, is much more likely to be the dominant concern in modern academic philosophy departments. And yet it would be a bold critic who claimed that the British empirical tradition was now defunct or that Franco-Germanic thought was now the only effective intellectual force in philosophical debate. A particularly vigorous form of pragmatism flourished in some American universities which is not dissimilar in its methods, if not in its premises, to that of the British tradition, and the work of philosophers such as Quine suggests that scientism in one form or another is always going to be with us.

What should be said is that philosophy represents a very much more pluralistic body of thought now than it did in the days of the Wellek–Leavis exchange, and that it is likely that some current philosophical positions are now much more in tune with the position Leavis is thought to be defending than was the case in the 1930s. This is indeed the position of Michael Bell, who, in an impressive recent book on Leavis, argues that to look selectively and in the right spirit at Heidegger's thinking on art and language is to construct a framework of philosophical reference points which facilitates certain kinds of inter-translation between the phenomenological tradition and Leavis' own thinking on the nature of art, language and the role of criticism.[15] While I think Bell takes a considerable risk of misrepresenting Leavis' work in this way – the nature of which might be indicated by saying that Leavis would almost certainly have disapproved of his project on the grounds that it presents him as some kind of philosopher manqué – it is undeniable that a thinker such as Heidegger is operating on an intellectual wavelength more attuned to that of Leavis' own than that, say, of Russell or Ayer, and it is possible – but not likely – that such a thinker would be more receptive to what Leavis has to say about literature as a 'necessary kind of thought' than philosophers of a more scientific persuasion. In other words, important shifts have taken place in recent times in professional philosophy which make an accommodation between the activities of literary critics and those of philosophers seem more likely than hitherto.

But this is not to say that the intellectual ethos fostered by the analytic tradition is dead, nor that the kind of assumptions that govern most philosophical practice in this country at the most basic of levels – assumptions about the pattern and type of valid arguments for instance – are fundamentally different from what Leavis believed them to be. Leavis was very conscious of his own vulnerability in this respect; his later work is posited around a central image of the risk-taker, the sea-captain of the *The Secret Sharer*, taking an unpopular and in some respects incomprehensible stand on behalf of his own beliefs (*LP*, pp. 45–8). Some such type of risk Leavis believed himself to be taking when he characterised himself as 'an anti-philosopher' and came forward in public to postulate the existence of an institutionalised (though not of course explicit) resistance to literary thought originating in the practice of professional philosophy as such, a position that he was very conscious could only too readily be dismissed – as it predictably has been – as paranoid or just ignorant and ill-informed. And yet such serious trial of his position as has been made by the philosophically qualified does not in fact show him up in this light. On the contrary the impression is that his argument has still to be tested in ways appropriate to it, ways that necessitate a firm grasp of the premises from which he works, premises outlined in the Wellek exchange but subsequently refined and expanded over many years of reading, thinking and closely attending to the works of writers such as Dickens, Blake, Conrad, Eliot and, particularly, D. H. Lawrence. Without such recognition no amount of philosophical expertise, even when reinforced with good-will and a declared sympathy with Leavis' position, is likely to rescue the attempt from embarrassment. Such is the conclusion one draws from Leavis' subsequent exchange with Michael Tanner, an-other philosophical 'interrogator' of his on the subject of criticism and its relationship to philosophy.

Tanner's two exchanges on this question with Leavis in succeed-ing issues of *New Universities Quarterly* (1975–6) deserve to rank in classic status with that of Wellek's forty years earlier. Tanner was responding initially, in an article called 'Literature and Philosophy', to the appearance of *The Living Principle*, and after a rejoinder from Leavis to this article, he then produced a second article, 'Mutually Necessary – a rejoinder', which ended the public debate.[16] Tanner writes as a professional philosopher contemplating the complexion of Leavis' general claim in that book that, while it is essential for a literary student to have some understanding of the evolution of post-renaissance philosophy, it is impossible to get the right kind of understanding of this from professionally trained philosophers. Like Wellek, Tanner is keenly appreciative of Leavis' critical abilities but is more aware, because more informed, of the philosophical sophis-tication of Leavis' position: 'Leavis' instinct for where the danger-zones in philosophy are for someone who wants to hold his view of the relations between thought, language and objectivity is extra-ordinarily sound and his ideas about coping with them are also those of a first-rate philosophical intelligence'.[17] None the less he finds it impossible to take some of Leavis' arguments seriously, largely because of the choice of philosophical reference points. In-stead of looking to Marjorie Grene and Michael Polanyi to justify his position, 'he should have gone to Wittgenstein' for the kind of sup-port and illumination that he needs. As a result of his failure to do so 'the undoubted truths of the philosophical section of his new book may well be ignored or scoffed at because of the support that he has chosen to rally'.[18] Of especial importance in this respect is Leavis' view of Polanyi as an epistemologist who has 'solved' the problem of mind/body dualism. Tanner smiles at this as simplistic in its innocence , suggesting that Polanyi has missed the nub of the prob-lem by positing its solution as purely one of incarnation:

While freely granting that my mind is the mind of my body, and vice-versa, I may still be puzzled (and this *has* been the major perplexity of philosophers of mind) as to how they are connected with one another. How, if at all, can my mind act on my body and vice-versa? It is no help at all, although it has been canvassed by other, and in my opinion much more distinguished philosophers than Polanyi, to say that the basic concept is that of a person, who has both mind and body.[19]

But Leavis' reply chooses to ignore Tanner's point, insisting instead on reiterating his general recommendation of Polanyi and Grene as practical resources in the critic's need to get recognition for that 'other kind of thought' which is the focus of his book, thus apparently confirming Tanner's point about the inadequacy of his philosophical content, and, by implication, revealing a line of weakness in his argument (*MN*, pp. 186f.).

The argument between Tanner and Leavis is both sensitively tuned and closely-woven, yet far-ranging and complex in its scope, so any attempt to summarise it in detail would have to be for another occasion. Nonetheless, to characterise it as a debate in which Tanner exposes Leavis' philosophical ignorance would be seriously to misrepresent it. It is clear from the exchange as it stands that both writers misunderstand each other's position. Leavis grotesquely attributes to Tanner views which he patently does not hold or express, such as a *parti pris* for Lord Robbins, or a religious partiality for 'Four Quartets', and his startling rebuke to Tanner for not correcting the 'conventionally slack way' Ian Robinson goes about his reviewing is just bizarre. On more substantial points Leavis also appears wayward. He mounts what is in effect a radical critique of the methodology of the social sciences in *The Living Principle* but then seems surprised that Tanner takes this for what it is, an attack on the validity of social science. He is also remarkably obtuse about Tanner's reading of Eliot, finding in Tanner's carefully and warily phrased exposition of Leavis' argument on 'Four Quartets' a 'dismissal of my placing valuation' of the poem and an attribution to himself of the 'liar paradox' which Tanner had merely used to illustrate the nature of Leavis' argument. 'Mutually Necessary' is not an essay in which Leavis' forensic skills show to advantage.

It is arguable, however, that the greater misconception lay on Tanner's side. To illustrate this is not easy because he is responding to a book in which, as he claims, Leavis deploys a philosophical position of great power and sophistication, the opening part of which alone occupies fifty pages of unorthodox and challenging argument. To be sure that one has grasped this position is not necessarily a good sign, for it might lead to one being classified alongside those 'lazy reviewers' whom Tanner identifies as wholly missing the point of what Leavis is trying to do, such is the difficulty of the idiom in which *The Living Principle* is written. Furthermore, in so far as Leavis' argument is a philosophical one, Tanner is not only better equipped in terms of professional training than most to evaluate this, but he is disposed to look very sympathetically upon Leavis' enterprise as a whole anyway. In a generous and open spirit he invites Leavis to contribute to the clarification of some knotty aesthetic problems. So to respond by claiming that these are in fact the very conditions of the misunderstanding in question might appear perverse.

But any reading of the opening essay of Leavis' book, together with the supplementary essays, can only confirm that Leavis is quite deliberately and insistently claiming this. He is postulating adverse effects for the literary understanding of any philosopher whose notion of culture is one fostered by the native philosophical tradition. He is also claiming that there are disabling effects for the English student who is exposed to this tradition; that the philosophical tradition that prevails here is one inscribed within an objectivist epistemology and discourse; that this orientation is central to that governing the practice and development of the human or social sciences in this country; and that as long as this is the case any true understanding of society and the individual will be out of reach. This is so because the vital factor in such understanding is missing; there is no capacity in such thought for a recognition of the specific, distinct and unique dimension of what Leavis predicates as 'the human world', the self-defining product of which is language. Philosophy, understood in a large and general sense but certainly including professional philosophy, appears to Leavis to be a constituent of an ideology of misconception, a component of a culture of anti-perception, a seminal presence in the practice of moulding thought in general – and linguistic thought in particular – into patterns closed to a meaningful representation of what the postulated 'human world' could imply for an understanding of literature. He agrees philosophy need not, ideally, reinforce or contribute to such activity but as a matter of experience this is how in fact it appears.

It is this large and general sense of what philosophy represents for Leavis that Tanner ignores, either because he considers it too crude and general a point to deal with, a wild misconception, or because he interprets it as irrelevant to himself. But to take the last point first, it has to be said that in his discussion of how a creative writer makes or utters 'statements', he largely confirms Leavis' point that he has not grasped what the essence of the argument is, that notwithstanding his claim to understand – and share – of Leavis' view of critical judgement, he is still failing to grasp that for Leavis art is not primarily a matter of intellectual paradoxes or puzzles:

> I am sure Leavis will agree with me [about] the most perplexing dilemma for the critic: the power of great art to undermine one's most strongly-held beliefs, at least temporarily. . . . All I was saying in regard to *Four Quartets* was that the problem they present the sensitive reader with is not significantly different from that presented by a very large number of works of art.[20]

Leavis did not publish a reply to this so unless he correspond with Tanner privately it is unlikely that his comment on this could be known. But one's initial reaction is that this is far from what Leavis would have agreed to. The whole burden of the case he builds up in the first chapter of *The Living Principle* emphasises the continuity between language, as the created achievement of a community, and the creative achievement of the artist. The artist does not create a vision *ab initio*, out of nothing other than a private experience; it is the degree to which he or she is attuned to a body of living experience – which *is* language as created by the 'human world' – that determines the greatness or otherwise of the art in question. To lay the stress on art's paradoxical qualities as its distinguishing – and most distinguished – feature is to miss the thrust of Leavis' case. He wants us to see art as remarkable to the extent that it confirms, expresses and further develops that even more remarkable element inherent in language, its capacity to create *human* meaning and significance. Art will have special features, paradoxical or puzzling characteristics, only to the extent that its audience are oblivious and insensitive to its roots in ordinary language, the language of active human meanings. This aspect of art is not expected to catch the critic by surprise; insofar as the critic is a *literary* critic, so Leavis' argument runs, he or she will be conscious that art has the capacity to challenge preconceptions and to send us back to interrogate our experience at the profoundest level. To characterise this as 'undermining one's most strongly-held beliefs' is to misrepresent the process. To phrase it in this way is to lend art the semi-mystical properties of a revelation, to emphasise its features as an 'aesthetic' experience, rather than to present it as Leavis did as a special but integral part of the universal process of uncovering latent meaning. Of course it is the case that modern art has unique problems in this respect; the living body of the language is not as robust as it was, indeed in some respects its condition is pathological, and this poses special problems for the critic (which is why, for Leavis, Eliot is such an important case), but this should in no way change our understanding of the essential relationship of art and language.

A puzzling feature of Tanner's commentary is that there are times when he talks as though he fully understands this point and can comment:

> The overwhelming truth that emerges from that valuable though disfigured part [Ch. 1] of *The Living Principle* is the priority of language in what makes us distinctively human, and therefore the continuity of the artist's activities with those of everyone else, in so far as the rest of us use language responsibly. . . . Artists are dependent, no matter how great their genius and originality, on non-artists. So great creative work is bound to be a sign of spiritual health.[21]

This communicates a quite different sense of appreciation of Leavis' argument that the lines quoted above. If this had been part of an opening statement designed to describe that argument, and then to discuss it in a way which showed that a grasp of the position also led to an appreciation of its implications and larger meaning, which would have meant, incidentally, an acknowledgment of the force (if not the conclusiveness) of Leavis' 'anti-philosophy' argument, then little more than expressions of gratitude would have been in order. In fact Tanner's comments appear as part of some concluding remarks about the book which, appreciative as they are, stray disconcertingly off into abstruse ponderings about what the problematics of 'sharing meanings' are. A philosopher, so Leavis might have said, needs to consider it as such (that is why he is a philosopher), but a critic needs to recognise it, not as a problem for fine excogitation, but as a fact of language, the meaning and implications of which are there to be acted upon in terms of reading and interpreting literary texts. Tanner does not seem to grasp that, for Leavis, it is not crucial whether or not the figurative expression 'sharing meanings' is rationally valid or not; what matters is: does it work as a tool of literary-critical thought? Does it effectively advance understanding of the art-language-human-meaning matrix ('thought' here being understood in Leavis' rather pointed sense of a much larger entity than that to which 'rational' alone could apply)? In other words, intelligent and sympathetic as he is in response to *The Living Principle*, Tanner fails to grasp that what is being offered there is not a programme for philosophical enquiry, a survey of interesting and intellectually testing questions, but a blueprint for cultural action (the establishing of an educated public) based upon certain basic *perceptions* about the nature of literature and language offered for *recognition*, acceptance and active follow-through, not high-minded discussion. For many people this is not a congenial mode of intellectual procedure, it requires far too robust an attitude to complex and difficult questions, an attitude in some respects approaching that of religious belief and conviction rather than that of philosophical enquiry. So it is not wholly surprising that Tanner refuses to adopt this position as his own, but it is what Leavis understands as the mode required by and central to literary criticism as a *sui generis* discipline. 'This is so, is not it?' is an invitation to *collaborate* first and foremost, and collaboration entails a degree of assent, a degree of shared perceptions, well in excess of the mere ready interest and sympathy that Tanner evinces.[22]

A clinching demonstration of this emerges in Tanner's incomprehension about 'statement' in relation to Eliot's poetry. He quotes Leavis to the effect:

> I had better say at once that early in my acquaintance with *Four Quartets* as a completed work I experienced a decided arrest at
>
> *human kind*
> *Cannot bear very much reality,*
>
> divining that this was an intimation of something basic in Eliot's 'answer' that I couldn't endorse.

to which Tanner responds: '[If] Leavis would not want to say that it was a *statement* that Eliot was making that he found unendorsable, then I can only say that I don't see why.'[23] The answer is because it is not a statement; it is an expression which acquires such meanings as it has by virtue of its place in a poem, a place which gives it quite different properties to that of a 'statement'. Leavis describes it as 'an intimation of something', the meaning of which phrase, no doubt, Tanner feels confident could be assimilated to the term 'statement'. It's a fair bet, however, that Leavis would not in any sense agree. One could offer for Tanner's benefit to gloss this 'intimation' in ways that would perhaps suggest that 'statement' is an inappropriate term: that what Eliot is doing here is framing a meaning which simultaneously is being undone by its own vacuity, its own incapacity to endorse what is presented as an authoritative pronouncement, and that in local terms we have here what Leavis finds endemic in Eliot's *oeuvre*: a pervasive ambivalence of position which is indicative of a larger lack of confidence in his own creativity. But if the extended and detailed commentary on the *Quartets*, which Leavis provided in the book and which Tanner had read, could not enlighten him as to the nature of the conceptual division, which leads him to talk of 'statements' in poetry and brings Leavis strenuously to reject such terms, then it is hardly likely that a few expository lines would help.

Michael Tanner is a far more intelligent, perceptive and well-informed interlocutor than Wellek was, and yet inevitably the conclusion has to be – as it was in the case of the latter – that Tanner has not understood and grasped Leavis' case to the extent that one can say his critique is justified. Notwithstanding Leavis' own erratic and perverse reactions to Tanner's often judicious and always courteous and appreciative commentary, it has to be said that the case that *The Living Principle* outlines, particularly in its first chapter, escapes recognition as far as Tanner is concerned. Whether this is because he is philosopher, as Leavis repeatedly claims – and which of course Tanner rejects – is clearly not a matter for limited debate. But what can be said is that being a philosopher gives Tanner no advantages when it comes to explaining, interpreting or criticising Leavis' argument for the simple reason that he treats it as a philosophic rather than a literary one. He has identified Leavis as a critic of unusual ability whose instinct for philosophical questions of central importance is remarkably incisive and sure, and who has a view of language, and its relation to art, the complexity of which entitles him to be regarded as a philosophical thinker in his own right. All of this Tanner concedes. What he cannot concede, because he does not accept the premise, is that to call Leavis a philosopher is not a compliment. For Leavis philosophers are rivals to literary critics because they set out their stalls in the same market place, selling – apparently – the same wares. But these are not the same wares; they

are fakes, spurious versions of 'human' meanings with the essential
ingredient that makes them human left out. This ingredient, a proper
understanding and regard for language, is an understanding drawing not on philosophically originated currents of ideas (such as those
from Wittgenstein) but on literary critical experience built out of
reading and interpreting creative work produced by major writers of
literature over several centuries. For Leavis this work is a creative
achievement of cognition and intellect, as well as imagination; it
represents a body of thought, a body of meaning, quite different in
implication and significance to that deriving from the post-renaissance philosophic tradition but just as entitled to respect as *thought*
as that which is of a more recognisably philosophic character. This is
spelt out clearly in the first chapter of *The Living Principle,* but it is not
there for Tanner, in spite of his own testimony to the scrupulousness
of his search for it.

> I have sought to examine the rhetorical form of Leavis's literary
> criticism in its function as an existential critique. In so far as
> literature is a creative and exploratory enactment of irreducible
> significances and values, what is at stake for him in the work
> cannot be expressed in terms more fundamental than those of the
> work itself, and hence the ostensive procedure which lies, quite
> consciously, at the heart of his practice. But the 'object' to be
> displayed is not, as it were, the 'text' on the page so much as the
> participatory act of reading it. Reading has an analogical relation
> to the act of composition in that it is a re-creation. Reading de-
> pends on the reader and is more comparable to musical perform-
> ance than it is to musical connoisseurship. By a demonstrative
> reading Leavis tries to define the quality of being for which the
> language of the text is the irreducible index. And his belief that
> poetic language is not merely the instrument for expressing some-
> thing but is in some sense the very being that is in question, leads
> him to resist any tendency in his own discourse to become an
> independent, potentially rival, structure of ideas. Instead he leans
> on the resources of the common tongue to reflect the struggle of
> the artist towards new significance.[24]

In this extract from the conclusion to Michael Bell's book on Leavis,
selected in part for the precision, penetration and comprehensive-

ness of its summarising quality, there is clear evidence of the shift that has taken place in the kind of thinking and discussing that is now devoted to Leavis' literary criticism. There is a noticeable colouration of philosophical terminology: 'function as an existential critique', 'ostensive procedure', 'analogical relation' and so on. More importantly, there is an explicit use of concepts derived from an identifiable philosophical tradition: 'existential critique', 'quality of being' and 'the very being that is in question' are notions drawn from a tradition of phenomenological thought and argument traceable to the work of Husserl and exemplified, for Bell's purposes, in Heidegger's philosophy of art and language. In so far as they are accurate – and there is a prior requirement to be in command of such thinking if one is to challenge their accuracy – they might be thought to add a noticeable intellectual 'stiffening' to the kind of case that Bell is developing in defence of Leavis.

The 'philosophical' case is professionally and, so far as one can judge, expertly assembled and presented. Anyone seriously interested in Leavis' criticism cannot but feel that they could and should read Heidegger as a constructive step in the difficult task of becoming more inward with his thought. Yet, throughout the argument, and not just in those parts directed to philosophy as such, one is conscious that there is a tactical dimension to Bell's position. He is writing with what Leavis called in another connection 'one eye on a standard'. The standard, or standards in this case are those adopted by, and insisted upon by what one surmises is his intended audience, an audience no longer made up primarily of practising teachers of English, critics who see their main task as the reading, understanding and interpretation of literary works, but that of the ever-burgeoning band of critical theorists whose focus is, at best, the expansion of 'ideological awareness' about literature or, more generally, the promotion of various kinds of political stance. For this readership the parameters of once traditional critical apologetics – those post-renaissance tenets established and developed over three centuries which conditioned argument through appeals to a detailed knowledge of literary work, and which Leavis made the cornerstone of his own critical practice – are of purely historic, that is to say, diagnostic interest. This audience can no longer take these tenets seriously as working principles of critical thought, any more than Leavis himself can be taken seriously as a critical thinker. Hence the need for Bell's approach: his attempt to make Leavis' position not congenial (who could do that?) but perhaps comprehensible to those contemporaries sufficiently disinterested to want to know what the past used to look like.

It would be difficult to find a better book extant on Leavis than this one, and it is a book that can be wholeheartedly recommended by anyone who thinks that Leavis' work and thought is important. But as remarked earlier, the risks of misrepresentation entailed in such a 'tactical' approach as this are considerable and not effectively avoided by the writer. That Bell is aware of this is suggested by the way his concluding chapter attempts to undo many of the implications his preceding argument has set up: 'that the weight of [literature's] considered experience is not measurable by its philosophical premises'; that Leavis' ability 'to give himself to the work resists abstract definition';[25] that a philosopher who attempted to describe Leavis' criticism in Benthamite terms only 'confirmed Leavis' essential point about the *trained* incapacity to read' [my italics];[26] that 'by using Heidegger . . . I have not meant to suggest that Leavis needs Heidegger. . . . Indeed, in many ways, Leavis underwrites Heidegger rather than the reverse.'[27] Bell struggles better than most to square this particular circle but the crucial admission comes in an explicit avowal that:

> It would have been possible to conduct the present exposition, at least in its positive aspects, using simply Leavis' own statements and terms. One reason for not doing so is that, while Leavis could hardly be matched as a polemical expositor of this own convictions, it is notorious that these have repeatedly failed to convince a substantial body of readers; including especially those who invoke 'philosophical' or 'theoretical' criteria.[28]

This fails to convince, if only because Leavis' role as a polemicist is the least impressive, and important, side of his criticism and because it is ducking the issue of one's own critical idiom and discourse which Bell himself unwittingly highlights as a central question in any appreciation of Leavis' work.

What matters as far as appreciation is concerned is the 'thought' that Leavis was struggling to get recognition for, and which he himself spent a good part of his life trying to bring into a more exact focus and articulation. As Bell acknowledges, this was essentially a matter of discourse, of developing an appropriate critical idiom, but it is important to stress that Leavis' discourse developed and shaped itself into a critical lexis attentive to, and fed by, not 'convictions' as such but the kind of convictions attendant upon and only generated by an inherently evaluative form of perceptual experience, the kind of convictions that are inseparable from bearing witness: 'this is so, is it not?' By using an existential context to explain, and legitimise, Leavis' emphasis upon the perceptual character of critical experience, the evaluation character which is central to this gets lost or at least overlooked; the moral dimension of the Leavisite idiom is underplayed. In the present climate of a conceptual ferment fostered by the theory industry a stress in this direction is understandable; Leavis' discourse was an expressive system designed to incorporate the most delicate and the most unyielding of recognitions: not assertions, not postulates, not propositions, not even concepts or convictions, but recognitions. It is a discourse that is fully intentional in that it refuses to be reflexive, having always the focusing of the object in view. In this respect a comparison with the phenomenological tradition can seem justified. But to leave the stress there is to miss the point of the exercise: it is the *nature of the object*, the evaluative and moral order incorporated through language in the 'human world', which determines why this discourse is as it is. The character of the discourse is fitted to the nature of the object, an object whose reality cannot be in doubt for Leavis but the perception of which, together with its meaning and significance, is in continual danger of being neglected or missed. Any attempt to translate this discourse into terms other than its own, to 'condition it' so to speak that it becomes an idiolect inter-translatable with the multitude of other, theory-driven discourses, ruptures its continuity with that object, that literature which gave it its own meaning and substance, its integrity, or, in the special sense which Leavis used, its 'sincerity'.

Bell knows this, and, up to a point, gives it recognition in his argument. It is a matter of stress that is in question. But there can be no shirking of the central issue: Leavis' idiom is a moral one, a language chosen for its capacity to respect, recognise and as far as possible reproduce the evaluative insights of the literature which is its object. This is its *raison d'être*, its moving force. It is, we might say, the only form in which, for Leavis, criticism of literature is possible, because it is the only idiom in which the appropriate recognitions can take shape, can find expression. That is to say, if we follow Leavis' argument that one's choice of critical discourse becomes a moral choice: either one chooses a language in which such recognitions can take place, or one doesn't. It follows that for the reader or critic of Leavis one large choice soon emerges: either we accept the premise of his position, in other words the priority, centrality and *reality* of the meaning located in the phrase 'the human world', or we don't. If we accept the premise we accept the essential terms of his discourse (which does not mean adoption of his stylistic idiom); we accept that the reason why certain terms, phrases, emphases, idioms, or formulations occur and re-occur in the way they do is because those are the results of the efforts made by one of the keenest intellects of our century to bring the meanings and significances, the judgements, of literature within the bounds of common understanding and speech. Leavis' criticism is the nearest thing we have, in the modern period, to a presentation of literary experience in terms other than itself, and as such represents one of the major creative achievement of our time. If one recognises this one recognises also the difficulty, in some senses the impossibility, of escaping from the field of these terms, and unless one has the talent to go beyond Leavis by initiating a new level of human critical discourse, one is obliged to reflect this in the deployment of one's own critical approach.

It is not appropriate to close on a note of hagiography. Leavis knew he was a remarkable man whose achievement was considerable, yet his own work was entirely aligned towards the even more remarkable achievement of creative insight and vision that for him was English literature. He saw it much more steadily and much more wholly than the rest of us, but it is still along the direction of his gaze that we are exhorted to look rather than at the gaze itself. What makes that gaze distinctive is its capacity to bring to sharp focus what for most of us is at best hazy and at worst invisible, and we are naturally impressed by optics that have such power. But the point of the effort that went into fashioning such aids is in the perceptions enabled, not the craft of the instrument, and once convinced that this lens is less distorting, less obscuring, than virtually any other available to us at this time, we are clearly obliged to set out on or continue our own task of clarifying further what we have been brought so expertly to see.

NOTES

1. F. R. Leavis, 'Literary Criticism and Philosophy', *Scrutiny,* vol. VI, no. 1 (June 1937), pp. 59–71 and p. 63. This essay is also to be found in *The Common Pursuit* (Harmondsworth: Penguin, 1962) pp. 211–22.
2. C. Belsey, *Critical Practice* (London & New York: Methuen, 1980).
3. Ibid., p. 12.
4. Ibid.
5. Ibid., p. 14.
6. F. Mulhern, *The Moment of Scrutiny* (London: New Left Books, 1979).
7. Ibid., p. 169.
8. T. Eagleton, *Criticism and Ideology* (London: New Left Books, 1976).
9. Ibid., p. 16.
10. F. R., Leavis, *The Living Principle* (London: Chatto & Windus, 1975) esp. ch. 1; hereafter referred to as *LP*, with page references given in the text; and 'Mutually Necessary', in G. Singh (ed.), *The Critic as Anti-Philosopher* (London: Chatto & Windus, 1982); and 'Thought, Meaning and Sensibility', in G. Singh (ed.), *Valuation in Criticism and Other Essays* (Cambridge: Cambridge University Press, 1986).
11. R. Wellek, 'Literary Criticism and Philosophy', in *Scrutiny,* vol. V, no. 4 (March 1937) pp. 375–8. F. R. Leavis, 'Literary Criticism and Philosophy'; hereafter referred to as *LCP*, with page references given in the text; and R. Welleck, 'Letter', *Scrutiny,* vol. VI, no. 2 (September 1937) pp. 195-7.
12. Welleck, *Literary Criticism and Philosophy,* p. 376.
13. Ibid., p. 378.
14. A relevant observation would be that the Leavis/Welleck debate took place against a philosophical background largely dominated by Logical Positivism, a particularly virulent form of sceptical realism.
15. M. Bell, *F. R. Leavis* (London: Routledge, 1988) pp. 35–54 and ch. 4 passim.
16. M. Tanner, 'Literature and Philosophy', *New Universities Quarterly,* vol. XXX (Winter 1975) pp. 54–54. F. R. Leavis, 'Mutually Necessary', ibid., vol. XXX (Spring 1976), but the text used here is that available in G. Singh (ed.), *The Critic as Anti-Philosopher,* pp. 186–208; hereafter referred to as *MN*, with page references given in the text. M. Tanner, '"Mutually Necessary": A Rejoinder', *New Universities Quarterly,* vol. XXX (Summer 1976) pp. 313–23.
17. Tanner, 'Literature and Philosophy', p. 62.
18. Ibid., p. 67.
19. Ibid., p. 62.
20. Tanner, '"Mutually Necessary"', p. 318.
21. Tanner, 'Literature and Philosophy', p. 63.
22. This is another point at which Leavis' use of the *Secret Sharer* is relevant; one takes the risk that one's conviction may not be right but one has to act as though it is.
23. Tanner, '"Mutually Necessary"', pp. 316–17.
24. Bell, *F. R. Leavis,* p. 130.

25. Ibid., p. 133.
26. Ibid., p. 135.
27. Ibid., p. 136.
28. Ibid., p. 135.

16

Raymond Williams and Post-Modernism

TONY PINKNEY

'And', of course, as Raymond Williams knew in a series of titles that begins with *Culture and Society*, passes through *The Country and the City* and *Marxism and Literature*, and culminates in *Politics and Letters*, both separates *and* connects.[1] There are accordingly two hermeneutic possibilities tucked away in my title. 'Raymond Williams and Post-modernism' may in fact mean Williams *on* Post-modernism. A worthy project, to be sure. One of the draft plans for Williams' last and unfinished book, *The Politics of Modernism*, shows that he was planning a chapter entitled 'Modernism to Post-modernism'; and perhaps by scavenging about among earlier writings, gleaning the odd allusion or aside here and there, one could reconstruct the faint outlines of that lost essay. I'm not at all sure of the form Williams' analysis would have taken had he lived to write that chapter, but many of his admirers are. Here, for instance, is Fred Inglis, apodictically declaring in one of the editorial notes in *The Politics of Modernism* that 'Post-modernism was for him a strictly ideological compound from an enemy formation, and long in need of this authoritative rebuttal.'[2] Whether this robust confidence quite accords with Williams' own famous or infamous sense of difficulty, ambiguity, complexity, may, however, be doubted.

I do not intend to structure this essay around a lost manuscript, though that would be an appropriately post-modernist ploy and the temptation, as in Eco's *The Name of the Rose*, to play Jorge the monk to Williams' missing treatise is a strong one. For my title can be inflected differently: suppose the 'and' connects rather than separates, so that in place of Williams *on* post-modernism we have Raymond Williams *as* post-modernist. A project more scandalous than worthy, it might be objected; and in fact, since embarking upon a book *Raymond Williams: Postmodern Novelist*,[3] this is precisely the

214 The British Critical Tradition

kind of pained or outraged objection I've been hearing from friends
on the literary Left for some time now. It is as if it were an act of self-
disarmament and despair to assimilate Williams to post-modernism.
Around the 'and' of our title, a whole series of loaded Derridean
binary oppositions at once spring up: Raymond Williams – whole-
some, Welsh-European, historical, political, inspiring, serious;
post-modernism – decadent, American, spatial, apolitical, dystopian,
frivolous. It's not only on general deconstructive principles that I
feel one should seek to challenge this too neat binary schema. For
Williams himself, in his later works, repeatedly seeks to open up his
thought to new and surprising interpretations, to reinscription in
contexts he cannot foresee, to a future which remains always open
and unpredictable. The clearest instance of this is what I have elsewhere called the 'third-generational' structure of his later novels,
where the central narrative of the novel is encased in a frame which
foregrounds the interpretative activity of a young 'reader': Jon Merritt
in *Loyalties*, Glyn Parry in *People of the Black Mountains*.[4] The latter
novel, indeed, is exemplary in this respect: the authoritative grandfather, Elis, has disappeared while trekking across the mountains –
a fictional gap into which Raymond Williams has himself now fallen
– and the grandchild must decipher and reconstruct the traces as
best he can. These narrative frames enjoin upon us the responsibility
of re-interpretation, recycling, of bringing to bear new hermeneutic
contexts they themselves do not foresee. Even if Raymond Williams
were *not* a post-modernist (and I believe he is), his own work implies
that post-modernism is a 'metaphor' a powerful contemporary interpretive framework, that we should in principle open-mindedly try
out in relation to his thought.

Is there any kind of *prima facie* case for suggesting that Williams
might, in a sense yet to be defined, be some kind of post-modernist?
A sense that there was arose, for me, in the very process of editing
The Politics of Modernism after its author's death. In an earlier essay
I argued as strenuously as I could, in polemic with a well-established
view of Williams as unregenerately 'empiricist' in theory and dourly
'English' and 'realist' in aesthetics and fictional practice, that he
was in fact more of a European modernist: his intellectual formation
as a student took place in a subculture deeply marked by the early
twentieth-century European avant garde; his earliest writings on
European film and drama extend these concerns; even his early
novels can be read as a critique of realism rather than its obedient

reproduction and his middle-period novels from *The Fight from Manod*[5] on soon begin to move away from realism altogether, and finally modernism re-emerges centrally as a cultural and political issue in Williams' work of the 1980s, that series of major articles which (as I did not then know) were destined to become *The Politics of Modernism.*[6]

That polemical emphasis, challenging the valuations of a post-1968 generation of Williams readers who, in the grip of a Bloomian anxiety of influence, had diminished the Europeanism and avantgardism of this commanding precursor so that their own might burn more brightly, still seems to me timely. Yet in the long run it bends the stick too far the other way, becoming as one-sided as the very view it sought to displace. Many of the critical assessments of modernism in both the very early and very late writings are indeed harsh ones. Moreover, in *The Long Revolution* Williams had declared that 'a new realism is necessary, if we are to remain creative';[7] and if his novels breaks from realism into mass-cultural forms such as detective fiction and political thriller after *The Fight for Manod*, they do none the less effect a reconciliation with it –albeit a nuanced one – in his last project, *People of the Black Mountains*. At which point, however, this dual-track stance, simultaneously for and against modernism, lauding its technical advances while lamenting its human costs, begins to look uncannily familiar; it is, in effect, structurally homologous with the formative impulses of post-modernism itself. Raymond Williams is not F. R. Leavis or Peter Fuller, despising the rootless cosmopolitan modernists and harking nostalgically back to a happy Hobbitland or unsullied Englishness incarnated in Samuel Palmer's paintings, George Eliot's novels or the village cricket green; but nor also is he a glib celebrant of Marinettian modernity, finding more beauty in a hurtling formula one racing car than in *The Victory of Samothrace*. And if Williams, characteristically, inhabits a 'border country' between these two extremes, then rather than tongue-twistingly tagging him as a realist-who-nonetheless-believes-there's-no-going-back-behind-modernism, we might as well come frankly out with the phrase: Raymond Williams, post-modernist.

In 1983 Williams wrote that 'there are many signs that the period of conscious "modernism" is ending'; and where, after that, could you go but into post-modernity? We would, however, he continues, with his notorious sense of complexity and qualification, need better understandings of modernism itself before we:

know what is meant by 'post-modernism'. Is it some new phase of innovation and experiment, distinct from that earlier phase for which 'modernist' is a period description? Is it a conscious rejection of some or all of those actual innovations and experiments, which can include a deliberate return to earlier methods? Or is it a move beyond the general theoretical positions which were congruent with all the phases of 'modernist' art but which may also be congruent with some of the forms of the 'post-modernist' development or rejection?[8]

Three questions, three eminently sensible discriminations, though they hardly set the blood racing; yet even so *none* of them are answered in the following toughly argumentative review, which shifts to quite different issues. And this paragraph, fence-sitting and elusive as it is, seems to be Williams' fullest statement on post-modernism. His uses of the term elsewhere are relatively perfunctory, implying that post-modernism is the undistinctive fag-end of modernism itself, the ideological and incorporated terminus of an avant garde that was once heroic and socially exposed, the exiles and emigrés of the earlier phase becoming the puppets and parasites of a later, multinational capitalism. It may well be, then, that Raymond Williams *on* post-modernism will not take us very far in the analysis of Raymond Williams *as* post-modernist. But far from invalidating the latter project, Williams' relative silence on post-modernism means only that the analysis must be conducted in terms of deep-structural analogues and parallels rather than overt declarations of affiliation – an analytic level which I find more compelling than that of conscious manifesto and which may, perhaps, point us to a version of the postmodern less ideological and more politically worthwhile than we find in the noisy proclamations of its conscious adherents. I want to explore these analogues around four headings: (1) populism (or historicism); (2) the city; (3) media, simulacrum and the sublime; (4) space and geography. Post-modernism, I propose, is everywhere and nowhere in the work of Raymond Williams, everywhere present as structural parallel yet nowhere present as overt statement of allegiance; it is, as Walter Benjamin once suggested of the crowd in Baudelaire's poetry, so ubiquitous as to be effectively absent.

The most familiar view of post-modernism is as a collapsing of the barriers between high and mass culture, and the overcoming of high-modernist elitism as classically exemplified in the architecture of Le Corbusier, Walter Gropius and Mies van der Rohe. The death of modernism can then be pinpointed to 15 July 1972, when the Pruitt-Igoe housing scheme in St Louis, Missouri, is partially blown up. Built according to the best principles of the 'International Style' – austerely functional, rectilinear, geometrical, rationalistic – Pruitt-Igoe had for years been defaced and vandalised by its under privileged black inhabitants. And as it collapsed into a pile of dynamited rubble, with it went the high-modernist dream that flat roofs, gleaming white surfaces, stringent impersonality, absence of ornament and what Charles Jencks terms 'clean, salubrious hospital metaphor', would impart similar virtues to their inhabitants, breeding a new race of men and women who would be fit subjects for their streamlined, high-tech, post-individualist modernity.[9]

1972, as it turns out, is a good date for periodising Raymond Williams' work too, but here I simply want to point out the congruence between some key post-modernist themes and manifestos, and the direction of Williams' own early work. Alongside the post-modernist populism catchily embodied in Robert Venturi and Tom Wolfe's titles – *Learning from Las Vegas* and *From Bauhaus to Our House* – we can set one of Williams' own seminal early slogans· 'Culture Is Ordinary', an essay first published in 1958. Tackling Leavisite cultural pessimism in *Culture and Society*, he famously declared: 'we live in an expanding culture, yet we spend much of our energy regretting the fact, rather than seeking to understand its nature and conditions' (*CS*, p. viii). The very discipline of 'cultural studies', as it emerges from the early work of Williams, Richard Hoggart and E. P. Thompson, might itself be seen as an archetypally post-modernist phenomenon, dismantling received binary oppositions between literature and mass culture; and Williams' own contributions to this field, from *Communications* in 1962 to and beyond *Television: Technology and Cultural Form* in 1974,[10] are too well known to need rehearsing here. Moreover, the charge of 'populism', both cultural and political, was a key one levelled against him during the Althusserian onslaught of the mid-1970s. No doubt Raymond Williams' populism doesn't exactly map on to Robert Venturi's or Tom Wolfe's, and retains a political cutting edge which the full-blown post-modernism of the latter,with its much-touted 'collapse of critical distance', has virtually abandoned: whereas Main Street, for Venturi, is 'almost right', for Williams, one imagines, it would be decidedly wrong. None the less, the parallels bear further development.

The avant garde artist, for high modernism, is always right; the punters – readers of poems or users of buildings – always wrong, bogged down in aesthetic subjectivisim or localism rather than devoted to an austere, state-of-the-art functionalism. This aesthetic dichotomy, which receives its clearest expression in modernist architecture, is just one local instance of the general relationship between universal Enlightenment reason and traditional or regional cultures: whereas the former aspires to the transcendental truths of pure reason, the latter remain, from the viewpoint of Enlightenment, mired in history, trapped in the antiquated prejudices and superstitions which constitute their all-important 'tradition' or 'heritage'. Post-modernism, by contrast, while not simply abandoning the project of modernity, none the less returns to tradition, Nature, popular tastes, the myriad historical styles of the past, with a new openness and respect. Unlike the free-standing, wonderfully arrogant architectural sculptures of a Le Corbusier, the post-modern building is also 'post-Enlightenment': populist, in that the tastes of its users have been consulted in its design and construction, historicist, in that it has abandoned the International Style's interdict on reference to local, vernacular or traditional architectural styles, and contextual, in that it will endeavour to fit reciprocally into (rather than splendidly negate, *à la* Gropius or Mies van der Rohe) its immediate urban neighbourhood. And we also find Raymond Williams, from one end of his work to the other, seeking to define a post-Enlightenment (but not anti-Enlightenment) rationality and culture. The invocation of Edmund Burke's critique of Enlightenment planning at the start of *Culture and Society* is one such instance: 'Burke is describing a process, based on a recognition of the necessary complexity and difficulty of human affairs, and formulating itself, in consequence as an essentially social and co-operative effort in control and reform' (*CS*, p. 7). No body of intellectuals claiming access to transcendental Reason, no political party claiming to monopolise the logic of Revolution and the Proletariat, and no aesthetic avant garde appealing to the impersonal science of function and materials, can arrogate this tangled, multi-faceted process to themselves; there is no such Archimedean stance, no such pinpoint of unsullied modernity, outside of a historical process which constitutes us as time- and place-bound beings. However, Williams continues, it is 'foolish for conservatives to suppose that such conclusions are any kind of argument against the most radical social reform' (*CS*, p. 7); and to enforce his point, to define a post- rather than mere anti-modernity, he brings William Cobbett into his argument, insisting that we weld together the latter's political abrasiveness and Burke's conservative organicism in a *single* thought. Exactly these issues are again broached in the great set-piece debates of Williams' last novel, *People of the Black Mountains*, where representatives of modernity and tradition battle it out to an exhausting stand-off. Neither is wholly endorsed, neither wholly rejected; and the reader must venture on to think the impossible, synthetic thought – a post-modernist *historicist* thought – which is beyond the historical capacities of either of the two characters involved; in the finest of such encounters, that long chapter on 'The Coming of the Measurer', Dal Mered, in Volume One, we are, I suspect, persuaded that we *have* thought it.

Once the post-modern building truly becomes populist, historicist and contextual, the very notion of 'building', premised as that is on a stark contrast between itself and surrounding urban fabric, in a sense disappears; we enter a world of shifting nodes, relations, networks, force-fields within the entire city, a realm of Saussurean differences rather than positive terms. Post-modern architectural thinking therefore swiftly moves from the question of the building to the thematics of the city, its current nature, its utopian or dystopian possibilities. Venturi's *Learning from Las Vegas* already pointed in this direction, offering as a model not the rationalised, sanitised spaces of the modernist city, but rather a city of vibrant mass-cultural energy and witty commercial cliché. At the same time, Rem Koolhaas and Zoe Zenghelis painted *The City of the Captive Globe*, an extraordinary vision of New York as mass-cultural, multi-ethnic metropolis, as fragmented as it is energetic, containing within itself the bustling styles and cultures of the entire globe. In 1974 Jonathan Raban proposed the notion of 'soft city' in a book of that title, arguing that the 'hard' city of modernist rational planning had had its day and that urban space was now a rich, crowded field for the production of signs, images, fantasy, style.[11] In 1975 Colin Rowe formulated the key concept of 'Collage City' as a challenge to the relentless logic of a Le Corbusian *ville radieuse*. He found a small-scale model for his concept in Hadrian's Villa, of which he writes:

the Villa Adriana attempts to dissimulate all reference to a single controlling idea . . . Hadrian, who proposes the reverse of any 'totality', seems only to need the accumulation of the most various fragments. . . . The Villa Adriana is a miniature Rome. It plausibly reproduces all the collisions of set pieces and all the random empirical happenings which the city so lavishly exhibited. . . . It is almost certain that the uninhibited aesthetic preference of today is for the structural discontinuities and the multiple syncopated excitements which the Villa Adriana enacts.[12]

Decentred and aleatory, Collage City is everything that Walter Gropius or Mies van der Rohe despise; and that the aesthetic preference of today was indeed for such multiple urban discontinuities seemed confirmed by a sudden cluster of post-modern novels featuring such cities: Donald Barthelme's *City Life* (1970), Italo Calvino's *Invisible Cities* (1972), the Berlin of Thomas Pynchon's *Gravity's Rainbow* (1973), and William Burroughs' *Cities of the Red Night* (1981).

Raymond Williams' *The Country and the City* (1973), by common consent his finest single book, seems very clearly to belong in this context, as part of the general wave of post-modern thinking about the city. The book has often been discussed in terms of its rapprochement with Marxism; for the first time, it is said, classical Marxist texts provide the very terms of debate, and a new tone of clearer, colder political anger makes itself felt, very different from the hesitant complexifying of the earlier volumes. I don't want to disagree with that assessment so much as to reformulate it in a more nuanced way. For at the very moment that Williams gravitates towards Marxism, the latter in its turn gravitates – perhaps in the grip of the force-field of the post-modern – towards questions of the city, of 'the specificity of the urban'. In *Postmodern Geographies*, Edward Soja writes of 'the coalition of geographers, sociologists and political economists that had formed in the 1970s to develop a new critical interpretation of capitalist urbanization'.[13] Key works of this coalition would include Henri Lefebvre's *La Révolution urbaine* (1970) and *La Pensée marxiste et la ville* (1972), Manuel Castells' *La Question Urbaine* (1972) and David Harvey's *Social Justice and the City* (1974). It is, then, this kind of Marxism, that I would be inclined to call (following Soja) post-modern Marxism, for which questions of space have a new theoretical saliency and political urgency, and to which Williams' *The Country and the City* belongs.

While much of that volume is concerned with demystifying ideological concepts of city and country, it also concludes with a few visionary recommendations of its own. Williams finds in both Marxism and the utopian socialist tradition the intellectual resources for challenging the modernist technopolis, for thinking through the abolition of the stark binary opposition of city and country. But it's not altogether clear from *The Country and the City* why this should be a post- rather than anti-modernist solution to the problems of capitalist urban crowding and alienation. The last chapter of the book points us in the direction of the decentred socialist 'garden city' of William Morris' *News from Nowhere* rather than, say, Fritz Lang's *Metropolis*; yet Williams' anti-Morrisian stress elsewhere that achieved socialism will be vastly more *complex*, not vastly more simple, than capitalism seems inadequately registered here. To find the truly post-modern city in his work, we must remain faithful to another key post-modernist tenet and deconstruct the opposition between creative and theoretical writing – a task in which we shall find that Raymond Williams' footprints were already there in the sand many years ahead of us. For it is in his fiction that many of the post-modern hints, pointers and parallels in his work receive their fullest elaboration; and given the general neglect of his novels, even among devoted Williams admirers, it's not surprising that the notion of Williams *as* post-modernist seems more unfamiliar than it should be.

To the list of post-modern fictional cities given above, we should add one more, the Manod of Raymond Williams's *The Fight for Manod* (1979), a city as truly invisible of any of Calvino's because it is as yet only planned, not built. The critique of Enlightenment planning first broached in *Culture and Society* thus comes once more to the fore; but so too do the very contents of the plan, the nature of the post-Corbusian city itself. It is indeed a 'soft city' in Jonathan Raban's sense, open to all kinds of unconscious investment on the part of the Matthew Price, its ageing Master-Builder. It is a decentred, deconstructed city, in which the old divisions between town and country are fading away into irrelevance. It is made up of small towns, even, one would say, villages. Modernist functionalism is thereby overcome, and the 'irrational' admitted creatively back into the very structures of human settlement. So far, so Morrisian; but the break with the last chapter of *The Country and the City* comes when we grasp that the new Manod will be a truly post-modernist because *post-Fordist*, city, 'conceived, from the beginning, in post-industrial terms and with a post-electronic technology', 'new communications and transport technologies; a working model of a different kind of city: a dispersed city' (*FM*, p. 77). This post-modern vision, in the view of Peter Owen, who is appointed alongside Price as a government consultant on the scheme, is only the latest ruse of capitalism, a seductive smokescreen behind which ruthless class-interests continue to operate unabated. Matthew Price, while certainly aware of the political dangers, rejects this easy dismissiveness, and works for a utopian possibility lodged at the heart of the capitalist scheme which he believes might, just might, be liberated from it. Which is to say, in effect, that the literary or cultural critic, trying to come to terms with this baffling new phenomenon, the post-modern, is actually the hero of *The Fight for Manod*. If Peter Owen represents a knee-jerk Marxist dismissal of the new culture, Price, though the older man, embodies the more interesting (and surely likely) stance, seeing a precarious but exciting tangle of hope and danger in the unprecedented epoch which is coming into being all around him. It is, in the end, to Williams' novels we shall have to turn to glean what he has to say *on* post-modernism as well as to see him in action *as* post-modernist.

Emerging first in architecture, the post-modern motifs of populism and historicism lead swiftly into general issues of the city; but there is a second version of the post-modern which only partly overlaps with such concerns. This post-modernism is signalled by the slogans of Guy Debord and Jean Baudrillard – 'society of the spectacle' and 'precession of simulacra' – rather than those of Robert Venturi and Tom Wolfe. It points to the extraordinary proliferation of mass culture in our century, all the way from Charlie Chaplin to the Teenage Mutant Turtles, and to the accompanying development of a whole panoply of technologies of cultural reproduction: film, radio, television, tape-recording, videos. Whereas in the good (but stodgy) old days, such technologies simply obediently reproduced a reality which confidently pre-existed them, in the bad (but exhilarating) new ones, the image shoulders aside reality, constituting rather than passively reflecting it, so that the supposedly 'real' turns out to be the mere reflection *of* a reflection; Baudrillard's simulacrum now precedes that upon which it was supposed to be modelled. In such a culture, nature is abolished, and the post-structuralist 'death of the subject' sets in with a vengeance. My occasional desire to get my dumb-bells out from under the bed and pump some iron, which I consciously take to be a purely 'natural', naive response to the weedy state of my biceps and shoulders, turns out to be unconsciously imprinted in me by all the Stallone and Schwarzenegger movies I've watched. Roland Barthes' 'death of the author' isn't quite the Ayatollah Khomenei's, but it does reduce that previously god-like figure to a rag-bag or lumber-room of mass-cultural clichés and unconscious determinations of all kinds.

If 'Culture is Ordinary' was the Williams slogan to match Wolfe's and Venturi's, then 'dramatized society' is his equivalent of the

'society of the spectacle' or of the simulacrum. He coined it in his
Cambridge inaugural lecture of 1974, 'Drama in a Dramatized Society', reprinted in *Writing in Society*. There Williams notes that with
the advent of television a qualitative cultural leap sets in: drama is
no longer a local or occasional production of images, but rather 'in
quite new ways, is built into the rhythms of everyday life. . . . Till the
eyes tire, millions of us watch the shadows of shadows and find
them substance.' Beyond the overt 'theatricality of our image-
conscious public world' we have, he claims, entered an unprecedented new phase of 'the dramatization of consciousness itself'.[14]
The most 'dramatized' or image-ridden of all societies is, no doubt,
the United States, and thus as visiting professor at Stanford University in 1972, Williams found himself ensconced in the post-modern
heartlands. It was here, where he sometimes seems, on his own
account, to have spent his time watching seven televised films a day,
day in day out, that be began work on *Television: Technology and
Cultural Form*, whose central concept of 'total flow' has been repeatedly invoked by later theorists of post-modernity.

Again it is to Williams' fiction that we must turn to see the full
development of these themes. A remarkable passage from *The Fight
for Manod* describing the frigidly beautiful Juliet Dance had already
broached the unnerving possibility that Wales might be peopled by
simulacra. Juliet is as lovely as a subtly painted porcelain doll, yet
the novel is no longer able to tell whether such dolls are modelled on
Juliet and her human precursors or, rather, 'whether the occasional
Juliet . . . was not a human repetition, an imitation in its turn, of the
dolls and the figurines' (*FM*, pp. 111–12). In the Wales of *The Volunteers*,[15] whose hero Lewis Redfern works as a consultant for an international satellite television agency, virtually everything is 'Julietised',
image rather than substance. The early chapters of the book are set in
the open-air Welsh Folk Museum in St Fagans, a Baudrillardian map
which precedes its territory, a simulacrum which constructs the very
history it claims merely to reflect; and which is also, of course, a
memorable instance of those 'theme parks' and 'heritage industry'
which have themselves been seen as a distinctly post-modernist
manifestation – a 'good' historicism turning sour once the consum-
erist image lays hands on it. What takes place in that museum – the
terrorist shooting of a Cabinet Minister – is itself no less simulacral.
Television here, as in general, does not passively echo but rather
actively constitutes the event; the shooting, as Redfern swiftly realises, was always already an event-to-be televised, it belonged from

its very inception to the society of the image (it is in fact carried out by a character who as a student worked on a closed-circuit undergraduate television service and who later becomes programme director on the new Channel Five).

In this 'dramatized society', constituted by a play of images and simulacra without depth, the typical aesthetic experience, as various theorists of post-modernism have insisted, is the *sublime*, that hoary term from Romantic aesthetics which has made so unexpected a comeback in contemporary theoretical debates. There are perhaps two versions of this, Fredric Jameson's 'hysterical sublime' and Jean François Lyotard's more classical Kantian sublime.[16] For Jameson, the sublime operates as a moment of Sartrean 'derealisation', when the indistinguishability of the post-modern simulacrum from its live spectators (his example is the statues of Duane Hanson) returns unsettlingly upon your very neighbours in the museum, reducing them to possible simulacra in their turn. My own instance of such post-modern derealisation is afforded by Ridley Scott's *Blade Runner* (a film whose close parallels to Williams' *The Volunteers* would be worth pursuing). Here the sublime takes the form of that ghastly moment when, as with Rachel, you realise that you're not after all your 'own' human being but rather somebody else's *robot*, a mere 'skin-job' or android; your most intimate memories and desires, far from being truly your own, are in fact programmed into you in advance by multinational capital. This 'negative' sublime is a frequent occurrence in both *The Fight for Manod* and *The Volunteers*, providing us with some of the most powerful passages of both novels. It sets in desolately when, for example, Matthew Price realises that the hopes and desires of the local hill-farmers, which he has seen as a political resource against the predations of the multinationals that are moving into the Afren valley, are in reality in the grip of those multinationals; they constitute, rather than challenge, its local operations. A similar moment arrives in *The Volunteers* when Lewis Redfern, through the operation of what he takes to be a politically neutral investigative acumen, unwittingly unleashes the full weight of the Establishment security forces upon Mark Redfern and his secret Volunteers, whose project Redfern broadly approves of. Far from being the autonomous, hard-nosed professional he's taken himself to be, Redfern finds out that he's unconsciously been the pre-programmed robot of authoritarian power, a 'replicant' rather than a blade runner.

Jameson's sublime overlaps with Lyotard's at some points, though its political inflection is decidedly more pessimistic: for both men, the sublime is the moment when you encounter the total system, which normally escapes figuration, but in Jameson's version you seem to glimpse it only to find yourself already hopelessly implicated in it, reduced by it to android status rather than finding in the encounter an impetus to political challenge.[17] Lyotard's sublime, which demands that the work of art 'present the unpresentable' and takes on the impossible task of giving sensory figuration to Kantian ideas of reason, which by definition can be conceptualised but not presented, seems, strangely, more politically upbeat; for the Ideas one cannot but present – totality, the simple – have a vaguely utopian edge to them. All of Williams' fiction is dedicated to the sublime in this sense, to finding sensory embodiment or Eliotic 'objective correlatives' for a vast historical and political process which exceeds any single perspective or telling. Whether he succeeds or not in this can, naturally, only be established by analysis of each novel in turn. All I can do here is to offer what seems to me an instance of Lyotard's post-modern sublime at work in Williams' fiction in a virtually pure state, in that remarkable passage where Lewis Redfern sloughs off his political defeatism and commits himself (though not in a simple voluntaristic way) to the Pontyrhiw Inquiry:

> To be there and to be telling it was a local moment, a significant moment, but the immense process continued and there was no available identity outside it: only the process itself, which could never properly told in any single dimension or any single place. There was only, now, the deep need to connect and the practical impossibility, for unregrettable reasons, of making the connections, even the known connections. Yet then, all the time, within this impossibility, were the inevitable commitments, the necessary commitments, the choosing of sides. Through the persistent uncertainty, within the overwhelming process, I had now chosen and been chosen, in what would be, in effect, a quite final way. (*V*, p. 267)

It is upon such passages that I am content to rest my case for Raymond Williams as post-modern novelist.

The final heading under which I wish to deal with Williams as post-modernist is space and geography, categories which subsume the earlier themes I have addressed. Perhaps the nearest that theorists of post-modernism come to a consensus, in what is inevitably a much-contested, perpetually shifting cultural field, is in the definition of post-modernity as a *spatial* culture, for both good and bad. Populism and historicism, it is argued, lead to a lightweight eclecticism, a play of stylistic surface without depth, glossy signifiers torn from a living past and thereby denied a meaningful future; the simulacrum, too, by both its defenders and detractors, is seen as entailing a new 'spatial logic' (Jameson's phrase) of social relations; and the centrality of architecture and the city in post-modernism both point to a more familiar concern with spatial forms. It is at this point, above all, that objections to describing Williams as a post-modernist are likely to become vehement: space freezes history, turning active revolutionary will into the reified surfaces of unchanging landscape, and thus hardly accords with that 'resource of hope' that Williams' work so eminently is. True enough, but we need also to attend to the spatial signals emitted by the titles of his first and last novels, *Border Country*[18] and *People of the Black Mountains*.

Space can indeed be ideological in some influential forms of post-modernism, but the framework I wish to invoke for thinking about it is the 'topian Marxism' sketched out by Edward Soja in his *Postmodern Geographies*. The theoretical and political insistence on space, place and geography is then a counter-assertion to the one-sided 'historicism' of modern critical theory, its belief that time, history, active human self-making, are always and everywhere the most relevant interpretative context for social action; and the political correlate of this is the view of the proletariat as a universal, because placeless, class. In place of old-style historical materialism, this new post-modern Marxist geography calls for a 'historico-geographical materialism', a 'socio-spatial dialectic' which would see space not simply as the echo, reflection or outcome of other, more fundamental social processes, but as itself bending back upon and formatively shaping such processes – a true dialectic, and neither an aspatial historicism nor an ahistorical spatialism (which some post-modernisms arguably are). Space structures reflect social process, and never more so than in our own epoch when, for complex reasons in Marxist economics, it can be argued that it is space rather than time, global reach rather than temporal speed-up in the immediate labour-process, which is the fundamental characteristic of post-Fordist capitalist restructuring. Soja lists Michel Foucault, John Berger and Henri Lefebvre as great precursors of what he terms the 'spatial turn' of contemporary social and cultural theory; and to his litany I believe we should add the name of Raymond Williams.[19]

A preoccupation with space could be traced through at many levels in Williams' work. There is a well-nigh Bachelardian fascination with rooms and containers, spatial rhythms and structures, throughout his novels, which accounts for much of their fictional density and resonance. A related obsession with rooms seems also to structure his work on turn-of-the-century drama: the stifling enclosed rooms of naturalism, the dissolving rooms of early modernist drama, where objective space and Gothic phantasmagoria pass uncannily into one another. There are the memorable geographies of the novels: Glynmawr valley in *Border Country*, the Afren valley in *The Fight for Manod*, the meticulously mapped border country of *People of the Black Mountains*. From these fictional concretions arises an articulated political position: 'a new theory of socialism,' Williams argued in 1984, 'must now centrally involve *place*'.[20] And against the aspatial universalism of Bolshevik politics, he adhered firmly to the principle of 'many socialisms', as many, presumably, as there are different geographies to shape and inspire them; this case is worked through movingly in the novel *Loyalties* as well as in his theoretical writings. But for all this, space and place are not, as Williams' critics sometimes assume, pre-given positivities to which we can simply appeal against modernist Reason; rather, like the utopian city in *Manod*, they are something that will only fully come into being on the other side of – not by cancelling out – advanced productive and communications technologies. Anyone who could declare himself a 'Welsh European' obviously did not have a pre-modernist sense of what place or regional identity consists in; and a profound sense of spatial disjunction, of baffling gaps, absences or overlays in the new 'hyperspace' of post-modern multinational capital, runs as deeply through Williams' work as it does through Fredric Jameson's (indeed, Williams was talking about 'cognitive mapping' long before Jameson invented the phrase). 'He's studying Wales,' Eira Rosser says of Matthew Price in *Border Country*, 'and he goes to London to do it' (*BC*, p. 271). There are thus 'space warps' as well as timewarps, bewildering distortions of a geographical field as imperial or multi-national space enter and remake locality or place. Postmodernist culture may indeed foreground space in new ways, and this has its salutory impact upon a spatially blind Marxism in thrall to Enlightenment modernity; but post-modernity also makes space and geography problematic in quite unprecedented ways, hollowing out whatever settled positivity they might once have had, perhaps way back in the good old days of that realist literary tradition to which Raymond Williams has so often been unthinkingly assigned.

Populism and historicism, the city, the media, simulacra and the sublime, space and geography: these have been my chosen topics for constructing Raymond Williams as post-modernist, though there are perhaps others. A brief essay like this can only provide suggestive pointers, not elaborated answers; but even if Raymond Williams were not a post-modernist, *we* are – we inhabit, live, act politically within this new epoch, even if we also maintain a wary distance from its more full-throated ideological celebrations. Post-modernism is now the interpretative framework through which all the texts of the past must be processed if they are to speak to us today. To spare Williams' work this encounter is to consign it to that very realm of theme parks and heritage industry that he so effectively diagnoses in *The Volunteers*. To read Williams through the force-field of the post-modern is, in my view, for him to tell us as much about it as it about him, and for us to begin to sketch (with a little help from Edward Soja and David Harvey) a politically productive rather than disabling postmodernity. At any rate, the wager of this essay is that, if we can no longer describe Raymond Williams as a 'realist', nor can we any longer speak of him as straightforward 'modernist'; and after that there seems only one interpretative move left to make.

NOTES

1. R. Williams, *Culture and Society, 1780–1950* (London: Chatto & Windus, 1958); hereafter referred to as *CS*, with page references given in the text; *The Country and the City* (London: Paladin, 1975); *Marxism and Literature* (Oxford: Oxford University Press, 1977); *Politics and Letters* (London: New Left Books, 1979).
2. F. Inglis, 'Introductory Note', in T. Pinkney (ed.), *The Politics of Modernism* (London: Verso, 1989) p. 31.
3. For a fuller development of the themes of this essay, see my *Raymond Williams: Postmodern Novelist* (London: Seren Press, 1992).
4. R. Williams, *Loyalties* (London: Hogarth Press, 1989); *People of the Black Mountains*, vol. 1: *The Beginning* (London: Chatto & Windus, 1989); vol. 2: *The Eggs of the Eagle* (London: Chatto & Windus, 1990).

5. R. Williams, *The Fight for Manod* (London: Hogarth Press, 1988); hereafter referred to as *FM*, with page references given in the text.
6. See my 'Raymond Williams and the "Two Faces of Modernism"', in T. Eagleton (ed.), *Raymond Williams: Critical Perspectives* (Oxford: Oxford University Press, 1989) pp. 12–33.
7. R. Williams, *The Long Revolution* (Harmondsworth, Penguin, 1965) p. 316.
8. R. Williams, 'The Estranging Language of Post-Modernism' *New Society* (16 June 1983) p. 439.
9. C. Jencks, *The Language of Post-Modern Architecture* (London: Academy Editions, 1977) p. 9.
10. R. Williams, *Communications* (Harmondsworth: Penguin, 1962) and *Television: Technology and Cultural Form* (Glasgow: Fontana, 1974).
11. R. Venturi, *Learning from Las Vegas* (Cambridge, Mass.: MIT Press, 1972); Koolhaas' and Zenghelis' painting, 'The City of the Captive Globe' is reproduced on p. 120 of Jencks, *The Language of Post-Modern Architecture*; J. Raban, *Soft City* (London: Faber & Faber, 1974).
12. C. Rowe cited in Jencks, *The Language of Post-Modern Architecture*, p. 111.
13. E. Soja, *Postmodern Geographies: The Reassertion of Space in Critical Social Theory* (London: Verso, 1989) p. 69.
14. R. Williams, *Writing in Society* (London: Verso, 1984) pp. 12 & 18.
15. R. Williams, *The Volunteers* (London: Hogarth Press, 1985); hereafter referred to as *V*, with page references given in the text.
16. See F. Jameson, 'Postmodernism or the Cultural Logic of Late Capitalism', *New Left Review* (July/August 1984) no. 146, pp. 76–9; and Jean François Lyotard, *The Postmodern Condition: A Report on Knowledge* (Manchester: Manchester University Press, 1984) pp. 77–9.
17. See my exchange with Jameson on this in 'Postmodernism and Utopia: Interview with Frederic Jameson', *News from Nowhere* (Spring, 1991) no. 9.
18. R. Williams, *Border Country* (London: Hogarth Press, 1988); hereafter referred to as *BC*, with page references given in the text.
19. On all this, see also my 'Space: The Final Frontier', *News from Nowhere* (Autumn 1990), no. 8, pp. 10–27.
20. R. Williams, *The Resources of Hope: Culture, Democracy, Socialism*, ed. R. Gable (London: Verso, 1989) p. 242.

17

Frank Kermode: History and Synchronicity

BARBARA HELM

The role of critic has always been a varied one. There are those critics who work in an investigative manner, who concern themselves in a personal and very intimate way with a text or writer. Their method is essentially an exploration of the techniques or mechanics of a piece; a particular, very close and intricately worked examination. This type of critic offers a detailed, constructive recognition, sympathetic or otherwise, of the elements that the original author or poet has produced; and because of the complexity of the involvement that is a necessary part of this critic's work, the gap that normally exists between writer and critic is at times so narrow that it can become difficult to differentiate between the critic's idea of what is happening in a writer's work and the writer's own intention.

Then there are those critics who concern themselves with much more than just the text they may be reviewing. There is in this instance an idea of an 'overall view' of a work, a much more general outlook, a macro as opposed to a micro examination. This type of critic is not concerned with empathy but with the objectiveness of his/her enquiry. With this type of critic one is always aware of the gap between the critic and the work. Obviously it is necessary to stand back from an object in order to view it in its surroundings: the closer the position, the narrower (in one sense at least) the view. A gap exists always between writer and reader but when a third party is introduced – the critic – yet another gap appears, taking the same form as the first, but occuring between the critic and his/her reader. So we have the following sequence:

Author   Critic   Reader

However, what is interesting is the position of the critic (and therefore the size of the gap) relative to the previous definitions.

TYPE A

               Author   Critic   Reader

TYPE B

               Author   Critic   Reader

Frank Kermode, as critic, falls into the latter category. His concern, as he says himself, 'is less with the how than with the why'.[1] His viewpoint – and it appears to be a fairly easily identifiable one – is ultimately contextual. The following opening sentence would certainly seem to suggest this.

> Around 1907 great changes, we may confidently announce, were either occuring or pending, both in English society and in the English novel. Joyce and Lawrence were already at work; so was Gertrude Stein. James was publishing his Prefaces, and Ford, who had worked with Conrad, was excogitating a new theory of the novel, Arnold Bennet was writing *The Old Wives' Tale* on what seemed to him sound French principles. 1907 wasn't a bad year for novels, for it saw the publication of both *The Secret Agent* and the *Longest Journey*. (*EF*, p. 33)

Now, if we adjust the model proposed for critical positioning we might well get something that looks like this:

Triangle of Interpretation

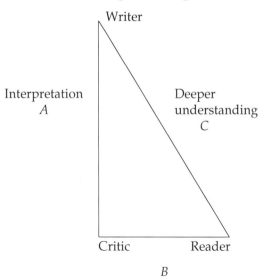

This, I propose, is how Frank Kermode positions himself as critic, so that $A + B = C$, i.e. Interpretation + Reinterpretation = Deeper understanding (as this critic defines it) for the reader. Using Pythagoras' theorem as a model for the interaction between writer/critic/reader helps to give a clearer insight into the process.

It does at first glance appear to be an almost ideal position for a critic of any description. Balanced between the two points of writer and reader, the critic receives the information from the writer and processes that information which s/he then transmits to the reader. However, it has to be borne in mind that this process is always a selective one and an investigation into this selective process could be useful in order to pin-point any effects this may have on the reader's acceptance of the re-interpretative input passed onto him/her from the critic.

Now it could be argued that this is the position adopted by all critics but I believe that Kermode's positioning at the radiating point of the Triangle of Interpretation, which is also the intersection of the diachronic and synchronic axes, could well prove illuminating. He positions himself far enough away from the writer – by use of external/contextual and often historical reference (the diachronic line) – to enable him to adopt an 'objective' stance. 'The requirement that art should edify, or at least it shouldn't disedify, is very old';[2] 'The canon seems to have begun to crystallise in reaction against an heretical attempt to impose a rigorously restricted list of sacred books on the church of the mid-second century' (*C*, p. 172); and 'Writing novels is more like history than we often choose to think' (*C*, p. 122).

His use of chronologically based reference provides the basis for his critical positioning. He also selects from writers using similar criteria: 'E. M. Forster in *Aspects of the Novel*' . . . goes back to neolithic, perhaps to paleolithic [time when] . . . the primitive audience was . . . only kept awake by suspense' (*EF*, p. 122) and 'Eliot, speaks of [the] "imperial imagination"; and [views] history as having a kind of perspectiveless unity, Virgil, Dante, Baudelaire and Kipling can exist within the same plane . . . but behind the temporal disaster of Babylon he knows that the timeless pattern of the eternal city must survive' (*C*, p. 74). This particular sentence expresses Kermode's understanding of the essence of literature and this includes the work of the critic. He is constantly searching for the right place (time) in which to fix his own ideas. But he is not so far removed from the writer that he is unable to form a valid criticism.

He is, however, closer to his own reader – along the synchronic axis: 'Miller obviously can write as Orwell claimed; but he rarely bothers to. Whether or not you think it worth rummaging through *Cancer* in search of those golden pages . . . really depends on how you like your wisdom served' (*C*, p. 160). The ideal, of course, would be a equidistant positioning of the critic, with the diachronic and the synchronic axes the same length, so that the critic, whilst using external referencing to aid his/her interpretation, did not allow an over-emphasis to occur.

Kermode's acknowledgement of the varied influences at work on any writer's output, while on one level assisting the reader with re-interpretation, on another checks a closer identification occurring between the writer and the reader. And, in fact, the diagonal between the writer and the reader is also the longest line in the Triangle. So whilst on the one hand Kermode appears to be contributing to the sum of knowledge available to the reader, his own type of intervention actually removes the reader that much further from the writer, at the same time as apparently opening up the work to him/her. It could be argued that this type of criticism can be a deliberate attempt to keep these two apart.

What is actually happening here is a control of the writer's presence, relative to the reader, by use of historical referencing. The tone of the referencing is even more interesting, often containing a theological or religious element. For example, in talking about myths: 'and it is the next step to make texts which actually provide for such exegis, as for example in the Gospels' (*EF*, p. 102) and 'Hermeneutic confusion and problematic closure are not breaches of contract but natural features of narrative, they are found in dreams, in romances, even in the Gospels' (*EF*, p. 108). An invitation to view the Gospels from a literary perspective is the implication here. Kermode talks of being 'obsessed by the chosen historical moment, as a theologian might mediate the Incarnation' and 'the sacramental aspect of art'.[3]

So the interpretation that the reader is being given, therefore allows for a theological as well as an historical strand, and it is necessary to ask what sense of the text is being communicated to the reader. Are all texts to be viewed through this historical or theological filter? The over-riding feeling with Kermode's type of criticism is his acknowledgement that the religious is at the heart of literature, 'the Bible is probably the most important single sourcee of all our literature'.[4]

Although appearing to be in a rather fixed position, historically,

Kermode does in fact allow for a progression in literary theory, but he also manages to view that in an historical context. 'The history of modernism could be written as an account of the conflict between excited catrastrophe theorists on one side and panic-stricken reactionaries on the other' (*EF*, p. 7). He is willing to acknowledge new theories and to some extent investigate them, for he is, above all, a mediator. 'I am interested in the record of both,' he says, talking about theoretical and traditionist approaches to literature (*EF*, p. 7).

Kermode seems to understand theory as being a variation on a theme rather than a completely new perspective. But even when discussing theories such as structuralism or transformational generative grammar and its effects on literary analysis he manages to do so in a contextual way, and in the Prologue to *Essays on Fiction, 1971–82* he maps his way quite neatly, and in chronological form, through the maze of new theorists. Always we are aware of an underlying acceptance of the rightness of traditional literary theory. 'In a sense he [Barthes] is saying, in a new way, something we have long known about the plurality of good texts' (*C*, p. 122). So although he does not actually use these theories as an investigative tool himself, he comments on them and assesses their usefulness as a continuation or development, rather than as a replacement, of what already exists. And he believes they owe their existence to the past in the same way that new novels/poems owe their existence to what other writers have created before them. He is always conscious of the need to express his belief in the continuity of all things. He sees literary theory as an evolutionary process rather than a finished product; theoretical processes are to be open-ended, and therefore always subject to revisions and adjustments, whilst at the same time retaining their traditionalist core. The theological, it would seem, is at the heart of everything, including the role of the critic. 'Performing it [interpretation], we have the comfort, if we take it to be so, of working in a long tradition, stretching back to the evangelists themselves, interpreters all – and, indeed, far beyond them' (*EF*, p. 200).

In his essay 'The Single Correct Interpretation (*EF*, p. 201), Kermode looks at the theories of both Gadamer and Hirsch through the work of yet another critic, P. D. Juhl, and one of the interesting ideas that this throws up is the similarity of Gadamer's hypothesis and Kermode's own brand of critical thought: that is, the concept of the 'fusion of horizons'.[5] In the prologue, Kermode explains his understanding of Gadamer's theory: 'It would be more accurate to say that he wishes to ask what it is to take into account the historical response to texts . . . when we formulate our own [response]' (*EF*, p. 27). And, of course, this is exactly what Kermode practises. He obviously feels a sympathy with Gadamer's ideas, he calls the theory 'attractive to common sense' (*EF*, p. 28). And then, naturally, and as we would now expect, he carries on to indicate that even this theory must be viewed through its own fusion of horizons, i.e. its predecessors in hermeneutics.

Kermode's critical work is a prime example of Gadamer's theory in practice, i.e. the meaning of a text going beyond its author, 'beyond' in Kermode's sense meaning the introduction of the historical legacy as supplied by him, as well as the experience each separate reader brings to a text. In fact we can again illustrate this by adapting the model used previously:

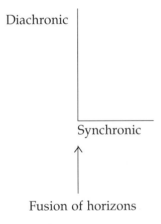

This intersection, which is also the point at which the critic (Kermode) positions himself, is now seen to be the very place where this fusion of horizons occurs. However, even if we allow for this fusion we have to try to be aware that this process is also selective, and whilst we cannot escape the 'givenness' of our condition we do only use information that we consider relevant, or in this particular instance, that the critic considers relevant. There would be no merit in a critic passing on information about food preparation in the mid-seventeenth century unless he had decided that the information was somehow relevant to a given work. And this is the key to the whole problem. Whilst there might be some consensus as to what constitutes the main body of acceptable information, there always remains a grey area governed by subjective opinion: and the fact that these areas do not conform to what we might consider the 'heart' of a work and its periphery only adds to the argument. So the point of fusion is now also divided into central and peripheral areas, and Kermode uses the peripheral area (which he himself identifies) as the place for storing all the 'theologically' historical information, which he considers to be necessary to a true interpretative reading of a particular work. He is quite clear about identifying the separate areas to his own reader, but it has to be remembered that the original identification of the areas is itself open to other 'interpretations'.

So, in fact, what is happening is that two very distinct but interdependent areas of interpretation are operating to produce a very highly personalised dynamic; 'The social world in which a work is produced and received evidently has a shaping effect on interpretation.'[6] The type of work produced by Kermode (and others who also use the diachronic to elaborate their work) turns out to be a very complex thing indeed. For the fusion that occurs for the critic, also occurs for the reader (at a different point along the synchronic axis). And the reader has somehow to disentangle one from the other, if any true understanding of an original work is to be effected.

It is difficult to categorise Frank Kermode's critical work, except in this very general sense. His work is useful and informative, and whilst I do not believe (and probably neither would he) that it would be possible for a reader of his criticism to feel a full recognition and understanding of a writer's work, the contribution made by this type of criticism is certainly to be welcomed and valued. It is illuminating, if only in a partial way; perhaps the ideal would be a combination of this critical method with a more textually based method (phenomenological, for instance).

Kermode now seems to have come full circle with the publication in 1982 of *The Literary Guide to the Bible*, which he contributed to and edited with Robert Alter. In this volume he discusses the Bible as a work of literature, using his expertise and experience as a literary critic to do so. So here literature is not viewed through a biblical or theological glass, but rather the Bible is now seen through a literary one. 'The language as well as the messages it conveys symbolizes for us that past. Strange and yet familiar, which we feel we somehow must understand if we are to understand ourselves' (*LGB*, p. 1).

NOTES

1. F. Kermode, *Essays on Fiction, 1971–82* (London: Routledge and Kegan Paul, 1983) p. 72; hereafter referred to as *EF*, with page references given in the text.
2. F. Kermode, *Continuities* (London: Routledge & Kegan Paul, 1988) p. 33; hereafter referred to as *C*, with page references given in the text.
3. F. Kermode, *Puzzles and Epiphanies* (London: Routledge & Kegan Paul, 1962) p. 4 and p. 31.
4. F. Kermode and R. Alter, *The Literary Guide to the Bible* (London: Collins, 1987) p. 2; hereafter referred to as *LGB*, with page references given in the text.
5. H. Gadamer, *Truth and Method* (London: Sheed and Ward, 1979) p. 269.
6. R. Selden, in R. Selden (ed.), *The Theory of Criticism from Plato to the Present* (London: Longman, 1988) p. 187.

18

Vanishing Point: On the Edge of Critical Breakdown

CLIVE BLOOM

Once education was driven by enquiry. Now it is driven by functional utility and consumptional circularity.

The profession of literary criticism as it is practised in the universities is in crisis. This is not peculiar to literary criticism, but to all the liberal and human sciences. It has been this way now for many years. Indeed, it may be said that this is now the natural state of the Humanities in the advanced cultures of the West. Why should this be? This essay is an attempt to come to grips with a problem central to educational practice in the humanities today and in a wider context the problems now endemic to cultural criticism as it is practised in the late twentieth century. I talk here of the crisis in Humanities subjects and the implications of that crisis.

If we wish to explore this critical moment we must lace our investigation with a little post-modernist theory. Jean Baudrillard's famous invocation of *simulacra* may be summarised thus:

> In *Simulacra and Simulations* Baudrillard extends, some would say hyperbolizes, his theory of commodity culture. No longer does the code take priority over or even precede the consumer object. The distinctions between object and representation, thing and idea are no longer valid. In their place Baudrillard fathoms a strange new world constructed out of models or simulacra which have no referent or ground in any 'reality' except their own. A simulation is different from a fiction or lie in that it not only presents an absence as a presence, the imaginary as the real, it also undermines any contrast to the real, absorbing the real within itself.'[1]

Umberto Eco makes a similar point about modern culture: 'To speak of things that one wants to connote as real, these things must seem real. The "completely real" becomes identified with the "completely fake".... The sign aims to be the thing, to abolish the distinction of the reference, the mechanism of replacement.'[2] In the land of supersaturation that we inhabit signification breaks down and systems with 'meaning' content cease to function 'naturally' and take on instead a strange half-life in which meaning systems *counterfeit* the roles they once had.

In this supersaturated world, in an age dominated by the pulse of electronic instantaneity, we find ourselves 'obesely' replicated in the consuming and consumed environment in which the object can no longer bear the full weight of its significance.[3] Instead, the object (as subject of analysis) weightlessly floats into the space of simulation. Simply, the intellectual space is overstocked and the currency devalued. The situation replicates capitalist excess in an age of driving inflation.

So, in our electronic age we simply have too much, too many images, too many inputs and all too *overtly* obvious. No need for the latent, the base, the hidden or the occulted: simply describe the obvious. The *thereness* of the object is the very thing we cannot cope with. It has the demonic force to drive us to all that metaphysics of the signified (as *the* hidden drive behind the thereness of the object). The consequence is that, as observers such as Baudrillard and Eco note, we now live in an age where reality begins to imitate its imitations.

Such a moment, always already backdated, ends mimesis, ends imagination, ends the idea of an imaginative *elsewhere*, for elsewhere is our own ordinary lives lived as imitation. This is the age of hyperreality – a cybernetic universe of *ungrounded* interchanging informational flows that no longer relate to each other as original to copy, sender to message, image to object.[4]

In literature this period sees the end of the age of *genre*: the end of techno-genres such as science fiction and genres of reason such as detective fiction. It also signals the end of formal genre divisions and the collapse of the classic novel (as form regardless of content). Whereas the novel once, at its outset, stood for a radical instability in form (the formal destruction of all written processes via the total field of the novel's inclusiveness) it later stood for a radical bourgeois stability (stability here is radical, during the period 1780–1820 on the axis Anne Radclyffe–Jane Austen). This stability in form has

remained. The novel qua novel, regardless of experimentation, was
the major informational art form of bourgeois life to which all other
classes had to conform in their representational desires.

Nowadays this is no longer so. The novel is a collapsed form. Its
structure is dry, for novels no longer perform the functions allotted
them – stabilising in grammatical prose the taxonomies of bourgeois
experience. Informational flows via electric powerlines produce flows
and meshes; they act holographically, internationally and across
classes. Their procedures are that at the level of the byte and the
interface, *destabilising* the very formalities codified in novels. Such
processes signal the end of the project not merely of novels but of
Literature in general and its formal control by castes and classes. The
codification of values in novels or in philosophy is a project that is,
in these terms, historically finished. Such codification here stands for
eternality and acts as such – codes act not merely as eternal signifiers
but they can be seen as acting as the signified qua signified. The
age of codes qua codes as eternally grounded in their own procedures is something that belongs to a long dead past (say 1955 for
English literature). This condition of encodedness is one that stands
for universal homogeneity, reinforcing local and national signs of
recognition (*self* recognition and the condition of belonging). One
text, Leo Sherley-Price's 1955 introduction to Bede, tells us 'We are
transported back into the fens and forests, highlands and islands of
Celtic Britain and Saxon England, and we feel strangely "at home".
These are our own people.'[5] This was only just tenable in 1955. In
Britain it was invalidated less by immigration and the beginnings
of a multi-racial nation and more because information technology
(television) and information flow – consisting of radical breaks, su-
tures and discontinuities – denies the very stability and 'at homeness'
Leo Sherley-Price found in Bede. Curiously, Leo Sherley-Price's
comments are also disturbed by Bede's own project – recording the
everlasting will of Christ's Church during a period of extreme instability, war and devastation.

But we must look further for a cause to hyperreality's disturbing
cultural dimension. Michael Grade, talking of TV's deregulation, has
said that technology has outstripped that which it can produce and
transmit; scriptwriting becomes a conservative nostalgia for print.
Baudrillard says that in a hyperreal culture the tools and technology
of investigation outstrip the raw material, we might say until the
raw material no longer signifies *sufficiently* to be recorded at the level
of the technology.

The technology then simply diversifies: deconstruction finds it can investigate popular culture and Anglo-Saxon at one and the same time and the pace of technological change (deconstruction gives way to post-modernism) heats up so that technological absorption outstrips those consumers who receive and use the technology. Indeed, the pace proportionally speeds up as technological literacy slows down. Technology then feeds off older technologies (post-modernism on deconstruction) and then off itself. The tools speak to themselves. Moreover, the speed of technological *replacement* necessarily lessens the time between technologies and thus the technological expert (someone who has been educated over a long period into a profession) ends up a media pundit.

The academy functions as the sharp focus and residual ark of these disposable ideas. And at the academy we encounter the generations of students who live its ungrounded reality. That is why the universality of knowledge that Leo Sherley-Price holds to as a national mean is no longer tenable. We teach 'illiterate' students, deeply outside the codes of universal *literate* knowledge, outside its procedures even. They literally cannot *read* the (cultural) conditions governing their nostalgia for reading and literature. They no longer function naturally as arbiters of culture. Thus they are illiterate and cut off from their teachers, who come from a liberal (bourgeois) humanist background. All teachers 'conform' necessarily to this for they all recognise the *same ground* for debate. Students no longer can. This is a profound disjunction.

We may clarify the position if we say that lecturers live in a museum culture and students in a heritage-centre culture. We speak outside each other's appropriate language and fail to communicate. The traditional Humanities subjects function within the system of the museum. In the debates over the canon and over popular literature, literary departments have opened the doors of the ark for the last time and admitted writers hitherto excluded. The question of literary values was never a debate over greater democratic availability of working class, feminist or popular genre texts but a recuperative exercise on behalf of history itself. The whole debate was about the validity of history. At such a point history as a subject becomes a museum exercise in recuperating its own practices. All the traditional humanities subjects: English, Philosophy, History, Psychology and Sociology belong to a museum culture which believes in *grounded* taxonomic values and judgemental systems grounded in origins and *authenticity*. We might also include Business Studies grounded in the authenticity of authority. Such grounding is displaced when it meets the students.

The whole Humanities project founders at this point – seemingly the end of the liberal bourgeois humanist project. All the disciplines crash, and all the recuperations (feminism, grounded in gender as authentic coded place, or black studies, grounded in ethnicity as authentic coded place, and studies in popular culture, grounded in genre and class distinction) fail also. All these, instead of being radical departures, are the conservative historical project of demands for authenticity. Such is the end of nineteenth-century positivism in the programmes of modern humanity degrees. We are all paleantologists now! Ironically this is why all really different thought is generated from Humanities, from the crisis of a dead project. Moreover, this is why all radical politics end as conservative recuperations. Terry Eagleton's notion of discourse itself becomes an idealisation of grounding – a grounding within coded systems – but all codes qua codes are decipherable into other systems that act as a grounding and give authenticity. The *new* is programmatically ungrounded – hence all political action will from now on be conservative and idealistic – a wholesale attempt to hold back technology and return it to the area of values, authenticity and human intention.

We need not, however, fear for the continuity of Humanities subjects. In a heritage society the archaic functions *as the present*, and the present unites the archaic to function as if always new: Baudrillard's totally saturated society. New technologies will *always* allow for the escape of outdated systems to function archeologically. Such residuality is faced by the Humanities subjects which function to hierarchise museum culture over heritage culture and which signify, for the moment, political and cultural *stability* and the retention of class. The Humanities expert will stand for the eternal values of scientific objectivity and humanistic truth; he will stand for the grounding function of textuality as *authenticity* itself. Here, to be literate and to be able to read is to 'be' *read* by others as a mythic figure (the professor or the doctor). This allows for the reinforcement of stabilities, but this is bought at a price, for our nostalgia for the project of literature and the project of the literary professional expert will prepare a change in labour practice. The old teaching project of distribution and exchange leading to student absorption and contemplation will be replaced by the procedures of circulation and disfunction, by the *act* and by the notion of production.

The end of Humanities in its old positivist sense and the rise of the new ungrounded residual sense is comparable to the replacement of one symbolic icon, the aeroplane, by the helicopter – from departure and destination to circulation and return. The Humanities will survive as a place where a ritualised priesthood will circulate the tokens of their indifference to change. The Humanities will suddenly return to contemplation of their eternal civilising missions, but unlike before, when they existed within history, they no longer will mean anything. What will be important is that they exist.

NOTES

1. Mark Poster, in introductory remarks to Jean Baudrillard, *Selected Writings*, tr. Mark Poster (Oxford: Basil Blackwell, 1989) pp. 5–7.
2. Umberto Eco, *Travels in Hyper-reality*, tr. William Weaver (London: Picador, 1987) p. 7.
3. Jean Baudrillard, *Fatal Strategies* (London: Pluto, 1990) p. 27 onwards.
4. Method is not the simulacra of reality, but the fantasy whereby the metaphoric becomes the world. It does not describe an authentic and prescribed reality, but an, as yet, unknown reality. It is the space of the real (but we mistake that space for the description of an already given state). Method as simulacrum is not a substitute for reality nor a mirror, nor model nor a passive description of reality, but where reality *is* (an abstract fantasy space where the real is found in adventurous abundance). It is therefore *prior* to reality as reality's origin. Nevertheless, this 'origin' cannot exist beyond or before the production of the real. It thus connotes a space in which it itself is enveloped by a quest for origination (in the reality of the world). Hence, the methodological simulacra is the real, the real originates in its mimetic other: itself realised in the myth of methodology. Thus, does the imitation have priority over the original.
5. Leo Sherley-Price, in introductory remarks to Bede, *A History of the English Church and People* (Harmondsworth: Penguin, [1955], 1988) p. 24.

Index

Index

251

Carlyle   10–15, 18, 20–3
literary taste   1, 6, 29–30
literary value   6
  functional   217–18
  'good' literature   31–2, 33–5, 58–9,
    81–2, 141
  Orwell's attitude   140–2, 146–8,
    150–1
  Woolf's attitude   95–6, 97
  see also aestheticism
literature:
  and cultural life   31–2, 33
  and human nature   81–3, 86–90
  and ideology   30, 34, 84
  and language   86–7, 128–30, 154,
    204, 207
  and politics   104–5, 142–3, 144–5,
    149, 151
  and religion   9, 29–30, 32–3, 42–3,
    44–7, 75, 174, 236
  as academic discipline   30, 31, 84,
    172, 182, 188, 238–43
  definition   32, 33, 141–3
  descriptive   142–3
  drama   33, 67–74, 75, 76–8, 223
  evolutionary theory of   85–6
  fiction   33, 81, 86–90, 95–102, 104,
    106–10, 214–15, 219, 221–8,
    239–40
  'good'   31–2, 33–5, 58–9, 81–2, 141
  humane texts   82
  national   33
  poetry   32–4, 60, 103, 104, 127,
    128–32, 141, 154–9
  pornographic   115
  prescriptive   142–3, 144, 145–6
  prose   141–2
  readerly   60
  writerly   60
  theory of   172–5
The Living Principle (Leavis)   191, 196,
    199, 220–6
Lodge, David, Twentieth-Century
    Literary Criticism   186–7
logic, and grammar   163–4, 166
logical positivism   134, 135, 197, 211
loneliness:
  in literature   119–20
  see also individuality
Long Revolution, The (Williams)   215
Loyalties (Williams)   214, 227
Lyotard, Jean François   224

Macbeth (Shakespeare)   70, 75, 77–8

McFarlane, James, The Mind of
    Modernism   85
Machine Stops, The (Forster)   80, 86–90
Marx, Karl   69, 71, 85
Marxism and Literature (Williams)   213
Marxist criticism   170–1, 173–8, 191,
    220–1, 227–8
mass culture   31, 217, 219, 222–3, 238–9
  effects of   1–2, 6–7
  populism   217
  technological change   240–1
  television   217, 223–4, 240–1
  see also social structure
masturbation, in literature   115
materialist theories   68–9
meaning, and language   127, 128,
    135–6, 157–9, 162, 201–2
Meaning of Meaning, The
    (Richards)   127, 128, 135–6, 139
Measure for Measure
    (Shakespeare)   158–9
the media   217, 222–4
men:
  as novelists   101, 102
  see also gender
Merchant of Venice (Shakespeare)   185
metaphorical expression   see
    symbolism
metaphysics, in Carlyle   17, 20–3
metonymy   160–1, 162
Mill, J. S.   112
  On Liberty   113
Miller, Henry:
  and Orwell   145, 233
  Tropic of Cancer   145, 233
mimetic theory   52, 53–4
Mind of Modernism (McFarlane)   85
Modern Essay, The (Woolf)   106
Modern Fiction (Woolf)   96
modern poetry   131–2
  see also poetry
modernism   215–17
  and Forster   85–6
  and Woolf   96–7
  post-modernism   1, 2, 3, 213–28
Moment of Scrutiny   (Mulhern)
    189–90
Moore, George E.   98, 123–4, 125, 135,
    138, 196
  and Richards   125, 126
Morris, William   221
Mother Courage (Brecht)   71
The Moths   see The Waves (Woolf)
Mr Bennett and Mrs Brown